ISBN 978-1-331-10114-7
PIBN 10144955

1 MONTH OF
FREE
READING

at
www.ForgottenBooks.com

By purchasing this book you are eligible for one month membership to ForgottenBooks.com, giving you unlimited access to our entire collection of over 1,000,000 titles via our web site and mobile apps.

To claim your free month visit:

www.forgottenbooks.com/free144955

English
Français
Deutsche
Italiano
Español
Português

www.forgottenbooks.com

Mythology Photography **Fiction**
Fishing Christianity **Art** Cooking
Essays Buddhism Freemasonry
Medicine **Biology** Music **Ancient
Egypt** Evolution Carpentry Physics
Dance Geology **Mathematics** Fitness
Shakespeare **Folklore** Yoga Marketing
Confidence Immortality Biographies
Poetry **Psychology** Witchcraft
Electronics Chemistry History **Law**
Accounting **Philosophy** Anthropology
Alchemy Drama Quantum Mechanics
Atheism Sexual Health **Ancient History**
Entrepreneurship Languages Sport
Paleontology Needlework Islam
Metaphysics Investment Archaeology
Parenting Statistics Criminology
Motivational

THE GOLDEN BOOK OF VENICE

A Historical Romance of the 16th Century

By

MRS. LAWRENCE TURNBULL

'This noble citie doth in a manner chalenge this at my hands, that I should describe her . . . the fairest Lady, yet the richest Paragon, and Queene of Christendome.'

Published by The Century Co.
New York · · · · · · 1900

THE DEVINNE PRESS.

AS A TRIBUTE TO HIS GIFT OF VIVID

HISTORIC NARRATION WHICH WAS

THE DELIGHT OF MY CHILDHOOD,

I INSCRIBE THIS ROMANCE TO THE

MEMORY OF MY DEAR FATHER.

ACKNOWLEDGMENT

I desire gratefully to acknowledge my indebtedness to many faithful, loving and able students of Venetian lore, without whose books my own presentation of Venice in the sixteenth century would have been impossible. Mr. Ruskin's name must always come first among the prophets of this City of the Sea, but among others from whom I have gathered side-lights I have found quite indispensable Mr. Horatio F. Brown's "Venice; An Historical Sketch of the Republic," "Venetian Studies," and "Life on the Lagoons"; Mr. Hare's suggestive little volume of "Venice"; M. Léon Galibert's "Histoire de la République de Venise"; and Mr. Charles Yriarte's "Venice" and his work studied from the State papers in the Frari, entitled "La vie d'un Patricien de Venise."

Mr. Robertson's life of Fra Paolo Sarpi gave me the first hint of this great personality, but my own portrait has been carefully studied from the volumes of his collected works which later responded to my search; these were collected and preserved for the Venetian government under the title of "Opere di Fra Paolo Sarpi, Servita, Teologo e Consultore della Serenissima Repubblica di Venezia" and included his life,

Acknowledgment

letters and "opinions," and all others of his writings which escaped destruction in the fire of the Servite Convent, as well as many important extracts from the original manuscripts so destroyed and which had been transcribed by order of the Doge, Marco Foscarini, a few years before.

FRANCESE LITCHFIELD TURNBULL.

La-Paix, June, 1900.

PRELUDE

Venice, with her life and glory but a memory, is still the *citta nobilissima*,—a city of moods,—all beautiful to the beauty-lover, all mystic to the dreamer; between the wonderful blue of the water and the sky she floats like a mirage—visionary—unreal—and under the spell of her fascination we are not critics, but lovers. We see the pathos, not the scars of her desolation, and the splendor of her past is too much a part of her to be forgotten, though the gold is dim upon her palace-fronts, and the sheen of her precious marbles has lost its bloom, and the colors of the laughing Giorgione have faded like his smile.

But the very soul of Venetia is always hovering near, ready to be invoked by those who confess her charm. When, under the glamor of her radiant skies the faded hues flash forth once more, there is no ruin nor decay, nor touch of conquering hand of man nor time, only a splendid city of dreams, waiting in silence—as all visions wait—until that invisible, haunting spirit has turned the legends of her power into actual activities.

THE GOLDEN BOOK
OF VENICE

THE GOLDEN BOOK
OF VENICE

SEA and sky were one glory of warmth and color
this sunny November morning in 1565, and
there were signs of unusual activity in the Campo
San Rocco before the great church of Santa Maria
Gloriosa dei Frari, which, if only brick without,
was all glorious within, "in raiment of needle-
work" and "wrought gold." And outside, the deli-
cate tracery of the cornice was like a border of
embroidery upon the sombre surface; the sculp-
tured marble doorway was of surpassing richness,
and the airy grace of the campanile detached it-
self against the entrancing blue of the sky, as one
of those points of beauty for which Venice is
memorable.

Usually this small square, remote from the cen-
tres of traffic as from the homes of the nobility,
seemed scarcely more than a landing-place for the
gondolas which were constantly bringing visitors
and worshippers thither, as to a shrine; for this
church was a sort of memorial abbey to the illus-

trious dead of Venice,—her Doges, her generals, her artists, her heads of noble families,—and the monuments were in keeping with all its sumptuous decorations, for the Frati Minori of the convent to which it belonged—just across the narrow lane at the side of the church—were both rich and generous, and many of its gifts and furnishings reflected the highest art to which modern Venice had attained. Between the wonderful, mystic, Eastern glory of San Marco, all shadows and symbolisms and harmonies, and the positive, realistic assertions, æsthetic and spiritual, of the Frari, lay the entire reach of the art and religion of the Most Serene Republic.

The church was ancient enough to be a treasure-house for the historian, and it had been restored, with much magnificence, less than a century before, —which was modern for Venice,—while innumerable gifts had brought its treasures down to the days of Titian and Tintoret.

To-day the people were coming in throngs, as to a *festa*, on foot from under the Portico di Zen, across the little marble bridge which spanned the narrow canal; on foot also from the network of narrow paved lanes, or *calle*, which led off into a densely populated quarter; for to-day the people had free right of entrance, equally with those others who came in gondolas, liveried and otherwise, from more distant and aristocratic neighborhoods. This pleasant possibility of entrance sufficed for the crowd at large, who were not learned, and who preferred the attractions of the outside show to the philosophical debate which was the cause of all this agreeable excitement, and which was presently to take place in the great church before a vast assembly of nobles and clergy and representatives from the Universities of Padua, Mantua, and Bologna; and outside, in the glowing sunshine, with the strangers and the confusion, the shifting sounds and lights, the ceaseless unlading of gondolas and massing and changing of colors, every minute was a realization of the people's ideal of happiness.

Brown, bare-legged boys flocked from San Pantaleone and the people's quarters on the smaller canals, remitting, for the nonce, their absorbing pastimes of crabbing and petty gambling, and ragged and radiant, stretched themselves luxuriously along the edge of the little quay, faces downward, emphasizing their humorous running commentaries with excited movements of the bare, upturned feet; while the gondoliers landed their passengers to a lively refrain of "*Stali!*"· their curses and appeals to the Madonna blending not discordantly with the general babel of sound which gives such a sense of companionship in Venice—human voices calling in ceaseless interchange from shore to shore, resonant in the brilliant atmosphere, quarrels softened to melodies across the water, cries of the gondoliers telling of ceaseless motion, the constant lap and plash of the wavelets and the drip of the oars making a soothing undertone of content.

From time to time staccato notes of delight added a distinct jubilant quality to this symphony, heralding the arrival of some group of Church dignitaries from one or other of the seven principal parishes of Venice, gorgeous in robes of high festival

3

and displaying the choicest of treasures from sacristies munificently endowed, as was meet for an ecclesiastical body to whom belonged one half of the area of Venice, with wealth proportionate.

Frequent delegations from the lively crowd of the populace—flashing with repartee, seemly or unseemly, as they gathered close to the door just under the marble slab with its solemn appeal to reverence, "Rispettati la Casa di Dio"—penetrated into the Frari to see where the more pleasure could be gotten, as also to claim their right to be there; for this pageant was for the people also, which they did not forget, and their good-humored ripple of comment was tolerant, even when most critical. But outside one could have all of the festa that was worth seeing, with the sunshine added,—the glorious sunshine of this November day, cold enough to fill the air with sparkle,—and the boys, at least, were sure to return to the free enjoyment impossible within.

A group of young nobles, in silken hose and velvet mantles, were met with ecstatic approval and sallies deftly personal. Since the beginning of the Council of Trent, which was still sitting, philosophy had become the mode in Venice, and had grown to be a topic of absorbing interest by no means confined to Churchmen; and young men of fashion took courses of training in the latest and most intellectual accomplishment.

Confraternities of every order were arriving in stately processions, their banners borne before them by gondoliers gaudy and awkward in sleazy white tunics, with brilliant cotton sashes—habiliments

which possessed a singular power of relieving these
sun-browned sons of the lagoon of every vestige of
their native grace. On such days of Church festival
—and these alone—they might have been mistaken
for peasants of some prosaic land, instead of the
graceful, free-born Venetians that they were, as,
with no hint of their natural rhythm of motion, they
filed in cramped and orderly procession through the
avenue that opened to them in the crowd to the door
of the church, where they disappeared behind the
great leather curtain.

It was a great day for the friars of the Servi,
who were rivals of the Frari both in learning and
splendor, and the entire Servite Brotherhood, black-
robed and white-cowled, was just coming in sight
over the little marble bridge, preceded by youthful
choristers, chanting as they came and bearing with
them that famous banner which had been sent them
as a gift from their oldest chapter of San Annun-
ziata in Florence, and which was the early work of
Raphael.

A small urchin, leaning far over the edge of the
quay and craning his neck upward for a better view,
reported some special attraction in this approaching
group which elicited yells of vociferous greeting
from his colleagues, with such forceful emphasis of
his own curling, expressive toes, that he lost his bal-
ance and rolled over into the water; from which he
was promptly rescued by a human ladder, dexter-
ously let down to him in sections, without a mo-
ment's hesitation, by his allies, who, like all Vene-
tian boys of the populace, were amphibious animals,
full of pranks.

5

But now there was no more time for fooling on the quay, for at the great end-window of the library of the convent of the Frari it could be seen that a procession of this body was forming and would presently enter the church, and the fun would begin for those who understood Latin.

A round-faced friar was giving obliging information. The contest would be between the Frari and the Servi; there was a new brother who had just entered their order,—and very learned, it was said,—but the name was not known. He would appear to respond to the propositions of the Frari.

"Yes, the theses would be in Latin—and harder, it was said, had never been seen. There were the theses in one of those black frames, at the side of the great door."

"But Latin is no good, except in missals, for women and priests to read."

The gondolier who owned the voice was undiscoverable among the crowd, and the remark passed with some humorous retaliation.

Hints of the day's entertainment sifted about, with much more,—each suggestion, true or otherwise, waking its little ripple of interest,—as some nearest the curtain lifted it up, went in, and returned, bringing reports.

"The church is filled with great ones, and Mass is going on," a small scout reported; "and that was Don Ambrogio Morelli that just went in with a lady—our old Abbé from the school at San Marcuolo—Beppo goes there now! And don't some of us remember Pierino—always studying and good for nothing, and not knowing enough to wade out of a *rio?* The Madonna will have hard work to look after *him!*"

"Don Ambrogio just wants to cram us boys," Beppo confessed, in a confidential tone; "but it's no use knowing too much, even for a priest. For once, at San Marcuolo—true as true, faith of the Madonna!—one of those priests told the people one day in his sermon that there were no ghosts!"

The boy crossed himself and drew a quick breath, which increased the interest of his auditors.

"Ebbene!" he continued, in an impressive, awestruck whisper. "He had to come out of his bed at night—Santissima Maria!—and it was the ghosts of all the people buried in San Marcuolo who dragged him and kicked him to teach him better, because he wanted to make believe the dead stayed in their graves! So where was the use of his Latin?"

"Pierino will be like his uncle, the Abbé Morelli, some day; they say he also will be a priest."

"I believe thee," said Beppo, earnestly; "and that was he going in behind the banner, with the Servi."

The little fellows made an instant rush for the door, and squeezed themselves in behind the poor old women of the neighborhood for whom festivals were perquisites, and who, maimed or deformed, knelt on the stone floor close to the entrance, while with keenly observant, ubiquitous eyes they proffered their *aves* and their petitions for alms with the same exemplary patience and fervor—"Per l'amor di Dio, Signori!"

The body of the church, from the door to the great white marble screen of the choir and from

7

column to column, was filled with an assembly in which the brilliant and scholarly elements predominated; and seen through the marvelous fretwork of this screen of leafage and scroll and statue and arch, intricately wrought and enhanced with gilding, the choir presented an almost bewildering pageant. The dark wood background of the stalls and canopies, elaborately carved and polished and enriched with mosaics, each surmounted with its benediction of a gilded winged cherub's head, framed a splendid figure in sacerdotal robes. Through the small, octagonal panes of the little windows encircling the choir—row upon row, like an antique necklace of opals set in frosted stonework—the sunlight slanted in a rainbow mist, broken by splashes of yellow flame from great wax candles in immense golden candlesticks, rising from the floor and steps of the altar, as from the altar itself. From great brass censers, swinging low by exquisite Venetian chainwork, fragrant smoke curled upward, crossing with slender rays of blue the gold webwork of the sunlight; and on either side golden lanterns rose high on scarlet poles, above the heads of the friars who crowded the church.

On the bishop's throne, surrounded by the bishops of the dioceses of Venice, sat the Patriarch, who had been graciously permitted to honor this occasion, as it had no political significance; and opposite him Fra Marco Germano, the head of the order of the Frari, presided in a state scarcely less regal.

His splendid gift, the masterpiece of Titian, had

been fitted into the polished marble framework over the great altar, and never had the master so excelled himself as in this glorious "Assumption." The beauty, the power, the persuasive sense of motion in the figure of the Madonna, which seemed divinely upborne,—the loveliness of the infant cherubs, the group of the Apostles solemnly attesting the mysterious event,—were singularly and inimitably impressive, full of aspiration and faith, compelling the serious recognition of the sacredness and greatness of the Christian mystery.

The choir-screen terminated in pulpits at either side, and here again the Apostles stood in solemn guardianship on its broad parapet—but emblems, rather, of the stony rigidity of doctrines which have been shaped by the minds of men from some little phase of truth, than of that glowing, spiritualized, human sympathy which, as the soul of man grows upward into comprehension, is the apostle of an ever widening truth. And over the richly sculptured central arch which forms the entrance to the choir, against the incongruous glitter of gold and jewels and magnificent garments and lights and sumptuous, overwrought details—the very extravagance of the Renaissance—a great black marble crucifix bore aloft the most solemn Symbol of the Christian Faith.

The religious ceremonial with which the festival had opened was over, and down the aisles on either side, past the family altars, with their innumerable candles and lanterns and censers,—ceaselessly smoking in memorial of the honored dead,—the brothers of the Frari and the Servi marched in solemn procession to the chant of the acolytes, returning to mass themselves in the transepts, in fuller view of the pulpits, before the contest began. The Frari had taken their position on the right, under the elaborate hanging tomb of Fra Pacifico—a mass of sculpture, rococo, and gilding; the incense rising from the censer swinging below the coffin of the saint carried the eye insensibly upward to the grotesque canopy, where cumbrous marble clouds were compacted of dense masses of saints' and cherubs' heads with uncompromising golden halos.

Some of the younger brothers scattered leaflets containing heads of the theses.

There was a stir among the crowd; a few went out, having witnessed the pageant; but there was a flutter of increased interest among those who remained, as a venerable man, in the garb of the Frari, mounted the pulpit on the right.

The Abbé Morelli sat in an attitude of breathless interest, and now a look of intense anxiety crossed his face. "It is Fra Teodoro, the ablest disputant of the Frari!" he exclaimed. "The trial is too great."

The lady with him drew closer, arranging the folds of the ample veil which partially concealed her face, so that she might watch more closely. But it was on Don Ambrogio Morelli that she fixed her gaze with painful intensity, reading the success or failure of the orator in her brother's countenance.

"Ambrogio!" she entreated, when the argument had been presented and received with every sign of triumph that the sacredness of the place made decorous, "thou knowest that I have no understanding of the Latin—was it unanswerable?"

"Nay," her brother answered, uneasily; "it was fine, surely; but have no fear, Fra Teodoro is not incontrovertible, and the Servi have better methods."

"May one ask the name of the disputant who is to respond?" a stranger questioned courteously of Don Ambrogio.

"It is a brother who hath but entered their order yesterday," Don Ambrogio answered, with some hesitation, "by name Pierino—nay, Fra Paolo. He is reputed learned; yet if the methods of the order be strange to him, one should grant indulgence. For he is reputed learned——"

He was conscious of repeating the words for his own encouragement, with a heart less brave than he could have wished. But the information was pleasantly echoed about, as the ranks of the Servi parted and an old man, with a face full of benignity, came forward, holding the hand of a boy with blue eyes and light hair, who walked timidly with him to the pulpit on the left, where the older man encouraged the shrinking disputant to mount the stair.

There was a murmur of astonishment as the young face appeared in the tribunal of that grave assembly.

"Impossible! It is only a child!"

It was, in truth, a strange picture; this child of thirteen, small and delicate for his years, yet with a face of singular freshness and gravity, his youthfulness heightened by cassock and cowl—a unique, simple figure, against the bizarre magnificence of

II

the background, the central point of interest for that learned and brilliant assembly, as he stood there above the beautiful kneeling angel who held the Book of the Law, just under the pulpit.

For a moment he seemed unable to face his audience, then, with an effort, he raised his hand, nervously pushing back the white folds of his unaccustomed cowl, and casting a look of perplexity over the sea of faces before him; but the expression of trouble slowly cleared away as his eyes met those of a friar, grave and bent, who had stepped out from the company of the Servi and fixed upon the boy a steadying gaze of assurance, triumph, and command. It was Fra Gianmaria, who was known throughout Venice for his great learning.

"Pierino!" broke from the mother, in a tone of quick emotion, as she saw her boy for the first time in the dress of his order, which thrust, as it were, the claims of her motherhood quite away; it was so soon to surrender all the beautiful romance of mother and child, so soon to have done with the joy of watching the development which had long outstripped her leadership, so soon to consent to the absolute parting of the ways!

She had not willed it so, and she was weary from the struggle.

But the boy was satisfied; the presence of his stern and learned mentor sufficed to restore his composure; he did not even see his mother's face so near him, piteous in its appeal for a single glance to confess his need of her.

"Nay, have no fear," Don Ambrogio counseled, his face glowing with pride; "the boy is a wonder."

The good Fra Giulio, turning back from the pulpit stairs, saw the faces of the two whose hearts were hanging on the words of the child; he went directly to them and sat down beside Donna Isa-. bella, for he had a tender heart and he guessed her trouble. "I also," he said, leaning over her and speaking low, "I also love the boy, and while I live will I care for him. He shall lack for nothing."

It was a promise of great comfort; for Pierino—she could not call him by the new name—would need such loving care; already the mother's pulse beat more tranquilly, and she almost smiled her gratitude in the large-hearted friar's face.

Then Fra Gianmaria, his mentor, seeing that the boy had gained courage, came also to a seat beside Donna Isabella, with a look of radiant congratulation; for he had been the boy's teacher ever since the little lad had passed beyond the limits of Don Ambrogio's modest attainments. Although she had resented the power of Fra Gianmaria over Pierino, she was proud of the confidence of the learned friar in her child; already she began to teach herself to accept pride in the place of the lowlier, happier, daily love she must learn to do without. Her face grew colder and more composed; Don Ambrogio gave her a nod of approval.

"It *is* Pierino!" the bare-legged Beppo proclaimed, pushing his way between dignitaries and elegant nobles and taking a position, in wide-eyed astonishment, in front of the pulpit, where he could watch every movement of his quondam school-fellow, whose words carried no meaning to his unlearned ears. But his heart throbbed with sudden loyalty in seeing his comrade the centre of such a festa; Beppo would stay and help him to get fair play, if he should need it, since it was well known that Pierino could not fight, for all his Latin!

But the little fellow in robe and cowl had neither eyes nor thoughts for his vast audience when he once gathered courage to begin—no memory for the pride of his teachers, no perception of his mother's yearning; shrinking and timid as he was, the first voicing of his own thought, in his childish treble voice, put him in presence of a problem and banished all other consciousness. It was merely a question to be met and answered, and his wonderful reasoning faculty stilled every other emotion. His voice grew positive as his thought asserted itself; his learning was a mystery, but argument after argument was met and conquered with the quoted wisdom of unanswerable names.

One after another the great men left the choir and came down into the area before the pulpits, that they might lose nothing.

One after another the Frari chose out champions to confute the child-philosopher, but he was armed on every side; and the childish face, the boyish manner and voice lent a wonderful charm to the words he uttered, which were not eloquent, but absolutely dispassionate and reasonable, and the fewest by which he might prove his claim.

Again and again his audience forgot themselves in murmurs of applause, rising beyond decorum, and once into a storm of approbation; then his timidity returned, he became self-conscious, fumbling with the white cowl that hung partly over his face,

14

forgetting that it was not a hat, and gravely taking it off in salute.

The next day it was proclaimed on the Piazza, as a bit of news for the people of Venice—for which, indeed, those who had not witnessed the contest in the church of the Frari cared little and understood nothing—that "in the Philosophical Contest which had taken place between the Friars of the Frari and the Friars of the Servi, the victory had been won by Fra Paolo Sarpi, of the Servi, who had honorably triumphed through his vast understanding of the wisdom of the Fathers of the Church."

This was also published in the black frame beside the great door of the Frari and posted upon the entrance to the church of the Servi, while in the refectories of the respective convents it formed a theme of absorbing interest.

The Frari discussed the possibilities of childish mouthpieces for learned doctors, miraculously concealed—but low, for fear of scandal. The Servi said it out, for all to hear, "that it was a modern wonder of a Child in the Temple!"

But Fra Gianmaria hushed them, and was afraid; for often while he taught he came upon some new surprise, for he perceived that the boy's mind held some hidden spring of knowledge which was to him unfathomable.

"It is most wonderful," he said one evening to Fra Giulio, as they talked together in the cloister after vespers; "I solemnly declare that it hath happened to me to ask him a question of which I, verily, knew not the answer; and he, keeping in quiet thought for some moments, hath so lucidly responded that his words have carried with them the conviction that he had made a discovery which I knew not."

"It is some lesson which Don Ambrogio hath taught him."

"Not so—for Don Ambrogio hath little learning; but Paolo will cover us with honor. In learning he is never weary, yet hath he an understanding greater than mine own, and in docility he hath no equal. In his duty in the convent and in the church he is even more punctilious."

"Is it strange—or is it well," asked Fra Giulio with hesitation, "that in this year he hath spent with us he asks not for his mother, nor the little maid his sister, nor seemeth to grieve for them? For the boy is young."

"Nay," answered Fra Gianmaria, sternly; "it is no lack, but a grace that hath been granted him."

"Knowledge is a wonderful mystery," Fra Giulio answered; but softly to himself, as he crossed the cloister, he added, "but love is sweet, and the boy is very young."

The boy was kneeling placidly before the crucifix in his cell when Fra Giulio went to give him his nightly benediction; but the good friar's heart was troubled with tenderness because of a vision, that would not leave him, of a hungering mother's face.

II

MANY years later one of the great artists of
Venice, wandering about at sunset with an
elusive vision of some wonderful picture stirring
impatience within his soul, found a maiden sitting
under the vine-covered pergola of the Traghetto
San Maurizio, where she was waiting for her
brother-in-law, who would presently touch at this
ferry on his homeward way to Murano. A little
child lay asleep in her arms, his blond head, which
pitying Nature had kept beautiful, resting against
her breast; the meagre body was hidden beneath
the folds of her mantle, which, in the graceful fash-
ion of those days, passed over her head and fell
below the knees; her face, very beautiful and ten-
der, was bent over the little sufferer, who had for-
gotten his pain in the weariness it had brought him
as a boon.

The delicate purple bells of the vine upon the
trellis stirred in the evening breeze, making a shim-
mer of perfume and color about her, like a sugges-
tion of an aureole; and in the arbor, as in one of
those homely shrines which everywhere make part
of the Venetian life, she seemed aloof as some ideal
of an earlier Christian age from the restless, voluble
group upon the tiny quay.

There were *facchini*—those doers of nondescript

smallest services, quarreling amiably to pass the time, springing forward for custom as the gondolas neared the steps; *gransieri*—the licensed traghetto beggars, ragged and picturesque, pushing past with their long, crooked poles, under pretence of drawing the gondolas to shore; one or two women from the islands, filling the moments with swift, declamatory speech until the gondola of Giambattista or of Jacopo should close the colloquy; an older peasant, tranquilly kneeling to the Madonna of the traghetto, amid the clatter, while steaming greasy odors from her housewifely basket of Venetian dainties mount slowly, like some travesty of incense, and cloud the humble shrine. Two or three comers swell the group from the recesses of the dark little shop behind, for no other reason than that life is pleasant where so much is going on; and some maiden, into whose life a dawning romance is just creeping, confesses it with a brighter color as she hangs, half-timidly, her bunch of tinselled flowers before the red lamp of the good little Madonna of this *traghetto benedetto*, whose gondoliers are the bravest in all Venice! Meanwhile the boatmen, coming, going, or waiting, keep up a lively chatter.

And under the trellis, as if far removed, the sleeping child and Marina of Murano bending over him a face glorified with its story of love and compassion, are like a living Rafaello!

"The *bambino* is beautiful," said the artist, drawing nearer, but speaking reverently, for he knew that he had found the face he had been seeking for his Madonna for the altar of the Servi. "What doth he like, your little one? For I am a friend to the *bambini*, and the *poverina* hath pain to bear."

She was more beautiful still when she smiled and the anxiety died out of her girlish face for a moment, in gratitude for the sympathy. "Eccellenza, thanks," she answered simply; "he has a beautiful face. Sometimes when he has flowers in his little hand he smiles and is quite still."

But the radiant look passed swiftly with the remembrance of the pain that would come to the child on waking, and she kissed the tiny fingers that lay over the edge of her mantle with a movement of irrepressible tenderness, lapsing at once into reverie; while the artist, full of the enthusiasm of creation, stood dreaming of his picture. This Holy Mother should be greater, more compassionate, nearer to the people than any Madonna he had ever painted; for never had he noted in any face before such a passion of love and pity. In that moment of stillness the sunset lights, intensifying, cast a glow about her; the child, half-waking, stretched up his tiny hand and touched her cheek with a rare caress, and the light in her face was a radiance never to be forgotten. The Veronese's wonderful *Madonna del Sorriso* leaped to instant life; a *smile* full of the pathos of human suffering, tender in comprehension, perfect in faith—this, which this moment of inspiration had revealed to him, would he paint for the consolation of those who should kneel before the altar of the Servi!

She was busy with the child, putting him gently on the ground as a gondola approached; he, with his thought in intense realization, fixing the peculiar beauty of these sunset clouds in his artist memory as sole color-scheme of his picture; for this grave, sweet face, with its pale, fair tones and profusion of soft brown hair, would not bear the vivid draperies that the Veronese was wont to fashion—the mantle must be a gray cloud, pink flushed, with delicate sunset borderings where it swept away to shroud the child; the beauty of his creation should be in that smile of exquisite compassion, and this wonderful sunset in which it should glow forever!

It was a rare moment with the Veronese, in which he seemed lifted above himself; the revelation of the face had seized him, translating him into the poetic atmosphere which he rarely attained; the harmonies of the vision were so perfect that they sufficed for the over-sumptuousness of color and detail which were usually features of his conceptions.

Some one called impatiently from the gondola in rude, quick tones, and the artist woke from his reverie. The maiden lingered on the step for a word of adieu to this stranger who wished to give the little one pleasure, but she dared not disturb him, for he was some great signor—so she interpreted his dress and bearing—and she was only a maiden of Murano.

He was still under the spell of his great moment, and he was in the presence of one who should help him to make it immortal; he uncovered his head with a motion of courtly deference he did not often assume as he started forward over the rough planks of the traghetto. "Signora, where shall I bring the flowers to make the little one smile?"

"To Murano, near the Stabilimento Magagnati,

Eccellenza," she answered without hesitation, lifting the baby in her arms to escape the rough help of the gondolier, who reached forward to hasten his stumbling movements.

And so they floated off from the traghetto—the Madonna that was to be, into the deepening twilight, while the Veronese, a splendid and incongruous figure amid these lowly surroundings, leaned against the paltry column that supported the shrine, wrapped in a delicious reverie of creation; for he was unused to failure and he had no doubts, though he had not yet proffered his request.

"To-morrow," he said, "I will paint that face!"

.   .   .   .

"By our Lady of Murano!" the gondolier cried suddenly.   "He spoke to thee like a queen—and it was Paolo Cagliari!   What did he want with thee?"

"Not me, Piero; it was the child.   He wished to give him flowers.   I knew he must be great to care thus for our 'bimbo.'   It was really he—the Veronese?"

"The child!   Santa Maria!   He is not too much like a cherub that the great painter should notice him!"

The baby threw out his little clenched fist, striking against the protecting arms that held him closer, his face drawn with sudden pain; for a moment he fought against Marina, and then, the spasm over, settled wearily to sleep in her arms.

"Poverino!" said the gondolier softly, while Marina crooned over him an Ave Maria, and the gondola glided noiselessly to its cadence.

"Piero," she said, looking up with eyes full of

tears, "sometimes I think I cannot bear it! He needs thy prayers as well as mine—wilt thou not ask our Lady of San Donato to be kinder to him? And I have seen to-day, on the Rialto, a beautiful lamp, with angels' heads. Thou shouldst make an offering——"

The gondolier shook his head and shrugged his shoulders; he had little faith or reverence. "I will say my aves, *poveriello*," he promised; "but the lamps are already too many in San Donato. And for the bambino, I will go not only once, but twice this year to confession—the laws of our traghetto ask not so much, since once is enough. But thou art even stricter with thy rules for me."

She did not answer, and they floated on in silence.

"To-morrow," said Piero at length, "there is festa in San Pietro di Castello."

She moved uneasily, and her beautiful face lost its softness.

"It is nothing to me," she answered shortly.

"It is a pretty festa, and Messer Magagnati should take thee. By our Lady of Castello, there are others who will go!"

"It would be better for the bambino," he persisted sullenly, as she did not answer him. His voice was not the pleasanter now that its positive tone was changed to a coaxing one.

"One is enough, Piero," she said. "And for the festa of San Pietro in Castello—never, *never* name it to me!"

"Santa Maria!" her companion ejaculated under his breath; "it is the women, the gentle *donzelle*, who are hard!"

He stood, tall, handsome, well-made, swaying lightly with the motion of the gondola, which seemed to float as in a dream to the ripple and lap of the water; the blue of his shirt had changed to gray in the twilight, the black cap and sash of the "Nicolotti" accentuated the lines of the strong, lithe figure as he sprang forward on the sloping footrest of his gondola with that perfect grace and ease which proved him master of a craft whose every motion is a. harmony. If he were proud of belonging to the Nicolotti, that most powerful faction of the populace, he knew that they were regarded by the government as the aristocrats of the people.

Marina arranged the child's covering in silence, and stooped her face wistfully to touch his cheek, but she did not turn her head to look at the man behind her.

"L'amor zé fato per chi lo sa fare,"

he sang in the low, slow chant of the familiar folksong, the rhythm blending perfectly with the movement of the boat in which these two were faring. His voice was pleasanter in singing, and song is almost a needful expression of the content of motion in Venice—the necessary complement of life to the gondolier, a song might mean nothing more. But Piero sang more slowly than his wont, charging the words with meaning, yet it did not soften her.

"Love is for him who knows how to win!"

He could not see how she flushed and paled with anger as he sang, for it was growing dark over the water and her face was turned from him; but she straightened herself uncompromisingly, and he was watching with subtle comprehension.

He could not have told why he persisted in this strange wooing, for there had been but one response during the two years of his widowhood, while his child had been Marina's ceaseless càre. Marina had loved the baby the more passionately, perhaps, for the sake of her only sister Toinetta, Piero's child-bride, who had died at the baby's birth, because she was painfully conscious that Toinetta's little flippant life had needed much forgiveness and had been crowned with little gladness. Marina was now the only child of Messer Girolamo Magagnati, which was a patent of nobility in Murano; and she was not the less worth winning because she held herself aloof from the freer life of the Piazza, where she was called the "donzel of Murano," though there were others with blacker eyes and redder cheeks. Piero did not think her very beautiful; he liked more color and sparkle and quickness of retort—a chance to quarrel and forgive. He was not in sympathy with so many aves, such continual pilgrimages to the cathedral, such brooding over the lives of the saints—above all, he did not like being kept in order, and Marina knew well how to do this, in spite of her quiet ways. But he liked the best for himself, and there was no one like Marina in all Murano. During all this time he had been coming more and more under her sway, changing his modes of living to suit her whims, and the only way of safety for him was to marry her and be master; then she should see how he would rule his house! His own way had always been the right way for him—rules of all orders to the contrary—whether he had been a wandering gondolier, a despised *barcariol toso*, lording it so outrageously over the established traghetti that they were glad to forgive him his bandit crimes and swear him into membership, if only to stop his influence against them; or whether it had been the stealing away of a promised bride, as on that memorable day at San Pietro in Castello, when he had married Toinetta—it was never safe to bear "vendetta" with one so strong and handsome and unprincipled as Piero.

Gabriele, the jilted lover of Toinetta, over whom Piero had triumphed, soon became the husband of another *donzel*, handsomer than Toinetta had been—poor, foolish Toinetta!—and the retributive tragedy of her little life had warmed the sullen Gabriele into a magnanimity that rendered him at least a safe, if a moody and unpleasant, member of the traghetto in which Piero had since become a rising star. A man with a home to keep may not "cast away his chestnuts," and so when Piero, in that masterful way of his, swept everything before him in the traghetto—never asking nor caring who stood for him or against him, but carrying his will whenever he chose to declare it—to set one's self against such a man was truly a useless sort of fret, only a "gnawing of one's chain," in the expressive jargon of the people.

Piero finished his song, and there was a little pause. . They were nearing the long, low line of Murano.

25

"It is not easy," he said, "when women are in the way, 'to touch the sky with one's finger.'"

She turned with a sudden passionate motion as if she would answer him, and then, struggling for control, turned back without a word, drawing the child closer and caressing him until she was calm again. When she raised her head she spoke in a resolute, restrained voice.

"Since thou wilt have it, Piero—listen. And rest thine oar, for we are almost home; and to-night must be quite the end of all this talk. It can never be. Thou hast no understanding of such matters, so I forgive thee for myself. But for Toinetta—I do not think I ever can forgive thee, may the good Madonna help me!"

"There are two in every marriage," Piero retorted sullenly, for he was angry now.

"It is just that—oh, it is just that!" Marina cried, clasping her hands passionately. "Thou art so strong and so compelling, and thou dost not stop for the right of it. She was such a child, she knew no better, poverina! And thou—a man—not for love, nor right, nor any noble thing"—the words came with repressed scorn—"to coax her to it, just for a little triumph! To expose a child to such endless *critica!*"

Only a Venetian of the people could comprehend the full sting of this word, which conveyed the searching, persistent disapproval of an entire class, whose code, if viewed from the moral point of view, was painfully slack, though from its own standard of decorum it was immutable.

"It has been said, once for all—thou dost not forgive."

"It is the last time, for this also, Piero; I meant never to speak of it again, but those words of thine of the festa in San Pietro in Castello made me forget. It came over me quite suddenly, that this is how thou spendest the beautiful, great strength God gave thee to make a leader of thee in real things. But whether it be great or small, or good or ill, thou always wilt have thy way!"

"It 's a poor fool of a fellow that would n't keep himself uppermost, like oil," he cried, hesitating only for a moment between anger and gratification, and choosing the way that ministered to his pride. "Santa Maria! I'll butter thy macaroni with fine cheese every time!"

"Nay, spare thy pains, Piero, and be serious for one moment. There is no *barcariol* in all Venice who hath greater opportunities, but thou must use them well. They spoil thee at the traghetto; and if a man hath his will always, it will either spoil him or make him noble."

"What wouldst thou have me to do?" he questioned sullenly.

"They would be afraid of thee—thou couldst quiet these troubles in the traghetti—thou must use thy strength and thy will for the good of the people. It is terrible to have power and to use it wrongly."

Piero moved back to his place again and took up his oar, throwing himself in position for a forward stroke. "Forget not," he said, poising, "that I need not listen to thee if I do not choose. I may not stay *in casa* Magàgnati—not any more, if thou art always scolding."

"I shall scold—always—until thou dost quiet this disorder of the traghetti," she answered, undaunted.

27

"And thou wilt return; for there is always the bambino."

"If I come back," he said in a softer tone, responding to the appeal for his child, "I must speak of what I will."

"Of all but one thing, Piero;" for it was not possible to misunderstand him, and she was resolute. "If this is not the end I shall speak with my father—and the bambino——"

They were both silent. He knew that no one could ever care for his invalid child as she had done; and all that he owed her and must continue to owe her restrained him under her chiding, for the baby could not live away from her. Sometimes, too, there were moments of strange tenderness within him for this helpless, suffering morsel of humanity that called him "babbo!" He did not know what might happen if the wrath of the redoubtable Magagnati were to be invoked against him, for this quarrel could not be disposed of as those small matters with the gondoliers had invariably been. So far from threatening this before, Marina had hitherto shielded Piero, in her unanswerable way, from everything that might hasten the rupture that seemed always impending between these two dissimilar natures; and Messer Magagnati had two thoughts only, his daughter and his *stabilimento*— the great glass furnaces which were the pride of Venice.

Piero had no suspicion that Marina always touched the best that was in him; he thought she made him weaker, and it was not easy to yield the point that had become a habit. No one else had ever moved him from any purpose, but now he perceived that there would be no reversal of that sentence—that he should continue to come to see his child, and that he must continue to submit to Marina's influence. It was she who had, in some unaccountable way, persuaded him out of his unlawful trade of *barcariol toso*, and had forced his reluctant acceptance of the overtures that were made to him from the Guild of Santa Maria Zobenigo, where he had risen to be one of the *bancáli* or governors, his qualities of force and daring making him useful in this age when lawlessness was on the increase. He was beginning to feel a sense of satisfaction, not all barbaric, in the position he had won among men who had some views of order, and to perceive that there might be a lawful use, almost as pleasant, for those very attributes which had rendered him so formidable a foe outside the pale of traghetto civilization.

"*Ecco!*" he announced, with a slow, sullen emphasis which declared his unwilling surrender, while he plied his oar with quick, wrathful strokes. "It will take more than aves to make a saint of thee! And thou mayst hold thy head too high, looking for better than wheaten bread! But I'm not the man to wear a curb, nor to put up with thorns where I looked for roses! Thou hast no right to mind what chances to me—yet thou hast made me give up the old life."

"Because I knew thou couldst do better. See where thou standest to-day! It is not a little thing to be a governor of the Nicolotti!"

"It is a truth," Piero confessed, "upside down,

and not to boast of, for whoever tries it would wish it less. The bancali are 'like asses who carry wine and drink water,' for the good of the clouts, in days like these."

"I heard them talking to-day, Piero. The *barcarioli tosi* are worse than Turks; one must pay, to suit their whim, in the middle of the Canal Grande, or one may wait long for the landing! And there was a scandal about a friar of San Zanipolo, of whom they had asked a fare for the crossing; I know not the truth of it! And at Santa Sofia the great cross with the beautiful golden lustre is gone, and one says it is the 'tosi.'"

Piero winced, for, to an ancient "toso," or even to a "bancalo" of to-day, such enormities had not the exciting novelty that might have been expected, and Marina had a curious habit of seeming entirely to forget his past when she wished to exact his best of him.

"And Gabriele——"

"Fash not thyself for a man of his measure, that is fitter to 'beat the fishes' like a galley-slave than to serve an honest gondola!" Piero interrupted scornfully.

"But Piero, Gabriele hath sold his license to one worse than he, and there was great talk of quarrels along the Riva, and how that yesterday they sent for Padre Gervasio from San Gregorio to bring the Host to quiet them."

"Ah, the Castellani!" said Piero, with the contempt that was always ready for any mention of this great rival faction of the people whose division into one or other of these factions was absolute.

"But the Nicolotti have their scandal also," Marina asserted, uncompromisingly; "among themselves it is told they break the laws like men not bound by vows! Some say there will be an appeal to the Consiglio."

"Nay," said Piero, with an ominous frown; "the *bancali* and *gastaldi* are enough; we need no bossing by crimson robes."

This question of the traghetti and their abuses had lately grown to large proportions among the people, and it possessed a deep interest for all classes quite apart from the antiquity and picturesqueness of these honorable institutions of the Republic— since all must use the ferries and wish for safety in their water-streets. For centuries these confraternities of gondoliers who presided over the ferries, or traghetti, of Venice had been corporations, self-governing, with officers and endowments recognized by the Republic, and with a standard of gondolier morals admirably defined in their codes—those "Mariegole" which were luxuriously bound and printed, with capitals of vermilion, a page here and there glowing like an illuminated missal with the legend of the patron saint of the traghetto, wherein one might read such admonitions as would make all men wiser.

But of late there had been much unruliness among the younger members of the traghetti, and a growing inability among their officers to cope with increasing difficulties, because of these barcarioli tosi, who lived in open rebellion against this goodly system of law, poaching upon the dearly bought rights of the traghetto gondoliers, yet escaping all taxes.

And because of the abuses which had been gradually undermining the fair reputation of the established orders of the traghetti, the Republic, by slow encroachments upon ancient concessions, was surely reducing their wealth and independence.

"Santa Maria!" Piero ejaculated after a pause, during which his wrath had been growing. "The Consiglio hath its own matters for ruling; the traghetti belong to the people!"

They had reached the little landing of the first long waterway of Murano, where one of the low arcaded houses, with its slender shafts of red Verona marble, was the dwelling of Girolamo Magagnati; the others of this little block of three were used as show-rooms and offices for the great establishment which was connected with them, in the rear, by small courtyards; and the dense smoke of the glass factories always rested over them, although this was the quarter of the aristocrats of Murano.

The buildings looked low and modest if measured by the palaces of the greater city, and their massive marble door- and window-frames increased the impression of gloom. But here and there a portal more ornate, with treble-twisted cords deeply carved, or a window of fourteenth century workmanship relieved the severity of the lines; while in this short arcade, where the houses rose but a storey in height above the square pillars which supported the overhanging fronts, these unexpected columns of rosy marble, delicate and unique, on which the windows seemed to rest, gave singular distinction to these dwellings.

Often the people passing in gondola or bark glanced carelessly into the depth of the open window space framed between those polished marble shafts, for the familiar vision of a wonderful young face, beautiful as a Madonna from some high altar in Venice; often, too, this vision of a maiden bent above a child, with rare golden hair and great eyes full of pain.

There was a little lingering on the landing as they left the gondola; for the baby, waking from his long, refreshing sleep, had claimed his share of petting before the great dark man who tossed him so restfully in his strong arms went away. There was no one who could make the little Zuane laugh like "babbo," though the tremulous, treble echo of the full tones of the gondolier had a pathos for those who listened.

III

THE little Zuane had eaten his supper of *polenta*
and, in the painted cradle which his grand-
father Girolamo had bought for him from under
the arcades of the Piazetta, lay at last asleep, con-
signed to the care of all those saints and guardian
angels who make the little ones their charge, and
who smiled down upon him from the golden aure-
oles and clouds of rose and blue on the cradle-roof
while, slowly balancing, it charmed him into
dreams.

And now, at her window, Marina had the night
and the stars to herself, over the still lagoon and
down in its mirroring depths.

It was a sad little tale soon told, this tragedy
of Toinetta which had seemed so great to the dwell-
ers in that home three years ago. A pretty, wil-
ful child of fifteen, who had grown up impatient
of all needful home restraint, finding rebellion eas-
ier because there was no mother to control her—with
a love of motion, color, sunshine, sound, and laugh-
ter that made her an Ariel of Venice, as full of
frolic as a kitten and as irresponsible, choosing in
her latest caprice one from the many lovers who
were ready for the wooing with the seriousness
with which she would have chosen a partner for a

festa, since to-morrow, if something else seemed better, this lover also could be changed. But the opposition of the grave father and sister made their consent the better worth winning, and set the youthful Gabriele in a more attractive light. So the betrothal had been duly made in the presence of the numerous circle of friends and relatives who stand as witnesses at a betrothal feast in this City of the Sea, and who were as ready with their smiles and their felicitations for any event in the home life of the quarter, as they would be withering in their criticism should there be any failure of complete fulfilment of those traditional observances which are imperative in Venice. Thus the boy and girl were *spoza* and *novizio*, waiting the fuller bond in all that pretty interchange of tokens so faithfully prescribed in Venetian circles of every degree; but the period had been one of quarrels and forgivenesses, of fallings away from and returns to favor, as might have been expected from two capricious, foolish children.

To make part of the pretty pageant of the "Brides of Venice," which took place on Lady Day in San Pietro in Castello, the maidens, all in white with floating hair, their dower-boxes fastened by ribbons from their shoulders, had seemed to Toinetta, as she stood each year an onlooker in the admiring crowd, a happiness devoutly to be desired. The custom was a survival of an earlier time, fast losing favor with the better classes of the people; but to Toinetta its dramatic possibilities held a greater fascination than the more sober ceremonial of the usual wedding service, and, all persuasion to the

contrary, when the procession gathered in San
Pietro in Castello, Toinetta, with flushed cheeks
and sparkling eyes, was one of the twelve maidens.
Marina looked on with offended eyes; her father
consenting, yet only half-convinced, atoning for this
lessening of the family dignity by the elegance of
the feast he had provided, and all permitted bravery
in the gondolas that were waiting to take them
thence.

The ups and downs of her childish courtship had
culminated in more tears and jealousies than usual
on the previous day, but these were secrets between
the lovers, and quite unguessed by father or sister.
But when the wedding oration had been preached
over those twelve bridal pairs, and the wedding
benediction had been granted, it was *not* Gabriele,
the boyish betrothed of Toinetta, who brought the
blushing bride, partly in triumph and partly in
pique, to her father's side, but Piero Salin, the hand-
somest gondolier on the lagoons, the most daring
and dreaded foe of all the established traghetti.
It had been impossible for the spectators from the
body of the church to follow closely the movements
of the twelve white-robed maidens with their at-
tendant swains while the ceremony was progressing
in the dim recesses of the choir, and the surprise
and dishonor this unexpected *dénouement* brought
upon the home were nothing to the unhappiness in
store for the childish bride, whose latest and wild-
est freak brought neither wisdom for self-discipline
nor power to endure that relentless criticism which
ceased only when a little one lay in the place of
the child-mother, who had been too weak to cope

with the worries of the year that had followed upon that unhappy day in San Pietro.

The jilted Gabriele had accepted the situation with a parade of philosophical scorn which removed him beyond the pale of the sympathy Marina would have offered him; and Marina—whose exquisite sense of truth, decorum, and duty had been outraged to a degree beyond Toinetta's comprehension—forgot it all in the overwhelming compassion with which she took her little sister in her arms and tried to help her live her difficult life; she realized, as only a large nature could, that love was the only hope for this emergency, and, feeding on her measureless compassion, love, the diviner faculty, grew to be a power.

Slowly and very dimly she had helped the young wife to some vague comprehension of the duties she had so rashly assumed.   Hitherto, for Toinetta, there had been no difficulties, and now there were so many she was frightened and did not understand; now, when Piero scolded at her tears or temper she could not run away nor change him for a pleasanter companion, and she knew no other way to manage such a difficulty; and there was no pleasure in the Piazza because of that eternal critica. There was triumph still in a *canalazzo*, for Piero was so handsome and so strong, and in the gondola, on the Canal Grande, one could not hear the talking—besides, Venice was not Murano; but in the home the old friends came no more, and life was very sad—quite other than it used to be!

Even her father, who traced the disgrace that had come upon his house to his over-indulgence, was now proportionately severe, and to his stern sense of honor the lawless son-in-law was a most unwelcome guest. Through that slow year of Toinetta's life Marina was the veritable angel in the house, not conscious of any self-sacrifice, but only of living intensely, making the living under the same roof possible for these two strong men who looked at life from such different standpoints, soothing the wounded pride of her father by her perfect sympathy while striving to rouse Piero to nobler ideals.

And now that it was all over—was it all over?—there lay the poor little Zuane; and Piero, over the water at his traghetto, was a great care. But he should do his best yet for the people!

A deep voice with a ring of wistfulness came through the darkness:

"Doth he not sleep yet, the little Zuane? The evening hath been long, and I have somewhat to show thee."

"I come, my father," she answered very tenderly, as she followed him through the narrow, dark corridor, into a large chamber which served as a private office, but where the father and daughter often sat alone in the evening; for here Girolamo kept many designs and papers relating to his work, and they often discussed his plans together.

He unlocked an old carved cabinet and brought out a roll of parchments, spreading them upon the table and explaining: "I could not leave them while I went to call thee, for it is an order from the Senate—thou see'st the seal—and a copy of the letter of the Ambassador of the Republic to the Levant, with this folded therein—truly a curious scheme of

38

color, but very rich, and the lines are somewhat uneven. What thinkest thou of the design?"

"The outline is good," she answered, after a careful scrutiny, for she had been trained in copying his best designs. This was a pattern furnished by the grand vizier of the sultan for a mosque lamp of a peculiar shape, wrought over with verses from the Koran, in various colored enamels. "The outline is well; but the colors—mayst thou not change this yellow? there is too much of it."

"Nay, for the colors have a meaning; methinks this yellow is their sacred color. But the texts are fine; the broken lines of the characters have a charm, and the scrolls relieve the surface, making semblance of shadow. Yet I will make thee a prettier one for thine own chamber, with some thought of thy choosing."

She looked up at him with shining eyes; their trouble, combated and borne together, had brought them very near to one another.

"I have often wished for a lamp with the colors soft like moonlight; and the design shall be of thine own hand, and the verse upon it shall be an ave, and in it there shall be always a light. It shall be a prayer for the little one!" she said in quick response. "The Senate wished thee to make a lamp of this design? I have seen none like it."

"Nay, not one; there will be nine hundred, for the decoration of a mosque," and Girolamo's eyes sparkled with triumph. "It is not that it is difficult," he explained, for Marina's eyes wandered from her father's face to the design with some astonishment. "It is even simple for us. But when the Levant sends to Venice for these sacred lamps for her own temples it is her acknowledgment that we have surpassed our teachers. It is a glory for us!"

"Father, I thought the glass of Venice was even all our own!" Marina exclaimed in a tone of disappointment. "I knew not that our art had come from the East to us. Some say that it was born here."

"Ay, some; but thou shouldst know the story of thy Venice better, my daughter," Girolamo answered gravely, for to him every detail connected with his art was of vital import. "There may be some who say this, but not thou. In the time of Orseolo the mosaics were brought from the Levant for our old San Marco. Thus came the knowledge to us in those early days. But now there is no longer any country that shares it equally with Venice, for elsewhere they know not the art in its fineness. These, when they are finished, shall be sent as a gift from the Republic; it is so written in this order from the Senate."

"When came it to thee?"

"To-day, with much ceremony, it was delivered into mine own hand by one of the Secretaries of the Ten. For, see'st thou, Marina, it is a mark of rare favor that they have trusted this parchment with me, and have not brought me into their presence to make copy of it in the palace. If thou couldst lend me thy deft fingers——"

"Surely," she answered, smiling up at him.

He was standing over her with one hand on her shoulder; he rested the other lightly on her hair, looking down into her eyes for a moment with a caress still and tender, after his own grave fashion. "It will be safer so," he said, folding the parchment and the letters carefully and locking them away in his cabinet. "And to-morrow, Marina—for they have granted me but one day."

The chamber in which they sat was wainscoted with heavy carved woodwork stained black, and every panel was a drawer with a curiously wrought lock, containing some design or some order for the house of Magagnati; and these archives were precions not only for the stabilimento and Girolamo the master, but they would be treasured by the Republic as state papers, representing the highest attainment in this exquisite Venetian industry, which the Government held in such esteem that for a century past one of the chiefs of the Council of Ten had been appointed as inspector and supervisor of the manufactories. For further security the Senate had declared severest penalties against any betrayal of the secrets of the trade—a form of protection not quite needless, since the Ambassador of His Most Christian Majesty had formed a species of secret police with no other object than to bribe the glass-makers and extract from them the lucrative secret which formed no part of the courtesies that were interchanged between France and the Republic.

The large, low table, black and polished like teakwood, upon which they had been examining the vizier's design, was lighted by a lamp of wrought iron swinging low by fanciful chains from the high ceiling, making a centre of dense yellow flame from which the shadows rayed off into the gloom of the farther portions of the room, and a charming picture of father and daughter was outlined against the vague darkness. Another lamp, fixed against a plate of burnished brass, cast a reflection that was almost brilliant upon the glory of this chamber—a high, central cabinet of the same dark, carved framework, with a back of those wonderful mirror plates so recently brought to perfection by another stabilimento of which the good Girolamo was almost jealous, although against this luminous background the exquisite fabrications of the house of Magagnati reflected their wonderful shapes and colors in increased beauty.

Not yet had any plates of clear glass fine enough for the display of such a cabinet been realized, though it sometimes seemed to Girolamo that such a time was very near; but the solid doors of wood, with ponderous brass locks and hinges, stood open, and the inner silk curtain which protected these treasures from dust was always drawn aside by Marina's own hand when these evening lamps were lighted; they were so beautiful to see, if they but raised their eyes; the very consciousness of their gleaming was sometimes an inspiration to Girolamo, and at this hour they were quite safe, for the working day was over, and no one entered this sanctum save by invitation.

Girolamo Magagnati prided himself on being a Venetian of the people, and it was true that no member of his family had ever sat in the Consiglio; but in few of the patrician homes of Venice could more of what was then counted among the comforts of life have been found than in this less sumptuous house of Murano, while its luxuries were all such as centered about his art.   He was one of the magnates of his island, for his furnaces were among the most famous of Murano, and to him belonged secrets of the craft in his special field to which no others had yet attained, while in a degree that would scarcely have been esteemed by the merchant princes of Venice, who sat in the Consiglio, they had brought him wealth and repute.   But to him, whose heart was in his work, it was power and glory that sufficed.   No stranger whom it was desired to honor came to Venice but was conducted, with a ceremony that was flattering, while it was also a due precaution against too curious questioning, through the show-rooms of the factories of Murano; and often in this chamber had gathered a group of men whom the world called great, led by that special Chief of the Ten who was then in power at Murano, to see the treasures of this cabinet of which Girolamo was justly proud.

This first bit of the wonderful coloring which glowed and flashed when the light shot through it, as if some living fire were caught in its heart; or that curious, tortured shape, with its dragon-eyes of jewels, and its tongue forever thrusting at you some secret which it almost utters, yet withholds; this fragment of tenderest opalescence which is of no color, yet blending all, as if a shower of petals were blown across a rainbow in spring; that one—frosted in silver and gold—pink, with the yellow sunshine in its core; here the aquamarine, lucent as Venice's own sea!   And here, throned in regal state, in its quaint case of faded azure velvet, is that very masterpiece of the glass-workers of Murano which was carried in the first solemn procession of all the arts at a Doge's triumph in the thirteenth century. Its very possession was a patent of nobility in Girolamo's reverent esteem; and the most gracious letter of the Senate, conferring upon this piece of glass the distinction of first mention among all that were shown upon that day of triumph, is here also—a yellowed parchment, carefully inclosed in the little morocco case, securely screwed to the shelf beneath, and Marina had been present when it was opened for some rare visitor. It was a relic of those earlier days when there were no furnaces in Murano, though many of the finest workers came from this island and belonged to the corporation of the workers on Rialto, and it was almost a prehistoric record of greatness.

Marina had left the table and gone to the cabinet; her father followed her. "This I would show thee," he said, calling her attention to a whimsical shape, blown and twisted almost into foam. "This Lorenzo Stino brought me only yesterday; he is full of genius; I think none hath a quicker hand, nor a more inventive faculty. I have watched him in his working." He scanned her eagerly as he spoke.

"Yes, it is fanciful—wonderful," she added to please him, but without warmth, while her eyes wandered over the shelves. "Oh, father, here are some of the very mosaics that were made for San Marco; thou hast forgotten!"

She lifted eagerly a small opaque basin of turquoise blue and held it toward him; it contained a few bits of gold and silver enamel, the earliest that had been made in Venice, bearing their ancient date.

"Thou askest more of Venice than I," he said, well pleased with her enthusiasm; "but have a care lest they say I have not taught thee well, or that I do not know my art, or that I claim too much. At the time of the burning of San Marco these Mosaics for the restoration were from the stabilimenti of the Republic on Rialto—so early it came to us, this glorious art. And it was one Piero, a founder of our house, though the name was other than Magagnati, who was the master in that restoration. But the first mosaics in that old San Marco —ay, and the workmen," he added with a conscious effort, so much would he have liked to claim the invention for Venice, "came hither from the East. Thou shouldst know the history of our art; it is the story of thine ancestry and the nobility of thy house. Thou hast no other."

"I have thee, my father!"

IV

THE Veronese did not paint that beautiful face the next morning as he had planned; for the first time he had encountered difficulties. Slowly, as he wended his way through the many turnings of the narrow calle to Campo San Maurizio, carrying a beautiful Moorish box filled with the pearly shells which the Venetians call "flowers of the Lido," and a bouquet of aromatic carnations for the bambino, he recalled the figure and speech of his Madonna, and they were not those of the maidens whom one might encounter at the traghetto or in the Piazza; there had been a dignity and self-forgetfulness in such perfect harmony with the face that, at the moment, this had seemed entirely natural. But the tones returned to him as he pondered, filled with a deeper melody than the usual winning speech of the Venetian; with the grace of the soft dialect there was a rare, unexpected quality, as if thought had formed the undertone. He had never heard such a voice in the Piazza—it was rare even in the palazzo; it was the voice of some sweet and gracious woman with a soul too large for the world; it held a suggestion of peace and convent bells and even-songs of nuns.

Then, still more passionately, the desire overcame him to paint that face for his Madonna; he

46

would never give it up! Yet this maiden was not one of whom he could ask the favor that he craved, nor to whom he could offer any return.

He had come to San Maurizio to take a gondola from the traghetto, partly that he might be free to wander without comment wherever his search should lead, partly because he was always ready for a chat with the people; their experiences interested him, and he himself belonged by his artist life, as by his sympathies, to all classes. Perhaps, too, he had been moved with a vague hope that he might find the face he was seeking, for he was used to fortunate happenings. But there were no waiting Madonnas under the pergola, and the air of the early spring morning blew chill from the Lido, almost with an intimation of failure to his sensitive mood. He pushed aside an old *gransiere*, without the gift of small coin that usually flowed so easily from his hand, for service rendered or unrendered, as he impatiently questioned the gondoliers.

"One who knows Murano well!" he called.

There was an instant response from an old man almost past traghetto service, but his age and probable garrulity commended him.

"I will take thee and thy gondola, since thou knowest Murano," said the artist kindly; "but I must go swiftly, and I would not tax thee. Thou shalt have thy fare, but I will pay for another gondolier also from the traghetto; he must be young and lusty. Choose thou him—and hasten."

There was a babel of voices and a self-gratulatory proffer of lithe forms, while the old gondolier turned undecidedly from one to another, and the tottering gransiere ostentatiously protected the velvet mantle of the artist as he sprang into the boat. With an impatient gesture the Veronese indicated his choice, and they were soon on their way.

"Come hither, *vecchio mio*, and rest thine old bones; let the young one work for us both," the padrone commanded, as he flung himself down among the cushions. "Do they treat thee well at thy traghetto?"

"Eccellenza, yes; but I am scarce older than the others; it is the young ones who make us trouble; they keep not the Mariegole, and it is only the old one may depend upon."

"*Davvero*, the world is changed then! It used to be good to be young."

"Eccellenza, yes; when I myself was not old, and his excellency also had no beard."

"If age and wisdom might be traded for the time of youthful pranks," said the Veronese with twinkling eyes, "I doubt if there were wisdom enough left in Venice to cavil at the barter! Yet thou and I, having wisdom thrust upon us by these same beards, if trouble come to thee, or too soon they put thee at the gransiere service, we will remember this day passed together."

"Eccellenza, thanks; the gransiere has not much beside his beard to keep him warm, and the time draws near," the old man answered with pleasant Venetian insouciance.

"Tell me," said the Veronese, turning to the younger man, "why do you young fellows make Venice ring with your scandals? You are cutting off your own 'liberties.'"

"Yes, signore." The gondolier hesitated, glancing doubtfully at the artist's sumptuous attire, which might have indicated a state much greater than he kept; for the Veronese was famed throughout Venice, in quarters where he was better known, for an unfailing splendor of costume which would have made him at all times a model for the pictures he loved to paint. Recently, for bad conduct, the gondoliers had been gradually forfeiting their licenses, or "liberties," as they were called in Venice, and the thought crossed the young fellow's mind that this splendid stranger was possibly one of those government officials who were charged with the supervision of the confraternities of the traghetti.

"It is the first time I have the honor of conducting his Excellency; he is perhaps of the Provveditori al Comun?" These officials collected the government taxes and were viewed with jealous eyes by the gondoliers.

"Nay; I am Paolo Cagliari; I belong to a better craft. But please thyself, for there is much talk of this matter."

"Signore, one must live!" the young fellow exclaimed, with a friendly shrug of his shoulders and a gleam of his white teeth; for it was easy to make friends with the genial artist. "And between the governors and the *provveditori* one may scarce draw breath! One's bread and onions——" he added, with a dramatic gesture of self-pity. "It is not much to ask!"

"*Altro!* Nonsense!" the Veronese exclaimed, laughing, for the gondolier looked little like one who was suffering from hunger, as he stood swaying in keen enjoyment of the motion which showed his prowess, of the wind as it swept his bronzed cheek, of the talk which permitted him to exploit his grievances.

"There is the High Mass, twice in the month; there is the Low Mass—every Monday, if you will believe me! There are the priests, *for nothing*—Santa Maria, they are not few! The first fare in the day?—always for the Madonna of the traghetto. This *maledetto* fare of the Madonna suffices for the Madonna's oil, I ask you? Ebbene non! There are the fines—and these, it must be confessed, might be fewer, for the saints are tired of keeping us out of mischief. And little there is for one's own madonna, if one would make gifts!"

"This, then, for thine own madonna," said the artist pleasantly, tossing him a considerable coin. "And may she make thee wiser; for, by thine inventory, which it doth not harm thee to rehearse, thou hast a good memory."

"Eccellenza, there is more, if you be not weary. There is the government tax; it takes long to gather—ask the *gastaldo!* There are the soldiers for the navy; how many good men does that leave for the traghetto service? And a license is not little to buy for a poor barcariol who would be his own man; one pays three hundred *lire*—not less. Does it drop into one's hand with the first fare? One must belong to the Guilds—it is less robbery!"

"But for your gastaldo, your great man, for him it is much honor——"

"Eccellenza, believe it not. If the taxes are not

there for the provveditori, it is the gastaldo who pays. When the money is little it is the gastaldo who pays much. And the toso—all his faults blamed on the traghetti! Ah, signore, for the gondolier it is a life—Santa Maria!" He threw up his hands with a feint of being at a loss to convey its hardships.

"*Come non c'è altro!*" said the Veronese, laughing; "there is none like it."

"Ebbene—va bene!" the gondolier confessed, joining heartily in the merriment, his grievance, which was nevertheless a real one, infinitely lessened by confession.

Suddenly the old man rose and bowed his head, and both gondoliers crossed themselves. The Veronese also bared his head and made the sign of reverence, for they were passing the island of San Michele, toward which a mournful procession of boats, each with its torch and its banner of black, was slowly gliding, while back over the water echoed the dirge from those sobbing cellos. Here, where only the dead were sleeping, the sky was as blue and the sea as calm as if sorrow had never been born in the world.

Before them Murano, low-lying, scattered, was close at hand, the smoke of its daily activities tremulous over it, dimming the beauty of sky and sea.

"His Excellency knows Murano? The Duomo, with its mosaics? Wonderful! there are none like them; and it is old—'ma antica'! And the stabilimenti?—it is glory enough for one island! Ah, the padrone wishes to visit the stabilimento Magagnati?"

Paolo Cagliari had not known what he would do

until the old man's suggestion seemed to make his vision less vaguely inaccessible, and before they reached the landing he had learned, by a judicious indifference which sharpened his companion's loquacity, that Messer Girolamo lived there alone with his daughter, who went about always with a bambino in her arms—the child of a dead sister.

There could be no doubt; yet, to keep the old man talking, he put the question, "She is very beautiful, the donzella?"

"Eccellenza"—with a pause and deprecatory movement of the shoulders—"*cosi*—so-so—a little pale—like a saint—devote. For the poor? Good, *gentile*, the donzel of Messer Girolamo. *Bella*, with rosy colors? *Non!*"

With the Venetians there could be no sharp distinction between the decorative and the fine arts, as the fine arts were employed by them without limit in their sumptuous decorations; and that which elsewhere would have been merely decorative they raised, by exquisite quality and finish, to a point which deserved to be termed art, without qualifications.

The Veronese, who had been knighted by the Doge, could scarcely go unrecognized to any art establishment in any quarter of Venice, and with unconcealed pleasure Girolamo bowed low before this master who had come to do him honor; displaying all that the initiated would hold most precious among his treasures—that design, faded and dim, almost unrecognizable, of those early mosaics of the Master Pietro—he held nothing back. It was a day of honor for his house, and the two were alone in his cabinet.

The Veronese had a gift of sympathy; his heart opened to those who loved art and had conquered difficulties in her service, and the talk flowed freely. "I believe," he said, as together they laid away the parchment, "that in our modern mosaics we should keep to the massive lines of these earlier models—greater dignity and simplicity in outline and coloring. It is a mistake to attempt to confound this art with painting."

"It is good, then, for our art, Messer Cavalière, that at San Donato, our mother church, we workmen of Murano have our Lady in that old Byzantine type; there is none earlier—nor in all Venice more perfect of its time—and the setting is of marvelous richness and delicacy."

"It is most interesting," said the Veronese. "Sometimes a question has come to me, if an artist cannot do the *all*, is he most the artist who stops below his limitation or beyond it? A question of the earlier hint, or the later realization."

"Between the mosaic and the painting, perhaps?" Girolamo questioned, greatly interested.

"Nay, not between the arts, but of that which is possible to each. It is not a Venetian question. Here all is warmth, color, beauty, joy; here art is the expression of redundancy—it hath lost its symbolism."

"I know only Venice—the Greek and the Venetian types. But I have heard that the Michelangelo was in himself a type?"

"He was a prophet," the Veronese answered reverently, "like the great Florentine—a seer of visions; but at Rome only one understands why he was born. He was a maker, creating mighty meanings under formlessness. His great shapes seem each a mystery, wrestling with a message."

"I had thought there was none who equaled him in form—that he was even as a sculptor in his painting."

"And it was even so. When I spake of 'formlessness' it was not the less, but the more; as if, *before the visions had taken mortal shape, he, being greater than men, saw them as spirits.*"

"Never before have I talked with one who knew this master," said Girolamo, "and it is a feast."

"Nay, I knew him not, for it was not easy to get speech with him, nor a favor a young man might crave. But once I saw him at his work in San Pietro, where he wrought most furiously and would take no payment—'for the good of his soul,' he said, that he might end his life with a pious work. The night was coming on, and already his candle was fastened to his hat, that he might lose no time. They had brought him a little bread and wine for his evening meal, for often he went not home when the mood of work possessed him; and beside him was a writing of the man Savonarola—this and the Holy Evangel and the 'Inferno' fashioned his thoughts. He lived not long after that, for we were still in Rome when they made for him that great funeral in Santa Croce of Florence, the rumor of which is dear to artist hearts. He was great and lonely, and he knew no joy; there hath been none like him."

"And the Tintoretto, at Santa Maria dell' Orto?"

"He, too, is a *furioso*, wonderful in form—and the Michelangelo had not the coloring of our Jacopo. But the terror of the Tintoretto is very terrible and very human. The Michelangelo fills a great gloom with phantasms—they question—and one cannot escape."

"It hath been a morning of delights," Girolamo said with grave courtesy when the talk had come to an end. "I thank the master for this honor."

"Nay," answered the knightly Veronese; "it is I who have received. And more, yet more would I ask. I know not if in this chamber of treasures I may leave the trifle which I came to bring for the bambino?" he added with hesitation, as he placed upon the table his little inlaid box of baubles and his bunch of spicy flowers. "Yet it was a promise."

And while Girolamo listened in astonishment he told abruptly the story of his meeting with Marina and the little one, unconsciously weaving his thoughts into such a picture as he talked, that Girolamo recognized the inspiration and was already won to plead his cause.

"This," continued the artist, unfolding a letter, "is the order which hath been sent me by Fra Paolo Sarpi, of the convent of the Servi, a man most wise and of high repute in Venice. 'The face,' this learned friar sayeth, 'must be full of consolation and one to awaken holy thoughts. And I, being not an artist' (which, because he is greater than so many of his craft, he hath the grace to acknowledge!), 'have no other word to say, save that it shall be noble and most spiritual, as befitteth our religion.' And such a face till now, Messer Girolamo Magagnati—so beautiful and holy—I have not found. But now it is a vision sent to me from heaven, quite other than any picture I have ever dreamed, and I will paint no other for this Madonna of the Servi. I also, like the Angelo, would give my holiest work for the good of my soul; for the days of man are numbered, though his blood be warm in his veins like wine! It would be a pious act for the maiden; and if she will most graciously consent, the picture shall be an offering for the altar of the chapel of Consolation in the Servi."

"I will ask her," said the father simply, and felt no surprise at what he had granted when he was left alone with his thoughts, for Paolo Cagliari, because of a way he had that men could not resist, already seemed to him a friend; for the rare mingling of knightly grace and artistic enthusiasm, overcoming spasmodically the usual assertiveness of his demeanor, seemed at such moments to mean more than when assumed by those who were never passionate nor brusque, and his very incongruities held a fascination for his friends.

V

MARINA came often to the studio of the Veronese in San Samuele, while the *Madonna del Sorriso* grew slowly into life; it was not that most perfect life of which the artist had dreamed, for hitherto beauty had sufficed to him and he had never sought to burden his creations with questions of the soul; but now the sadness of the unattainable that was growing within him looked out of the wonderful eyes of the maiden on his canvas, yet he tossed his brushes aside in discontent. "Her smile eludeth me, though it hath the candor of a child's," the master cried.

Within his studio his pupils came and went, some earnest to follow in the footsteps of the master, absorbed in their tasks; others, golden youths, painting a little because Art was beautiful—not overcoming.

In the inner chamber, which was the artist's sanctum, were only the Veronese and his brother Benedetto at work; his brother, who was architect and sculptor too, was putting in the background of an elaborate palace in a fine Venetian group upon which Paolo worked when not occupied with his Madonna; and a favorite pupil, the young nobleman Marcantonio Giustiniani, was in attendance upon the master. The lovely girlish face, of a spiritual type rare in Venice, seemed to the young patrician more beautiful than that of any of the noble, smiling ladies who were waiting to be won by him, and in those hours of blissful service he, too, made a study —crude and inartistic.

"Thy hand hath yet to learn its cunning," the master said, as in much confusion, one morning when they were quite alone, his pupil revealed his roughly executed head; "yet thou hast painted the soul! The heart hath done it, Signorino mio, for thou art not yet an artist. There is no other lady for Marcantonio Giustiniani; yet she comes not of a noble house."

"She makes it noble!" cried the young fellow, flushing hotly, "for she is like her face."

"Ay, for me and thee she is noble," said the Veronese compassionately, for he loved. the boy. "But for the noble Senator, thy father—of the Council of the Ten—he will not find this maiden's name in the 'Libro d'Oro.' I am sorry for thee."

"Master!" cried Marcantonio imploringly, "art thou with me?"

"Verily, but I can do naught for thee."

"Listen, then! One day the nobles shall find that name inscribed in the 'Libro d'Oro'; it shall be there, for mine shall suffice."

The master answered nothing, but bending over the sketch which his pupil had made he caressed it, here and there, with loving touches of his magic brush, while the young nobleman poured forth his vehement speech, forgetting to watch the master's fingers.

"Once in the annals of the Republic there is

noted such a marriage; a daughter of Murano, of the house of Beroviero—nay, not so beautiful as Marina—wedded with one of our noblest names; and the children, by decree of the Senate, were written every one in the 'Libro d'Oro.' "

"*This* have I done for thee!" said the master, moving away from the sketch and disclosing it to the young fellow, who gazed at it in silent amazement. "Only the eyes have I not touched," the Veronese explained; "for thou hast made them more soulful than even unto me they seemed, and thus have I read thy secret."

"Maestro mio!" cried Marcantonio at length, in ecstasy; "none among us may learn the marvel of thine art!"

"I have but touched thy sketch with the power that mine art could give," the master answered, well pleased. "Yet it is thou who hast read the secret of the face that was not revealed to me."

"We were speaking of the 'Libro d'Oro,' " the young patrician interrupted eagerly.

"It may be so, I know not," the Veronese answered indifferently, for he himself was not written in that noble chronicle. "My art deals little with these cumbrous records of the Republic."

"Thou art wrong to scorn them, caro maestro, for in them is chronicled the glory of Venice."

"The saying doeth honor—from a pupil to his master!" the artist burst forth with his quick, uncontrollable temper. "The Tablets of Stone were reserved for the highest dignity of the Law; and in that Sala dei Capi, where at this moment sits Giustinian Giustiniani—one of the chosen three of the Council of the Ten—my name is written largely with mine own hand, as artists write their names, *above* the heads of rulers for all coming time to see! The *Avvogadori* do not keep my 'Libro d'Oro'; the entrance to it is by divine right!"

He flung his brushes fiercely aside, in one of those moods that seemed all unwarranted in comparison with the slightness of the provocation— moods that alternated with the lovable, genial, generous impulses of an artist soul, overwhelming in energy and great in friendship; yet jealous, to a degree a lesser nature could scarcely pardon, of anything that seemed to touch upon his province as an artist and the claims of art to highest honor.

.   .   .   .

The day was drawing near when Marcantonio Giustiniani, the only son of Giustinian Giustiniani, a noble of the Senate and of the Council of the Ten, should present himself before the *Avvocato del Comun* to claim admission to the Great Council as a noble, born in lawful wedlock, of noble parents, inscribed in the Golden Book.

To the young fellow himself this twenty-fifth anniversary of his birth, when, by Venetian law, the ceremony must take place, approached with needlessly rapid footsteps; he was not yet ready for the duties it would bring, so much more did he incline to that measure of boyish freedom which had thus far been his, so unwilling was he to renounce his longing for some form of art life—the impulse to which fretted him almost unbearably, in view of the political career which opened mercilessly before him, threatening every dearer project.

Not that he felt himself born to be an artist—
Paolo Cagliari laughed at his studies while he en-
couraged his coming to the studio, telling him that
for one who had not chosen Art for his mistress
the drawings were "well enough"; and from the
Veronese the words were consoling. His mother
had been afraid of this taste for art, which, for a
short time, had exercised such sway over his fancy,
stimulated by his *culte* for the beautiful, that he had
plead with her to win his father's consent for an
art life. Yet he had himself acquiesced in her quiet
but inflexible showing of the futility of attempt-
ing such an overturning of Giustiniani traditions,
though he still went with dangerous frequency to
the studio of the Veronese, to which she had pro-
cured him entrance upon his promise that he would
not seriously consider that impossible possibility at
which he had hinted. There had been mention of
Pordenone and of Aretino, with a certain cool scorn
that was worse than censure, and as convincing,
there was the Titian, than whom, in art and sumptu-
ousness, one could not be greater; but, even for him,
Cavalière of France, there was no place in the
Consiglio!

Not that Marcantonio would voluntarily have re-
linquished his hereditary place in the state, his pos-
sible part in its glory—the dream which came to all
young noblemen of the portrait in that splendid
Sala di Consiglio of his own face grown venerable,
wearing the ermine and the ducal coronet, in token
of that supremacy so dear to each Venetian heart,
but jealously held by every noble of the Republic
within confines which lessened with each succession,

until the crown was assumed in trembling and igno-
minious restriction—if with external pomp and
honor that might befit a king.

But he wanted time; he wanted liberty to choose
his own life or enjoy his restlessness, and he realized
the more keenly, from the sense of power that was
so chafed in the curbing, that he was too young
to be forced into such ruthless service; and he could
not but acquiesce the less fervently because it was
not open to him to *give* himself, since the claim of
Venice was absolute and resistance was a crime.

But with quite other sentiments the preparations
for the fête were progressing in that ancient family
of Giustiniani, where the day was awaited with an
impatience which increased the fervor and the pomp
of preparation, but was not otherwise manifested
in any sign of undignified eagerness. No house
in Venice had held this right for more generations;
no house was princelier in its bearing, nor more
superbly republican! No member of that Supreme
Council was more esteemed than the stern Giustin-
ian, who had been again and again elected to the
most important missions of the state; no *donna
nobile* of all the Venetians was prouder, more highly
born, more beautiful, nor more coldly gracious than
the mother of Marcantonio.

In such an environment there was but one career
possible for the only son of the house, who had been
carefully trained, according to the traditions that
made culture for the young Venetian of those days;
he had even attended courses of those philosophical
conferences which had become the fashion since the
sittings of the famous Council of Trent, and which

had been conducted in various convents by distinguished professors from Padua and Bologna, and even by some of the learned men of Rome; it was a species of amusement creditable for a young nobleman—it would quicken the reasoning powers and give more subtlety in debate, when government problems should later absorb his gifts.

But if, like other golden youth of his time, he was like a Greek in possession of their liquid tongue and in a mastery of oratory that filled the soul of Giustinian Giustiniani with satisfaction, the young patrician himself had acquired this learning, less with a thought of one day shining in the Senate than because it pleased him as a touch of finish. He was, in some sort, a reaction from the proud and typical Venetian so ably represented by the elder Giustinian, who claimed unchallenged descent from the Emperor Justinian, upheld by the traditions of that long line of ancestry and by the memory of many honorable offices most honorably discharged by numerous members of his house. Marcantonio, on the contrary, was handsome, winning, pleasure-loving—after an innocent fashion, which brought some sneers from his compeers, the gay "company of the hose;" but he thought life not made for pain, nor ugliness, nor hardness of any sort; he was bred to luxury, yet his intellectual inheritance made learning easy for him; he was many sided and vacillating, an exquisite in taste and the science of trifles. His affectionate nature, repressed and chilled, refused absolute subjection to that purpose which the elder Giustinian held relentlessly before him; he wished to live for himself a little, and not wholly for Venice. He was an embodiment of that late time of Venetian culture when its magnificence, its artistic and intellectual development had touched their height, and the hint of decadence shadowed its splendor with a pathos unguessed except by the thoughtful few.

He had dabbled a little in costly manuscripts—a taste for an exquisite in those days, when Venice was the envy of the world for the marvels of her press; and already he possessed a volume or two, for his cabinet, from the atelier of Aldus Manutius— that famous edition of Aristotle, the first ever printed in Greek, with the Aldine mark of anchor and dolphin on the title-page. But a volume more precious still, with its dainty finish and piquant his- tory, conferred distinction, it was said, among the literati, upon its youthful owner; this was no less a treasure than that first copy of "Le Cose Volgare di Messer Francesco Petrarca," most exquisitely printed in type modeled after the poet's own elegant handwriting, and the volume had been superin- tended by many learned heads,—awaited with impa- tience, as a triumph for its makers,—and thought a thing rare enough to be offered, like a jewel, to the learned and illustrious lady, Isabella of Mantua. Marcantonio was no pedant, but these treasures sim- ply had their place in the richly painted cabinet, beside many other bits of exquisite workmanship, because rare things in every art were beautiful to our dilettante, and possessions of all kinds came to him easily.

There lay the golden necklace presented by Henry III. of France to a Giustinian who had been one of the young nobles set apart for the household of the king, when on his visit to Venice; and beside it a curious volume of songs, all in honor of France and of the king, entitled "Il Magno Enrico III., difensore di Santa Chiesa, di Francia è di Polonia Re christianissimo." Here was also preserved that still more curious allegorical drama which had been given at the grand fête at the Ducal Palace in honor of this over-adulated monarch. It was natural that some of these literary curiosities, of which the visit of Henry III. had been prolific, should have remained in possession of the masters of the palace which had been tendered for his residence. The volume, bound in azure velvet, embroidered with golden fleurs-de-lis and seeded with pearls, lay open at the page "Chapter in which the Most Holy Catholic Religion is introduced conversing with the most Christian, most powerful and most holy Henry III., the most glorious King of France and Poland."

The noble lady Laura Giustiniani, who looked with pride upon these costly trifles of the cabinet of Marcantonio, was a Venetian in every throb of her patrician veins—first a patriot and then a mother—she earnestly coveted for her son that he should render vast services to the state, receive in his early years the Patriarch's blessing upon his alliance with some ancient Venetian house, and close his noble career with the Doge's coronet. She admitted reluctantly to herself, although she would never have confessed it openly, that in these latter days of the Republic the ermine was not likely to be offered to one so stern and masterful as her husband; while she also knew, and the knowledge held its compensation, that Giustinian Giustiniani could not be spared from the Councils of his government. She knew her history well, and she realized that the days of the Michieli and Orseoli were over, and that the supreme honor was no longer for the strong but for the pliant; this had made her the more willing that her son should partake of the facile and gracious mood of this time of Renaissance, and had led her to shape his education more in consonance with his natural tastes than with her own views of fitness for a Venetian noble. She knew that this was weakness for a Giustinian; but it was hard to see the noble line pass down through the centuries without that coveted sign of honor—the minikin Lion of San Marco, the mighty symbol—carved upon their palaces.

Meanwhile, for a suitable alliance there were already schemes on foot, and mothers of noble young Venetian ladies paid frequent court to the stately Lady Laura in her palace on the Canal Grande; and fathers, in the Senate, in moments of unbending, discussed the probability of the immediate rise of the young Giustinian upon his admission to the Consiglio—he was competent and not positive, gracions and no fool, he could be made to see the wisdom of other people's opinions, which, with the elder Giustinian, was unheard of!

Among the maidens who should grace the banquet to be given on Marcantonio's birthnight, more than one had sat for hours in some high balcony of her palace, preparing for Venetian belle-ship with a patience worthy of a better cause—her long locks, mysteriously treated, streaming over the broad brim of the great, crownless hat which protected her fair face, while the sun bestowed its last touch of beauty in bleaching the dark tresses to that rich, red, burnished gold which the Venetians prized.

The young patrician was already esteemed a connoisseur in the most exquisite industries of Venice, and the Lady Laura had confided to her son the ordering of a set of goblets of *girasole* for the banquet—a new opalescent glass, with iridescent borderings, such as had never yet been seen at any Venetian fête.

Thus the gondola of the Giustiniani floated for long hours before the famous establishment of Girolamo Magagnati, so delicate and intricate was the work that had been ordered from him; and the gondoliers, meanwhile, in their splendid liveries, held converse with other gondoliers in lazily drifting barks, with hatchments of other noble houses embroidered on their sleeves; and their tones were strident and quarrelsome, or self-complacent and patronizing, as the quality of the silken sashes which displayed the color of their house was heavier or poorer than their own.

One boasts of the lantern, all of brass, "Wrought by Messer Alessandro Leopardi—'come no c'è altro!'—there is no other like it—which he, the favored gondolier, has been burnishing for the banquet of the Dandolo, to which he shall that night convey the noble lady of the Giustiniani!"

"It is less beautiful," retorts a gondolier of the house of Mocenigo, the fringes of his sash of rose sweeping the bridge of his gondola as it moves forward, slightly tilting on its side, with a quick, disdainful motion called forth by proper Mocenigo pride—so pliant are these barks of Venice to the moods of the gondolier: "It is less beautiful—by the Holy Madonna of San Castello!—than the lantern of wrought iron with the jewels of *rubino* that Messer Girolamo Magagnati makes this day, by order of the Eccellentissimo Andrea Mocenigo, with the jewels of the fine glass of Murano that shall be like roses flashing in the night!"

And he has sworn so great an oath, by that most ancient Madonna of Castello, and so well has he vindicated the honor and splendor of his house in thus early appropriating this recent glory of Venetian workmanship in its own family emblem, that there is no present need of distance between him and his rival, and resting upon his oar, as he stands with a proud and graceful bearing of victory, he allows the gondola to glide back into position with the lapping of the water.

For the gondoliers of the house of Giustiniani are unfolding, with quick, ringing, jubilant voices, vast confidential tales of the fêtes that are in preparation for the marriage of the young noble of the Council, their master, of which this banquet is only the precursor. "For of course there will be a *sposalizia!* Santa Maria! there is no room on the Canal Grande for the gondolas that come to the palazzo—from every *casa* in the 'Libro d'Oro'—to win the favor of the donna nobile of the Giustiniani, for some bella donzella who shall be chosen for their young master—who is like a prince, and will end one day in being Doge! Santa Maria di Castello, he does not wait that day to scatter his golden coins!"

If that question of "sposalizia" is not imminent there is truth enough for any Venetian conscience in the story of the ranks of princely gondolas at the bend of the Canal Grande, on the days when the donna nobile of the Giustiniani gives welcome to her guests—princely gondolas they are, with *felzes* of brocaded and embroidered stuffs, the framework inlaid with ivory and mother-of-pearl, with metal fittings curiously wrought, and all that bravery of pomp so dear to the Venetian heart, which calls forth surly decrees from those stern Signori of the Council—the much unloved "Provveditori alle Pompe," the sumptuary officers of this superb Republic.

Meanwhile, in this narrow water-street, sunk a few feet below the paved foot-path that stretches to the doors of the dwellings, there are sudden grumbling movements among the retainers of the patrician families, as they steer their gorgeous gondolas from side to side, to avoid humiliating contact with that slow procession of barges bringing produce from the island gardens of Mazzorbo; there are other barges laden with great, white wooden tubs of water from Fusina, fresh and very needful to these cities of the sea; and the dark hulks of barks curiously entangled with nets and masts and unwieldy tackle of sailor and fisher, show flashes of brilliant color as the water plays through the netted baskets swinging low against their sides, while the sunlight glances back from the gold and silver glory of the scales of living fish, crowded and palpitating within their meshes.

The fisherfolk who guide these barks are gray

and gnomelike in their coloring, tanned by sky and sea and ceaseless atmospheres of fish, into a neutral tint,—less vivid in hues of skin and hair, with eyes less brilliant, with less vivacity and charm of bearing than the gay Venetians,—but they are the descendants of those island tribes from which the commerce and greatness of Venice issued; there is almost a show of stateliness in the aggravating slowness with which their heavily freighted barks proceed, serenely occupying the best of the narrow waterway. They are not envious of the hangers-on of those palaces of the nobles, these free fisherfolk of the islands; they have only haughty stares for the servile set of gondoliers in lacings of gold and scarlet—who are not nobles nor fishers, nor people of the soil—and they pass them silently, with much ostentation of taking all the gondoliers of Murano into the friendliness of their jests and curses, as the barges touch and clash with some swiftly gliding gondolier of their own rank, who wears no bravery or armorial bearings.

Their homes—long, low, white-washed cottages—spread along the main channel and reach in lessening, dotted lines far off into the sea, where other islands lie in friendly nearness; but the Bridge, with the Lions of St. Mark on archivolt and parapet—the invariable official signet of Venetian dominion—stretches between that simpler quarter and this, which holds the great houses of Murano, whose masters, a sort of *petite noblesse*, have made their names illustrious by marvelous inventions in that exquisite industry in which Venice has no rival.

VI

THE "Madonna del Sorriso" now lacked only the finishing touches upon the exquisite central figure, which reached more nearly to the spiritual ideal than anything that had ever come from the brush of the Veronese, and already the Servite friars, in their long black robes and white cowls, had visited the studio with suggestions many and fruitless, serving only to arouse the artist's indignant protest and increase his determination to image more perfectly the poetic vision that had been vouchsafed to him.

"It hath not the beauty of the 'Venezia' in the palazzo," said one.

"And the church is dark," said another, "and the people like the red and blue of the colors of the true Madonna."

"And a frate, of the Servi—since it hath been painted for the convent—here—kneeling," suggested another, more timidly; for it was known that the Veronese was not always docile in these days, since he had become great.

"Nay, leave me," said the Veronese fiercely; "for this one thing I *know*, and this will I paint, for the good of my soul, as mine art shall prompt me and not otherwise. And if it please not him—Fra Paolo, who hath given the order—I will bestow it elsewhere."

Then a friar habited like the others, who had stood apart and had not spoken, came and threw back his cowl, dismissing the group with a gesture. The features thus disclosed were unimportant, apart from the domelike forehead, which might well belong to the most learned man of his learned age; but Fra Paolo's face owed its distinction to the rare impression it gave the beholder of invincible calm and self-mastery, with a certain mysterious hint of power and a promise of unswervingness. His gaze held no suggestion of concealment; yet for the deeper thoughts that move the spirit of man, to those who knew him well his mild blue eyes remained inscrutable, while his courtesy to all made one forget that his words were few, and that of himself he had revealed nothing.

"It is well," he said, "to *know* that we know. Serve faithfully the God who gave the gift and take no counsel from men who know not."

Then he stood silent for a while before the picture, as if he would learn its meaning, the artist watching anxiously, not guessing his thought.

"The pious wish hath made the offering noble," he said at length, in quiet, measured tones. "And for the face, it is holy—of the beauty that God permits—yet I pretend no criticism, since Art is not of mine understanding. I will not take the honor of the gift away from the giver, though I had meant it otherwise."

After Fra Paolo had left the studio the Veronese was still studying his picture, pleased and serious, feeling that this man, who was not an artist, had comprehended the deepest mood in which he had ever approached his art, when Marina entered.

"Fra Paolo hath found our offering worthy," he said very gravely; and suddenly remembering that Marina had come for the last time, "Benedetto hath need of me in the outer studio for some measurements," he said to Marcantonio, "but I shall soon return. Do thou, meanwhile, show the *damigella* thy sketch."

She turned inquiringly toward Marcantonio, who placed it silently before her. When he gathered courage to look at her she stood flushed and trembling with clasped hands.

"Marina!" he cried.

She moved suddenly away from him, drawing herself up to her full height, one hand slightly extended, as if to keep him from coming nearer; but her face, as she turned it frankly to his, was lighted with a smile the Veronese would never copy, and her eyes shone through her tears.

"Is it true, Marina?" he questioned radiantly, as he tried to seize her hand.

But she still moved backward—not as if she were afraid, but as though she would help him by a motion to understand.

"You have confessed me unawares," she said, "and shown me mine own secret, which I knew not. It is not to confess nor deny."

"Yet you move away, Marina, as if you would not have it so."

"Because only the renunciation of it is for us," she answered firmly. "For I am of the people, and you—of the Giustiniani!"

"As you shall also be!" he affirmed, undaunted.

"Marco, at Venice this is not easy!" The tone was a caress which she made no effort to withhold, yet he dared not try again to touch her hand; he already felt her strength.

"None the less, because it is not easy it shall be done. Reach me your hand, Marina, to prove that you trust my vow."

He was not wont to crave favor so humbly, but a new reverence had entered into his soul.

She hesitated for a moment, then her words came brokenly, yet with dignity.

"Marco mio, not yet. Because I am of the people, and because the others — your father and mother, who are of the nobles, and my father, who is of the people—may not consent, we will make no vows until this difficulty is conquered."

"They shall not keep us from it."

She shook her head sadly, but came no nearer. "Will Giustinian Giustiniani ask a daughter of the people? But Girolamo Magagnati is not less proud."

"I will return now with thee to Murano. Perhaps thy father will befriend us."

"No, no; without their consent it would be useless. I think I shall not tell him—it would be only a grief."

"Because it meaneth much to thee?" Marco questioned, luminous and ungenerous.

She did not answer.

"Thou dost verily make too much of the nobles and the people, Marina; we are all Venetians."

"Venice is of the sea and of the land—not like other cities; and the Venetian people is not one, but twain; my father hath often said it. Some other day, perhaps—I do not know—if it is needful for the picture, I may come again. Will you tell the maestro? I think he is our friend, and he will understand."

He would have followed her, but she waved him back.

The day had a melancholy cast in the narrow waterways of Murano, where clouds of smoke, dense and constant, rose from hundreds of glass-workers' chimneys, dimming the reflections in the lagoon· and obscuring that wonderful coloring of sky which is nowhere so radiant as at Venice.

Beyond the bridge, which the ubiquitous Lion guards with menacing, uplifted paw, beyond the Piazzetta of San Pietro where the acacia trees are growing, down by the main canal, where the breath comes freer—for it is broader than the one where the gondolas from the great houses of Venice gather and float lazily; past the line of low, whitewashed cottages bordering the narrow foot-path on either side, over the little wooden bridge that spans the lagoon, fifty feet across from bank to bank with its ugly traghetto at the farther end, a figure was often seen wending, with a child held in tender mother fashion, to the campo of the "Matrice," the mother church of San Donato.

To-day when Marina had returned from Venice she had caught the little Zuane to her breast with such a passion of tenderness that he looked up into her face with startled eyes; hers were brimming with smiles and tears, and with that wise child-knowledge, which is not granted to earth's learned ones, he put up his tiny hand with a wan smile and stroked her cheek.

75

"We will go to San Donato, Zuanino mio," she said caressingly, as he nestled closer, "and I have *thee*, my bimbo!"

She put the little one gently down as they entered the triangular field where the grass grew green and long—whiteness of sand gleaming in irregular patches between the clumps of coarse blades; but to her this poor turf was something precious associated with that island sanctuary, restful and strange, and she drew a long breath with a sense of suppressed pleasure; for sometimes the water, with its shimmering, uncertain surfaces, wearied her, and unconsciously she craved something more positive.

The child, with uncertain steps, tottered toward the standard of San Marco, which floated proudly from the staff that rose from the rude stone pillar in the center of the campo, where other little ones were playing; in the corner by the well groups of women, from the cottages that bounded the campo on one side, were waiting to draw water for the evening meal, putting down their jugs and going first into the Duomo to say an ave, that the good Madonna might bless the cup.

A few feet only from the Duomo the campanile drew her vision skyward; the film of smoke was lighter here, and the sky seemed nearer—bluer. She turned to her little charge with a beaming face—her moods were so easily wrought upon by phases of nature, but slowly moved by personal influences. "See'st thou, bimbo, how it is beautiful here by the Duomo?"

But the little fellow, in one of his sudden spasms

of pain, was striking the air impotently with small, clenched fists, frightening the children who were gathering around him, joining in his cries.

Her caress and passionate forgiveness were always ready for the paroxysm in which she was violently pushed away and combated with struggling feet and hands, before came the period of exhaustion in which he nestled close, panting from weakness. Then she carried him into the church, where, kneeling before the Mother of Sorrows, whose outstretched hands seemed to touch her own in responsive sympathy and gift of calm, she prayed and wept.

"O Holy Mater Dolorosa! Why need the children suffer?—they are so tender and so dear!"

She knelt with loving, protecting arms folded close about the little form now breathing softly and at rest, while an agony of questioning filled her prayer to that beseeching Mater Dolorosa, who, wrapped in the clinging folds of her long blue robe, still leaned forward from the marble background of the apse, compassionate for the suffering ones of earth, with imploring hands and ceaseless dropping tears, symbol of love abounding—a symbol, too, of the dignity of those who suffer and are pure in heart.

This sanctuary was almost a home to the maiden, who came hither to praise or question, for life was full of enigmas. Here, too, where she came from duty and deep devotion, with an intricate sensitiveness of conscience which often rendered her unintelligible to her confessor, she lingered for delight. For the tracery on the arches—the color,

77

the wonderful delicacy of the sculpture—were of that time when art was suggestive and faint, in tint and meaning, like a dream, and its message was always spiritual.

"It is not Thou, O Christ," she said, "who willest pain; but thy children, who are not always loving!"

For in her reverie she was comforted by that vision of a legendary time when the Holy Mother had stood, beautiful, compassionate, and commanding, in this field of flaming scarlet lilies; when a great emperor had obeyed her bidding, and San Donato, the Duomo of Murano, had arisen as a refuge for the sorrowing.

In tender language of the people it was the mother church—"Matrice."

She made a cushion of her cloak and laid the little one upon it, for he still slept and she would not waken him; and then, though the quaint, inlaid pavement was cold and bare, she knelt again, her rosary dropping from her hands as she shyly whispered the burden of her strange new confession to this ever-waiting, tender Mother—her confession more full of pain than joy, yet already dear, and a thing not to be surrendered, though it should bring her only pain.

But there was no other friend to whom she told it.

Soon, alas! the days grew over-full of pain, and Marina came more often to the Mater Dolorosa, for the little Zuane had not grown stronger with the coming of the spring; sleep came to him more easily, but it did not bring refreshment, and the roses on his cheeks were only signs of failing bloom.   Passionately Marina's loving prayers were breathed before the shrine of the Madonna San Donato, but the little one grew weaker every day, till, after a long night of watching, a sweet-voiced nun stood with Marina beside the cradle.

"The burden of the baby's suffering life is changed to blessing," she said.   "Earth held no joy for him; God hath been merciful beyond thy prayer, my daughter."

VII

FRA PAOLO SARPI—this friar so grave and great and unemotional—had been since he had entered the convent in his precocious boyhood the central figure, fascinating the interest of his community by the marvel of his progress, so that those who had been his teachers stood reverently aside, before he had attained to manhood, recognizing gifts beyond their leading which had already won homage from the savants of Europe and crowned the order of the Servi with unexampled honors. The element of the unusual in the young Paolo's endowments had transformed this Benjamin of the convent into a hero, and surrounded the calm flow of his studious life with a halo of romance for these Servite friars; yet the good Fra Giulio in those early days, having little learning wherewith to estimate his progress and watching over him like a father, had been grieved at his strange placidity. "He sorely needeth some touch of emotion," he said yearningly; "methinks I love the lad as if he were mine own son, and I feel something lacking in his life."

"Fret not the lad needlessly with those fanciful notions of thine," Fra Gianmaria had retorted with much asperity. "It is the most marvelous piece of mental mechanism that I have ever dreamed. Already he hath attained to larger knowledge than thou, with thy gray hairs, canst comprehend."

Fra Giulio had crossed himself devoutly, as if confessing to some earthliness. "I measure not my simple mind with that of a genius, my brother; for so God hath endowed our lad. Yet it may be that He meaneth man to garner other blessings besides knowledge. We received him as a child into our fold, and we are responsible for his development. But his condition is not normal."

"Genius is abnormal," Fra Gianmaria had responded shortly.

"He hath no wish but for this ceaseless mental labor; all natural youthful fancies, all joy in the things of beauty—for these he careth naught."

The elder friar's troubled utterance had stirred no tremor in his companion's stern reply. "Thou and I, my brother, have attained by penances and years of abnegation to that mood which hath been granted the boy as a gift to fit him for the cloister life. It were small kindness to implant a struggle of which he knows not the beginnings."

And now, after all these years, through which the good Fra Giulio had watched this son of his affections, whom he loved with a love "passing the loves of earth" he pathetically told himself,—"as if God thus made up to him for all the loves he had resigned,"—now that the name of Fra Paolo was uttered with reverence while his own was unknown, he still expressed his heart in many tender cares, providing the new cassock before the scholar had noticed that the one he wore was seamed and frayed, with such other gentle ministries as the convent rule permitted toward one who never gave a worldly thought to the morrow.

And still, after all these years, the fatherly friar often fondly recurred to a time when he had first seemed to catch some dim, shadowed glimpse of that inner self which Fra Paolo so rarely expressed. He had been endeavoring to rouse the lad to enthusiasm. "Never have I known one show so little pleasure in nature," he had said. They were standing on the terrace of a convent among the hills beyond the plains of Venetia, and the view was beautiful and new for the youth.

"What is nature?" the lad had responded quietly.

"Nature?" Fra Giulio echoed, startled at the question. "Why, nature is God's creation. Dost thou not find this bit of nature beautiful?"

"It is pleasant," the young friar had assented, without enthusiasm. "But hath God created anything nobler than the mind and soul of man? The earth is but for his habitation."

"Nay," the old man had replied, in a tone of disappointment, "it is more for me—much more for those whom we call poets."

"Poets are dreamers," the lad had said, turning to his old friend with a smile which seemed affectionate, yet was baffling, and went not deep enough for love. "I would not dream; I must *know*."

"A little dreaming would not hurt thee, my Paolo; for sometimes it seemeth to those who care for thee that thou needest rest."

"Rest is satisfaction," the lad answered quickly. "If there be a problem to be solved, I would rather think than dream. I would rather come in contact with the nobler activities—the mental and spiritual forces—through the minds and works of men. I would find such attrition more helpful than this phase of creation which thou callest 'nature,' whose unfolding is more passive, depending on its inherent law."

"This also is of God's gift, Paolo mio," Fra Giulio had said yearningly. "Sometimes thou seemest to find too little beauty in thy life, and when I brought thee hither I hoped it might move thy soul."

"What can be more beautiful," the young philosopher had questioned earnestly, "than the fitting of all to each, the search for hidden keys, the linking of problems that seemed apart? These are the things that move me. I must walk soberly, Fra Giulio, lest I miss some revelation, so sacred and so mysterious is knowledge! And the love of it leaves me no room for questions of outside beauty— this ordered beauty of hidden law is so wonderful!"

For one moment, as Fra Giulio had looked at him, he fancied that he had seen deeper into his eyes than ever before; then the veil had seemed to rise up from the boy's heart and close over its depths. If it had been a moment of self-revelation the young friar was again protected by that baffling calm as he glanced about him, turning affectionately to his old friend. "It pleaseth me that thou art pleased," he said.

Fra Giulio had answered with a sigh. It was hard for one who loved so truly to get so near, yet be no nearer. "I could wish that thou also shouldst take pleasure in this beauty, my Paolo, for thou art missing a joy that God permits."

Then the youthful scholar had turned his eyes upon him silently; and it had seemed to the old man, in his great love, that a sudden glory had transfigured the grave young face like a consecration. He still remembered the tones of that clear voice saying serenely: "My Father, when God speaketh a message in our souls, the peace and beauty which come to us as we follow its call, are in the measure which He hath decreed for us."

Now that the convent rang with his triumphs, and Fra Paolo was often absent from his cell on missions of honor, the old friar sometimes wondered how many of those philosophic and scientific truths which had made him famous as an original thinker had come to the lad in glimmerings on that first night among the hills, when, turning to his old friend and stretching out his hands with a solemn, imploring motion which seemed to confess a desperate need of isolation, he had said only, "Let me think!"

Had his seeming nearness to the stars in the convent *loggia* brought him a premonition of the later message which had made him the "friend and master" of Galileo?

Did he develop his "Laws of Sound" in that voiceful silence; or was it in that solitude he had first watched the gentle ebb and flow of his own life-current and learned the secret which Harvey, later, uttered to the world?

Or had he been wholly absorbed in those philosophical questions which he so brilliantly disputed at the learned Court of Mantua?

But to be near him was only to wonder more at the mystery which enveloped him; and Fra Giulio, now that the lad had reached his prime, often went reverently back to that night under the stars, when the gifted youth had first stood, distanced as it were from men, remote from human habitations and alone with the One whom only he acknowledged as Master—then, perhaps, he had first been conscious of his latent power; surely then the manifold message of his life must have whispered within him many premonitions!

The time was long past when a question could arise as to the right of the Augustinians to rich possessions in church and convent; and the priceless treasures of art, flung sometimes in atonement upon their quiet walls by a world-worn artist, or sent in propitiation for some unconfessed sin by a prince of Church or State, were found side by side with the gifts and legacies of the faithful, which, in sincere devotion, they often impoverished their families to bestow.

But none of these things had charms for Fra Paolo. Not even the beauty of the cloisters, where the low, gray arches rested on slender shafts of marble, wrought and twisted into as many devices, drew his thoughts from the ceaseless contemplation of his problems; not even the petted rose-tree, lovingly trained by the gentle Fra Francesco and lifting its pink glory to the crest of the colonnade, won his eyes to wander from the absorbing treasures of the great library where he passed his days. Here many a brother had taught himself patience over the fine, endless text of an ancient gospel, or wrought into the exquisite illumination of some missal which stood to him in the place of his daily living those yearning, torturing, hungering affections which had so enriched a gentle home—as a brother, less disciplined, had carved his unruly tempers into the grotesque figures of the reading desks. But for Fra Paolo the great library of the convent held no unsatisfied yearnings—only an infinite content and power to achieve.

From the days when those curious in philosophical research had flocked from the neighboring universities to see this professor of theology who could not be conquered in argument, and had been confronted by a smooth-faced lad of twenty, until now, he was still the glory of the Servi; and well might the friars watch in triumph, as one by one he gathered laurels for their order. A little human flush of triumph or of self-conceit would have added charm to his argument, but these notes were lacking; clearly, logically, unanswerably, he met each . question, convincing without emotion and hastening from the gay court, of which these intellectual tourneys were the delight, to the welcome seclusion of the convent. If he seemed to have missed a real childhood,—its follies, its innocent pleasures, its winsome affections,—so later, the temptations that would naturally beset a career so extraordinary fell harmlessly away from him, for a passion for knowledge burned within him, consuming all ignoble motives and keeping this young scholar, in friar's robes, in marvelous singleness of heart, in the midst of a flattering and luxurious court.

Always he had been a law to himself, both morally and intellectually; never before did it seem that genius had been cast in a mold so orderly and calm. In that state of intense concentration which was his habitual mood, he accomplished without apparent effort the things for which others paid by a lifetime of struggle; and morally he had no visible combats, not seeming to be even reached by the things which tempted other men. His wants were fewer than the simplest rule of his convent allowed, and it seemed less that he had triumphed over the usual earthly temptations than that he had been created abnormally free from them that his whole strength might spend itself in the solving of problems. In a certain sense he stood mysteriously alone, though his friends were many and devoted and among the wise and venerated of the earth; but there was always a door closed to them beyond the affection which he returned them. "Always," he said once, "we veil our faces": yet none doubted his sincerity.

From time to time, as the years sped, some echo of the jealousy which his phenomenal success and the boldness of his bearing naturally evoked, penetrated to the cloisters of the Servi; and more than once there had been a denunciation to the Inquisition to discuss; some one in authority had found fault with his theological opinions and denounced him for his reading of a passage in Genesis, upon which he based his argument—the affair was grave indeed.

"Ah, the pity of it—the pity of it!" Fra Giulio had exclaimed. "They should show mercy—he is still so young a man!"

"Ay, young enough to need much discipline,"

bravely muttered a friar who dared to disbelieve in their prodigy.

"Silence!" commanded Father Gianmaria, who was now the Superior, in a stentorian tone; for within these walls there was no appeal from his judgment or his temper. "The man who speaks only what he *knows* is old in wisdom;" and turning he addressed the company in great dignity: "It doth appear that Rome approveth Fra Paolo's rendering and hath gravely censured the Inquisitor who hath cited him, commanding him to meddle only with that of which he hath some understanding."

"There are then tale-bearers whose jealousy would ruin our Paolo!" Fra Giulio had exclaimed in anxiety.

"It was none other than Fra Paolo himself who carried the tale," the Superior retorted in scorn of the old man's weak affection. "Fra Paolo refused to appear before the Inquisitor who had cited him, who, he alleged, knew not Hebrew nor Greek, and had therefore no knowledge upon which to base his judgment; and on this ground Fra Paolo appealed to Rome."

"It were a pity," said a gentle-faced young friar, who had been listening silently, but with an expression of deep and affectionate interest, "that one of so rare learning should remain long in a position of danger to orthodoxy. Already the Court of Mantua hath been censured by the Holy Father for heretical opinions."

"Nay; but for harboring heretics, hunted and driven," Fra Giulio corrected warmly. "There be deeds of mercy that will be forgiven us."

A look of perplexity crossed the candid, boyish face of Fra Francesco.

"But the law of obedience is more simple," he said timidly; "and our Holy Father——"

"Thou, not yet out of thy novitiate, doest well, verily, to prate of obedience and doctrines," interrupted Father Gianmaria, less severely than he was wont to treat such breaches of etiquette; for Fra Francesco had deep, spiritual, loving eyes, in which an unuttered wonder sometimes seemed to chide, for all his gentleness; and his ways were winsome.

So, through the years, whether he were present or absent, the life of the convent had centered about Fra Paolo, who now, after many missions of importance, had once more returned to his old cell in the Servi, with another added for his books and labors, since often it suited him to be alone. The breath of jealousy still clouded the serenity of his sky, and he was not without some unfulfilled longings; but no scandal had ever touched him. He was great enough now to be smitten through his friends, and the good Fra Giulio had been the victim taken in his stead; upon Fra Paolo's last homecoming to the convent the loving, fatherly greeting had failed him.

"Ask the nuns, to whom he is father confessor; they will have no other, and refuse admittance to one of our order who hath been sent to take this duty upon him. And our good Fra Giulio hath been removed in humiliation, and languisheth in Bologna, by order of the Patriarch who hath been won by the tale of one who loveth thee not."

"There is no more to it than that?" Fra Paolo questioned.

"Nay, no more, my brother," Fra Francesco answered with conviction.

"The name then?" said Fra Paolo; and when it had been told him he recognized the man as one in whom trust was misplaced, and one who intrigued for power.

"The charge?" he asked again. And when he had patiently learned the details of which Fra Giulio's long and faithful service gave little hint, he gathered evidence wherewith to refute them, and journeyed swiftly back to Rome, returning, triumphant, to reinstate the good old friar with honor in the home and offices he loved—the manner of his return making amends to Fra Giulio for the pain he had suffered, so sweet it seemed to him to owe to this son of his affections all the gladness of his later days.

VIII

WHILE the little Zuane was failing, Marcantonio, seeing Marina but seldom, solaced himself in preparing a royal gift to offer to his mother on the occasion of his own birthday fête. The idea had come to him that night after the Veronese had touched his own faulty sketch into such rounded life; besides, he had thought but one beautiful thought since he had, as it were, been unconsciously brought to confession by that scene in the studio. And Paolo Cagliari had been most kind in accepting his commission with an enthusiasm which promised wonderful results. Great as was his fame in those days,—and the Veronese never lived beyond his fame,—still, as in his earlier years, he was eager for any new method of proving the genius in which his own faith was as unbounded as his capacity to achieve was vigorous and tireless. And the young noble's unique fancy for a superb goblet of crystal *da Beroviero*, with a miniature of Marina of Murano enlaced in exquisite gold borders and set round with costly pearls—a trifle fit to offer to a princess —not only pleased the artist's well-known taste for luxury, but seemed to him an object worthy of his skill. In the kindness of his heart he would make the lovely face so winning that the great lady should yield to the prayer that had prompted the gift.

Among all the elaborate gift-pieces that had come from the workshops of Murano, but one had as yet approached this, and it had been sent with the homage of the Senate, by a retiring ambassador of "His Most Christian Majesty," to the Queen of France, and it bore, from Titian's hand, the portrait of her royal husband. This goblet, then, must surpass that one in magnificence, for it was the Veronese's opportunity; and in his soul, genial as it was, some sense of rivalry, born of Titian's assumption of the highest place in Venetian art, would last forever, in spite of the great master's manifest affection. The suggestion of the pearls—an added touch—was indeed due to Paolo Cagliari's over-weening sumptuousness, and the eager young lover was scarcely more anxious for the completion of this gem, upon which his hope depended, than was the great artist who already had all Venice at his feet.

"I shall need no sitting," the Veronese had said, when they were planning for the work. "My picture is nearly completed, and it will suffice. Nay, ask her not, my Marco; she is a devote—she will not understand."

Marcantonio flushed like a boy. He knew it would be difficult to obtain her consent, and for that very reason he must win it, for he was a true knight.

"How shall I win my lady's favor," he cried hotly, "if I peril it by lack of chivalry! There is no prouder maiden among the donne nobile on the Canal Grande."

"*Altro! Altro!*" said the master quietly. "She also shall look down from the balconies in the palazzo Giustiniani."

But when the young patrician told her glowingly of his wish to give his mother, on his great day, the most beautiful gift in all the world, it was hard to make her yield.

"It is not fitting," she answered quite simply.

"Yes, yes, Marina—since I love thee!"

"Ah, no; it is only sad." Her eyes filled with tears and she moved away, so that he could not touch her hand.

"Trust me, Marina! The Veronese knows the world, and he says it is well. It is this that shall win the consent of my mother, and she will conquer my father. And in the Gran' Consiglio——"

He turned his eyes suddenly away from Marina lest she should trace the faintest flicker of a doubt within them, as the vision rose before him of that imperious body, so relentless in its decrees, so tenacious in its traditions, so positive in its autocracy; but the threatened invincibility of this force only nerved him to a resistance as invincible, and he turned back to her with a flashing face, almost before she had noticed the interruption.

"There also—in the Consiglio—it shall be arranged, and all will be well."

And where two were ready for the end that should be gained the pleading was not over-long, though the thought was very strange for this simple maiden of Murano; so the precious painting was finished and in the hands of the decorators. And meanwhile, during those days when Marina had been watching the flickering of the little Zuane's pale flame of life and there had been no spare moments for Marcantonio, he had tried to absorb himself, as far as possible, in the preparation of this gift—

since she would not let him go to her—and he had
come to regard it as the symbol of success; for
failure was never for an instant contemplated in his
vision of the future.   There were pearls to be se-
lected, one by one, in visits innumerable to the Fon-
daco dei Turchi, where the finest of such treasures
were not secured at a first asking, and in these his
mother was a connoisseur; but there were many
more anxious visits to Murano, to be assured that
no step in the fashioning of his gift was endanger-
ing its perfection.

But even for the most impatient, time may not
tarry indefinitely, and the lagging moments had at
last brought round that festa of San Marco which
meant so much for Venice, with its splendid pa-
geants for the Church, its festivities for the people,
its fluttering of doves in the Piazza, and of timid,
eager maiden hearts, waiting in a sort of shy assur-
ance for that earliest Venetian love-token, the *boc-
colo*—the rosebud which breathed the secret of many
a young Venetian lover to his *inamorata* under those
April skies, on the festa of this patron saint of
Venice.

And the next morning the stately lady of the
Giustiniani stood quite alone on the balcony of the
great palace at the bend of the Canal Grande, lean-
ing upon her gold-embroidered cushions to watch
the gondola that was just landing at the step of the
Piazzetta; the restless movements of her tapering
jeweled fingers were the only sign of an emotion she
rarely betrayed, though doubtless, under the fault-
less dignity of her bearing, there were often cur-
rents of feeling and thwartings hard to be endured.

She was thinking of her boy with a great and sudden tenderness, now that the moment had come in which she would be less to him and the world of men must be more, as from the distance she saw the gondola touch the landing and watched him until he passed out of sight, after pausing with his father for a moment before the great columns of San Marco and San Teodoro, looking up perhaps with a keener sense of the dread scenes they had witnessed than had ever before possessed him, though the sunshine streamed brilliantly over the water and life seemed full of promise for this only son of the Ca' Giustiniani, on his way to take the oath of "Silence and Allegiance to the Republic," as a "*Nobile di Gran' Consiglio.*"

Marcantonio had entered the gondola gaily, with a full, pleasurable sense of the beauty of life, and well content with that portion which had fallen to his lot; for he was easily affected, and the air of the palace was full of the excitement of his fête. The only forebodings that shadowed his sunshine were connected with Marina and the gift which he should offer to his mother upon his return from the Ducal Palace. But the day was one to banish every hint of failure, making him more conscious of his power than he had ever been before, and he felt himself floating toward attainment—whatever the difficulties might be. But with his first step upon the Piazzetta he forgot the glory of the sunshine flashing over the blue waters, and a sudden sense of fate possessed him, as his father made an almost ' imperceptible pause in his grave progress toward the Ducal Palace, and with the slightest possible movement of his hand seemed to direct his son's attention to the great granite columns which bore the emblems of the patron saints of Venice.

A hundred times, in crossing the Piazzetta, Marcantonio had been vaguely aware of them as appropriate emblems of barbaric force and splendor and allegoric Christian allegiance; but suddenly they stood to him for historic records—the echoes of dread deeds avenged there rolled forth from the space between the columns, and the jeweled eyes of the terrible winged Lion flashed defiance upon any who questioned, in the remotest way, the will or the act of the Republic. He glanced toward the elder man, some deprecatory comment rising to his lips as he strove to dissipate the symbolic mood which was surely possessing him, for he felt himself uncomfortably conscious of the meaning wrought into the very stones about him, and to-day this over-mastering assertion of Venice—always Venice dominant—was oppressive.

But his father, apparently unaware of Marcantonio's turbulent sensations, wore his usual reserved and dignified mien; even the motion he had seemed to make before the columns in the Piazzetta was probably only due to Marcantonio's imagination, and the young fellow's light rejoinder passed unuttered, intensifying his discomfort. He realized that he was not searching for this symbolism with a poet's appreciation, nor as an archæologist delighting in curios, but as a son of the Republic—to gather her history and her purpose, to make himself one with her, to put himself under her yoke—and in his heart he rebelled.

Yet it was he, this time, who paused, undeniably, before the great window on the Piazzetta. The sun streamed in broad flashes of light over the soft rose-tinted walls of the palazzo and over the splendid balcony from which the Doge was wont to view the processions and fêtes of the Republic; the richly sculptured decorations detached themselves at once in allegory, the figures all leading up to Venice enthroned, holding out to the world her proud motto, "Fortis, justa, trono furias, mare sub pede pono." (Strong, just, I put the furies beneath my throne and the sea beneath my foot.) He walked on under a spell, feeling that the coils were tightening around him; he was a noble, but not free; yet he would not have surrendered his opportunities for the freer life of the people who had no part in the Consiglio.

He quickened his pace that the moment of irresolution might be the sooner over.

"Wait!" his father commanded, as Marcantonio would have entered the palace gate; "haste ill befits thy grave and dignified purpose. Before thou enterest the Consiglio I would have thee reverently mark how, at the palace gate, Justice sits enthroned on high, between the Lions of St. Mark, while Courage, Prudence, Hope, and Charity wait upon her."

"And below," answered Marcantonio, because he could think of nothing else to say, and because he knew every angle and carving of the palace from the æsthetic point of view better than his father did; "below is the Doge Foscari, kneeling very reverently to our noble Lion."

97

His father slowly scanned him with his inscrutable gaze, but answered nothing, and they passed under the magnificent Porta della Carta quite silently. Under the deep shadow of the gateway the business of the Ducal Palace was already progressing. Secretaries at their desks were preparing papers for discussion, while their assistants came and went with messages from the various departments of the great body of workers within the palace; they were too absorbed to look up as this Chief of the Ten passed them, so oblivious were they of anything but their duty that the stir about them left them serene and undisturbed, not even penetrating the realm of their consciousness.

"There is no more learned nor devoted body of scribes in the world," said Giustinian, with pride; "they have not a thought beyond their papers, and most wonderfully do they sift and prepare them for the Council, working often far into the night."

"It is machinery, not life!" Marcantonio exclaimed, hastening beyond the portal.

The great courtyard, under the wonderful blue of the sky, was aglow with color; the palace façades, broken into irregular carvings, seemed to hold the sunshine in their creamy surfaces; the superb wells of green bronze, magnificently wrought and dimmed as yet by little weather-staining, offered a treasury of luminous points. Here, in the early morning, the women of the neighborhood gathered with their water-jars, but now the court was filled with those who had business in the Ducal Palace—red-robed senators and members of the Consiglio talking in knots; a councillor in his violet gown, a group of merchant-princes in black robes, enriched with costly furs and relieved by massive gold chains, absorbed in discussion of some practical details for the better ordering of the *Fondachi*, those storehouses and marts for foreign trade peculiar to Venice; some grave attorney, more soberly arrayed, making haste toward the gloom of the secretary's corner; a sprinkling of friars on ecclesiastical business, of gondoliers in the varied liveries of the senators waiting their masters' call; here and there a figure less in keeping with the magnificence around him, too full of his trouble to be abashed, going to ask for justice at the Doge's feet—the heart of Venice was pulsing in the court, and under the arches came the gleam and shimmer of the sea. Up and down the splendid stairway that opened immediately from the Porta della Carta the Venetians came and went—nobles old and young; the people, bringing wrongs to be adjusted, or favors to be granted, or some secret message for the terrible *Bocca di Leone;* the people, rich and poor, in continuous tread upon this Giant Stairway, guarded by the gods of war and of the sea; the winged Lion enthroned above, just over the landing where the elected noble dons the rank of *Serenissimo*—this kaleidoscopic epitome of the life of the Republic was bewildering.

"How was it possible that all these people could take part in it without emotion?" the young patrician asked himself, forgetting that in this familiar scene the emotion only was new for him.

At the head of the landing on the Giant Stairway the Senator arrested his son with a gesture of command. "Welcome," he said, "to the Consiglio, Marcantonio Giustiniani. Thou wilt not forget that thou comest of a house which has held honors in Church and State. May this day be memorable for Venice and for thee!"

The influences of their surroundings were strong upon them both; but the young fellow, in his bounding life, craved something more than this formal induction into the official life of his sumptuous state—he longed to feel the human throb beneath it, that the sense of its weight might be lifted; but he could not find his voice until they had passed through the loggia and reached the chambers of the *Avvogadori*, where sat the keepers of the Golden Book.

He stretched out his hand wistfully and touched the elder man.

"Father!" he cried, in a voice not well controlled. And again, more steadily, though no answer came, "Father, I will not forget!"

The finding of his name among the birth records of the nobles of Venice, the registration witnessed by the three solemn Avvogadori,—those officers of the law whose rulings in their department were inexorable,—the act of confirmation before the Imperial Senate, whither, in grave procession, they immediately fared, preceded by the sacred "Libro d'Oro," upon which the oath of allegiance was sworn with bended knee—the ceremony was soon over, and Marcantonio stood enrolled among the ruling body of the great Republic.

As they returned through the splendid halls of the palace, Giustinian paused frequently to exchange a greeting with some old senator who came forward to welcome the young noble to the grave circle of rulers, and they were followed with glances of interest as they passed through the Piazza. For it was whispered in the *Broglio* that there were reasons—valid and patriotic, as were all the arguments of Venice—for the fact that no member of that ancient and loyal house had worn the highest honor of the state. *"The Ca' Giustiniani was too old, too wealthy, too influential—too much a part of Venice itself."*

"Like the Orseoli!" said Morosini Morosini, who was a friend of the Giustiniani, and who, like many another strong-brained Venetian, knew the taste of unsatisfied longings, yet kept a brave heart for the records of the Republic. And as he spoke there came to some of them who knew their annals well a stinging memory of the tale—which was no legend—of that pathetic group in their island sanctuary—the brothers who were left, after the death of Otto, the exiled Doge, and of Orso, the noble bishop-prince, all of the house of Orseoli, who, with their abbess-sister Felicia, were wounded to the heart because for the crime of too great love and service the jealous and unrequiting Senate had banished them forever from the Venice so loyally served—had decreed the extinction of a family to whom, as Doge and Patriarch, the Republic owed the wisest and most self-sacrificing of her rulers!

"Nay," said another speaker quickly, a friend to Morosini the historian—for the Broglio had been known to have a voice as well as ears, and the subject was a dangerous one, not honorable to Venice—

"Nay, there are no Orseoli. But it is for honor to the Giustiniani that none hath been chosen for the Serenissimo. He is strong, grave, and very silent; but most wise in council, most prudent in resource. He is needed among the *Savii*."

"And the coronation oath hath grown over straight since the days of the Michieli," responded Morosini. "The Giustinian is not a man for our *promissione* which, verily, fitteth ill with the dignity of our Prince—a man of spirit may well find it hard to assume the beretta under such restrictions!"

IX

WITH the nonchalance that concealed a skill all Venetian the gondoliers of the Giustiniani guided them gracefully through the floating craft moored to the stakes which rose in sheafs before their palace, announcing the colors of their noble house. Barges bearing flowers and decorations for the fête, fruits and game, were unloading on the broad marble steps, and through the wrought open-work of the splendid gates a scene of activity was disclosed in the nearer court which served as an office for the various departments of the household: while the house-master had come down the steps from his cozy lodge beside the entrance, and stood dispensing orders to a group of eager domestics.

In the deep shadow of the entrance-court the open one, through which the light streamed radiantly, seemed far distant, and when the great bell sent clanging echoes from court to court, gondoliers in undress liveries, who were lazily lounging and chatting, sprang to a show of activity over all those finishing touches of polish and nicety which had been achieved long before; and the lithe figures coming and going, throwing themselves into graceful attitudes over their semblance of labor, exchanging joyous sallies in anticipation of the evening's revelry, awoke a contagious merriment. Marcan-

tonio rallied from the heaviness of the morning
and felt young again, as he yielded to their influence
and wandered among them, tossing compliments
and repartees with Venetian freedom.

In the midst of this harmless trifling the voice of
Giustinian Giustiniani sounded sternly.

"Marcantonio, these ancient arms have been bur-
nished in honor of this day; I have a moment to
remind thee of their history—if thou hast for-
gotten."

He was calling from across the open court, where
the sunshine seemed suddenly less, and Marcantonio
hastened to respond.

The seneschal called for lights, for the workman-
ship of these heirlooms was too fine to be appre-
ciated in the gloom which pervaded the far inner
court; two or three iron lanterns were brought and
hung up, and link-boys flashed flaring torches upon
the pieces on the wall near which their master stood.

"Surely thou dost recall this breastplate of the
General Taddeo Giustiniani, who forced the Aus-
trians to surrender Trieste, when Venice laid siege
to the city in 1369? It was wrought in the East,
no doubt, and the inlaying is of gold and precious;
but not for this do we keep it chained. It is a
priceless jewel in the history of our house, for
Trieste meant much for Venice."

He raised the heavy chain that fastened it, and
the links fell, clanging, against the stones of the
wall; for this hall, which served as an armory, was
like a prison in its construction,—as strong and as
forbidding,—and here, among the ancestral relics,
were kept the arms which every nobleman, by Vene-

tian law, was required to hold in readiness to equip
his household against uprisings of the populace,
who were, by this same law, debarred these means
of self-defense.

At a sign from the Senator a young squire came
forward, proudly bearing a sword with a jeweled
hilt, in an intricately wrought scabbard. Giustin-
ian drew it from its sheath, displaying a blade ex-
quisitely damascened with acanthus foliage, as he
turned to his son.

"This is especially thine own," he said, "in honor
of this day—thy maiden sword. So far as the
handiwork of Cellini may make it worthy of a son ,
of our house, it hath been worthily chosen for thee.
Yet, unless thou leavest it to those who come after
thee, enriched by the name of a Giustinian who hath
wrought of his best for Venice, it will be all un-
worthy of a place among these trophies.'

The torch-bearers flashed their lights over it, and
the squires of the household pressed forward to
admire it, but Giustinian cut short the enthusiastic
chorus of the young men-at-arms and Marcantonio's
eager words of appreciation, crossing the sombre
hall with stately steps; for to his mind this impor-
tant day held many ceremonies yet unfulfilled, and
the pomp with which he chose to surround them was
not a circumstance to be dilated on.

"This," he said, as he touched a quaint dagger,
"belonged to thine ancestor, Marco Giustiniani,
Ambassador to the Scaglieri; there were other en-
voys of our name in other Italian provinces, in Eng-
land and the Papal Court, for we have been great
in statescraft as well as in war. But I wrong thee

105

in *seeming* to think thou knowest not the history of thine house. Perhaps, in these latter days, a man may best distinguish himself in statesmanship, for the mind is a weapon not to be slighted—when it is builded with strength, sharpened with careful use, and so wielded"—his gaze fell full upon Marcantonio for a weighty moment—"so wielded that it hath no pliancy save at the will of its owner. For sometimes it chanceth"—again he paused for a moment—"that a mind hath more masters than one, and Venice brooks no rival."

His father had been pointing out one heirloom after another while he spoke, and the pauses which Marcantonio found irritating, because they seemed to indicate hidden meanings to be unraveled, might proceed only from his effort to carry several trains of thought at once; but it was a habit of the elder Giustinian which held not a less share in the education of his son because it was distasteful to him.

To-day the young patrician almost resented this persistent marshaling of the shades of his ancestors, though at heart he was proud of them, and the prestige and luxury of his surroundings suited him well; but he chafed under his father's scrutiny, which, it seemed to him, unveiled the differences of their temperaments to an almost indecorous degree. The thought of Marina was tingling in his pulses, but he would not yield it up until the propitious moment came; and the strong consciousness of this sweet new queenship made the constant assertion of the sovereignty of Venice not easy to endure. But the remembrance of his vow of allegiance, just rendered before the Senate, returned to him rather as the public investiture of his rights as a man than as a claim of self-surrender; and he vowed to himself to use that right, in all possible conflict between himself and the Republic, in questions personal and dear; for the pleasant freedom of his life thus far had left him less in awe of the senatorial majesty than Giustinian Giustiniani would have deemed possible. But how could he hope to win his father's consent to any unpatrician alliance!

He passed the elder Giustinian hastily and paused beyond the next group of armor—battered breast-plates, casques, and shields of the twelfth century— but his thoughts were elsewhere.

"These," said the Senator, inexorably recalling him, "were of the famous siege of Lepanto, where, but for the favor of the Holy Father, our house had been extinct."

The young fellow's soul stirred within him, for he knew the story well. How was it possible for a Giustinian to pause before this great stand of antique trophies of prowess and not call to mind visions of heroism and suffering in which the Giustiniani of those days—*every one who belonged to Venice*—had yielded up his life in this great struggle with the Turks!

Yes, every one who belonged to Venice. For the young Nicolò, the last survivor of their ancient name, was already set apart from the world by his priestly vows, amid the quiet groves of the island of San Nicolò. It was a pretty romance—all those noble councillors, trembling from fear of the extinction of this most ancient and princely house, framing humble petitions to the Holy Father; the

107

youthful monk, leaving the tranquil solitude of his island sanctuary, unfrocked with honor by a Pope's decree, to don the crimson robe of senator and wed the daughter of the Doge! And later, when sons and daughters many had risen up to call them blessed, the old haunting charm of the convent reasserting itself, the return of the Giustinian—this solitary link between the long lines of his noble house, before and after—to his lonely cell on San Nicolò; the retirement of the Lady Anna from the sweet motherhood of her home to reign as Lady Abbess in the convent of Sant' Elenà; the nimbus of sainthood for the pair when their quiet days were closed—it was a pretty story, leading easily to thoughts of Marina.

"To-morrow," said Giustinian Giustiniani, as if in answer to his thoughts, "at dawn of day, there will be Mass in the capello Giustiniani on Sant' Elenà; and later we must visit the shrines of San Nicolò and San Lorenzo. For in the Church also we have had our part. A Giustinian was first Patriarch of Venice; a saint was father to our else broken line—we have had our share in Church and State, and it behooves a member of the Consiglio to remember the honors of his house."

He stood for a moment looking up at the shield on which were blazoned the arms of the Giustiniani, as if he missed something that should have been there; then, slowly turning back to the central court, now flooded with sunshine, he began the ascent of the grand stairway which led to the banqueting hall. The gleaming marble panels bore a fretwork of sculptured foliage with symbols entwined—the mitre, the cross, the sword—in richest Renaissance; but in all the decorations of this lordly palace, of the most ancient of the Venetians, not once did the mighty Lion of St. Mark appear.

When they had reached the landing opening into the banquet hall the Senator, turning in the direction of his own apartments, released his son with a motion of his hand toward the great, splendid chamber from which issued ripples of girlish laughter; and Marcantonio stood for a few moments under the arches which opened into it, looking on unobserved, for here it seemed that the fête was already reigning.

The noble maidens who attended the Lady Laura, fresh and charming, were knotting loops of ribbon in pendant garlands or grouping flowers in great vases between the columns which crossed the chamber from end to end—darting up the stairway to the gallery to alter a festoon in garland or brocade. Sallies of laughter, snatches of song, and pelting of flowers, like a May-day frolic, made the work long in the doing, but full of grace; and now and again, as if any purpose were wearying for such light-hearted maidens, they dropped their garlands and glided over the polished floor, twining and un-twining their arms—a reflex in active life, and not less radiant, of the nymphs of Bassano on the painted ceiling, between those wonderful, gilded arabesques of Sansovino.

There was a little shriek of discomfiture as they suddenly perceived the young lord of the day, but the Contessa Beata Tagliapietra came saucily toward him as he was escaping.

"The Lady Laura hath charged me to ask the Signor Marcantonio whether the garlands be disposed according to his liking."

She swept him a mocking reverence, so full of grace and coquetry that the maidens all flocked back from their hiding-places to see how the young signor would receive it.

"I know not which pleaseth me best," he answered lightly; "the grace of the garlands, or the grace of the dance, or the grace of the *damigelle* who have so wrought for the beauty of this fête. Nay, I may not enter, for the Lady Laura will await my coming."

"Is this day then so full of gravity that one may not steal a moment to dance at one's own fête, Signor Consiglière?" she retorted, mockingly.

But the Lady Laura herself was coming toward them, with slow, stately steps, hiding her impatience—for the morning had seemed long.

At sight of her Marcantonio bent his knee with the knightly homage still in vogue, and gave his hand to conduct her to her boudoir.

"Signor Consiglière,"—she began, with a stately congratulation, when they were quite alone in her own boudoir; she had been planning, during the long morning, a speech that should be of a dignity to suit so great an occasion, but the words died away upon her lips; for once she forgot Venice and the Ca' Giustiniani, and the mother was uppermost. She folded her arms about him closely, and rested her head upon his shoulder in delicious abandon.

"Marco, my boy!" she murmured.

His heart overflowed to her in unaccustomed endearments, so rarely did she express any emotion, and to-day the rebound from the morning's repression filled him with hope and gladness. All fear of winning her aid was lifted. *"Madre mia!"* he cried, his face radiant with happiness.

"This day is not as other days," she said, half in apology for her weakness, as she recovered herself.

"I have a gift for thee, madre mia; let me bring it."

"I need no gift, Marco; for now hast thou everything before thee—every honor that Venice may offer to a Venetian of the Venetians! Forget it not, my Marco."

But he had already flown from her, with impatient, lover's footsteps. Now that the moment had come he could not wait.

"Mother!" he cried, with shining eyes, as he placed the costly case upon a table and drew her gently toward it.

She stood in mute astonishment before the faultless gift, this perfect bit of Beroviero crystal,—opalesque and lucent, reflecting hidden rainbow tints, enhanced by the golden traceries delicate and artistic—the beautiful young face framed in those sea-gems dear to the Venetian heart, each pearl a study of changing light.

"There is none like it in Venice!" she exclaimed; "nor hath there ever been. Thou hast treated me like a queen, my Marco!"

"I wished it so," he answered impatiently, for he could not wait. "And the face——"

"Never hath there been a more exquisite! It is the Titian's work?"

"Nay, of the Veronese; for the goblet is of mine own designing. And the master, for my sake, hath spent himself upon the face."

"He will be here to-night, and we will thank him," she answered graciously. "And for thee—thou hast excelled thyself."

But Marcantonio answered nothing to her praise; his eyes were fixed upon the miniature of the Veronese.

"If Paolo Cagliari findeth none so beautiful among the noble damigelle who will grace thy fête to-night as this face which he hath painted, we will forgive him," she said playfully. "But thee, Marco, we will not forgive. The time hath come when thou shouldst choose; thy father and I have spoken of this."

She came close to him and folded his hand caressingly. "The Contessa Beata Tagliapietra hath a wonderful charm; and there is the Lady Agnesina Contarini—a face for a Titian!"

"Mother! I pray thee——" Marcantonio interrupted.

"Nay, Marco—to-day it is fitting; for thy wedding should follow soon upon this fête. Thou art no longer a boy, and Venice looks to us to help thee choose a fitting bride; for there is none other of this generation of thy name, and thou,—I will not hide it from thee since thou needest heartening, —thou wilt be a fortunate wooer with these maidens, or—or elsewhere. But my little Beata is charming——"

"Mother," said Marcantonio, flushing like a boy, yet drawing himself up proudly, "I have already crowned her who shall be my bride with pearls; and for her face—thou hast named it exquisite." Then, unbending, he threw his arms around her and kissed her on the forehead.

The Lady Laura stood as if petrified.

"I know her not," she said, when she could speak. "Name her to me." Her voice was hard and strained.

"Do not speak so, madre mia! Love her—she is so charming! And she will not come to me unless thou love her too."

"How, then—if she is thy bride?" The words seemed to choke her.

"Nay, but my *chosen* bride—holding my vows with my heart; yet, unless thou plead with me for my happiness she will not wed me—she is so proud."

"Name her," the Lady Laura repeated, unbending slightly.

"Marina Magagnati."

She stood listening, as if more were to follow, then she shook her head. "I know not the name, unless—but it is not possible! She is not of Venice, then?"

"A Venetian of the Venetians, my mother, with the love of Venice in her soul—but not——"

"Marcantonio, explain thine enigma! How should there be a name of all our nobles unknown to me?"

"There are nobles of the 'Libro d'Oro,' my mother, and—nobles of the people, and she is of these."

"How canst thou name a mesalliance to me—Marcantonio Giustiniani, Nobile di Consiglio—on

this day, when thou hast given thy vows to Venice!
Thou dost forget the traditions of thine house."

"Nay, mother; Venice and the Ca' Giustiniani I
am not likely to forget," he answered, with sudden
bitterness. "One thing—quite other—am I much
more likely to forget; but for this have I sworn,
that which my heart teaches me for noble will I
do, and she whom I love will I wed—*or none other.*"

"Marco!" the word seemed a desperate appeal.

"That do I swear upon this sword which my
father hath given me to prove my knighthood—'to
enrich,' he hath said, 'the records of our house.'
And thou wilt help me, my mother, for I love thee!"
His voice had grown tender and pleading again.

"I also love thee, Marco," she answered more
gently, for none could resist his voice when this
mood was upon him; "but I may not help thee to
undo thyself and forget the honor of thine house."

"Mother," said Marcantonio, sternly, "charge me
with no unknightly deed! To love Marina is to
love a woman nobler than any of thy maidens; thou
knowest her not. I would bring her to thee to win
thee, but she will not come. It is thou, she saith,
who must send her sign of favor."

"I fear me it must be long in going, my Marco;
yet I love thee well. How should I send my favor
to a daughter of the people!"

"Those are the words of Marina Magagnati."

"She is wise then; she will help thee to forget."

"The vow of a Giustinian is never broken; that
hast thou taught me, my mother, from the legends
of our house. This sword, upon which I have
sworn it, I lay at thy feet. Bid me raise it in token

of thy favor and of thine aid in this one thing which I ask of thee."

They stood looking into each other's faces, her pride melting under the glow of the beautiful new strength in the face of the son whom she had thought so yielding; yet it was she who had striven to teach him knightliness.

She hesitated,—"If I cannot aid thee, what wilt thou do?"

"I must wait and suffer," he said; "for Marina will not yield."

"It is new for a maiden of the people to know such pride," she answered, scornfully.

"It is because none are like her, and her soul is beautiful as her face! My mother, there are none prouder in all this palace; the little Contessa Beata is a *contadina* beside her! Yet, it is not pride, I think, but love and care for my happiness," he added, grown suddenly bold. "She will not come to bring me sorrow; and she hath said that my duty being to Venice, she can wed me only with the consent of our house. And Messer Magagnati———"

"There is a father, then, who would treat with thee?"

"Mother—use not that tone; thou dost not understand! Ask the Veronese. Messer Magagnati knows not of this; for so tenderly doth his daughter care for him that, to save him pain of knowing that she suffers for lack of thy welcome, she hath not told him. Shall the Veronese plead with thee better than thine own son? For he knoweth the maiden well; and the father, who is most honorably reported in Venice for the wonder of his discoveries in his industry of glass. He is of the people—of the 'original citizens'—for of the days before the *serrata*[1] hath his family records; but he might well be of the Signoria, so grave he is and full of dignity. And his name is old—*Mother!*"

"Nay, Marco, lift thy sword; how should it lie there for lack of thy mother's favor? I will not have thee suffer, if I can give thee aid. But one may suffer in other ways—quite other—which thou hast no knowledge of, for to thee there seemeth to be, in all the world, nothing worthy but this wish of thine! But it is no promise; one must ponder in so great a matter, my boy!"

They broke down in each other's arms, clasping the sword between them.

The Senator's firm step resounded on the marble floor; they had scant time to recover themselves; but his eyes fell at once upon the magnificent goblet, and there was pleasure in his stern face.

"This, then, is of thy designing, Marcantonio," he exclaimed, as he stooped to examine it in its case of satin and velvet. "A veritable gift-piece! And already thou hast won the favor of the Senate, since it hath been reported to them by our Chief of the Ten, who hath the industries of Murano in charge, that at the exhibit given yestere'en a goblet more sumptuous than that prepared for his Majesty of France was of thy designing. The Secretary will bring thee this night a summons from the Ten to appear before them on the morrow to receive their

---

[1] An important constitutional act, limiting the aristocracy to those families who had, at that period, sat in the Council; always referred to as an era in Venetian history.

congratulations, because of the inspiration thou hast given to our most valued industry.

"It is a rare mark of favor that it hath been confided to me," Giustinian continued, still examining the goblet with pride, "since custom doth require that one should withdraw from the sitting of the Council when any matter touching his house is treated. But Morosini, by grace of the Signoria, hath been with me for a moment, that there may be no misgivings of fear upon this fête-day of our house. And to-night this summons to favor shall be presented, to honor the youngest member of the Consiglio. Marcantonio, I am proud of thee; the Ten will be here—every one! And verily the goblet is beautiful. It shall be well displayed in the great banquet hall."

"Here, in my boudoir, where my boy hath placed it," said the mother quickly, as the Senator would have lifted it, "since it is my gift. And, Marco"— She turned to him a face softened and beautified by the struggle, which had been very great, and her eyes were deep with a light which bound him to her forever.

"Marco mio, it shall be well displayed. For I will bid my maidens circle this table whereon it rests with a wreath of roses—white and very beautiful— in token of thy mother's favor."

X

MARINA, under the yellow glare of the lamp in the dark oak cabinet, worked fitfully, with broken, lifeless strokes, at the designs before her; while her father, feigning absorption in some new drawings which lay spread out within touch of his strong-veined hands, watched her furtively from the other side of the table.

"Thou art restless," he said, suddenly and sternly; "what aileth thee?"

Her lip quivered, but she did not look up, while with an effort she steadied the movement of her hand and continued her work. "My hand hath no cunning to-night, and it vexeth me, my father."

"It is poor work when the heart is lacking," he answered, in a tone charged with irritation. "I also have seen a thing which hath taken my heart from me."

The color deepened in her cheeks and the pencil strokes came more falteringly, but she answered nothing.

"Nay, then!" he exclaimed, more brusquely than his wont, as he stretched out his hand and arrested her movement. "What I have to say to thee importeth much."

She flushed and paled with the struggle of the moment, then a beautiful calm came over her face;

she laid down her pencil and, quietly dropping her hands in her lap, she turned to him with a smile that might have disarmed an angrier man—it was full of tenderness, though it was shadowed by pain.

It relaxed his sternness, and, after a moment's hesitation, he came around the table and sat down beside her.

"To-night is the fête at Ca' Giustiniani, for the young noble of their house."

He waited for her to speak, but she did not tremble now, though he was searching her face.

"Yes, father, I know."

"And, Marina—I do not understand—and it is a grief to me——"

She nestled to him closely and tried to slip one of her slender hands between his, which were tightly strained together in a knotted clasp, as if he would make them the outlet for some unbearable emotion.

The previous evening was the first they had not passed together since the death of Zuanino; her father had sent her word that he had matter which would occupy him alone, and all day Marina had been heavy-hearted, going at matins and at vespers quite alone to the Madonna at the Duomo, that she might take comfort and counsel.

Girolamo did not respond to her caress, though his tone softened a little as he proceeded with his tale and her arm stole round him.

"Yesterday, at the stabilimento Beroviero, we were summoned by a call of our Capo of the Ten to witness the approval that should be passed on the exhibit of that stabilimento; we all, of the Guild of Murano, were there as always. And foremost

119

among the productions, most marvelous for beauty,
was a fabric of their lucent crystal—thou knowest
it, Marina? My child—how came thy face there?
Thy face, Marina—set round with lustrous pearls!"

He folded her to his breast with sudden passion,
and stooped his head to her shoulder for an instant,
lifting it quickly that she might not feel the sobbing
of his breath which, even more than his broken
words, betrayed his anguish.

"Dearest father, it was because I loved thee so
much that I would not have thee suffer from my
pain, that I told thee not. Never again will I hold
aught from thee."

"Thy pain, Marina? and thy face—and for the
young noble, Giustiniani? I do not understand."

"Father, because I could grant him nothing and
he would give me everything, and because—because
God sent the love and the Madonna hath made me
feel that it would be sweet, I granted him only this
—my portrait—because he pleaded so one could not
resist; and because he said it would win the consent
of all to see that he treated me like a queen!"

"Nay; one comes not in secret to steal the love
of a queen."

"My father," answered the maiden proudly, for
he had drawn away from her, "there is no stealing
of that which I would gladly yield him, if it were
thy pleasure and that of the Ca' Giustiniani! And
there would have been no secret; but I—to spare
thee pain of knowing that I suffered—I would
not let him come to plead with thee."

"Why shouldst thou suffer?"

"It is hard to lose thy love when only I told
thee not because I would spare thee pain! Father—

I have only thee!" Her courage broke in a quick sob.

"Nay, then—nay, then," he faltered softly, stroking her bowed head; "he is no man to love, if he would let thee suffer; he should take thee—before them all—if he would be worthy——"

The low, intense, interrupted words were a brave surrender.

"Ay, my father, it is like Marco to hear thee speak!"

"Then let him come and make thee Lady of the Giustiniani, like a true knight!" exclaimed the old man fiercely.

"Ay, father, so would he; but I have told him that thou and I are not less proud than those of his own house, and without their consent it may not be."

"Nay, I care not for their house—only for thy happiness; he shall wed thee, and my home is thine; I have enough for thee and him; he shall not make thee suffer."

They were close together now, father and daughter—a beautiful group in the yellow lamplight against the dark background that surrounded them like an impassible fate; her face was a study of happiness, tenderness, suffering, and strength; her father wrapped her close in his protecting arms, and thus she could bear everything. They were silent for a while: he trying to accept the revelation in its strangeness, she planning how she should make him understand.

"I am glad thou knowest it, dear father," she said at length, very softly. "I have thy love—I can bear everything."

"Nay, thou shalt have nothing to bear! Thou

shalt be Lady of the Giustiniani—what means the portrait else?"

"It is like Marco again!" she cried, with a little pleased laugh. "He said—because I would make him no promise until all consented—that he would take me thus before all the world, and that should make them consent."

"Nay, let him come out from his house and take thee! I also, of the people, bear an ancient name, and I have kept it honorable. Pietro, the earliest master of our beautiful art, was thine ancestor. The Giustinian stoops not in taking thee."

"He is noble enough to be thy son, my father— and chivalrous as thou—but we are too noble to let him do aught unbefitting his noble house; for thou knowest the Giustiniani are like princes in Venice, and Marco is their only son. He oweth duty to the Republic; and this day, in the Ducal Palace, hath he sworn his oath of allegiance."

"First should it have been to thee!"

"Ay, first it was to me," she answered serenely; "he would not have it otherwise; it is only *my* promise that is lacking. This will I not give until the Giustiniani make me welcome, or there would be no happiness for Marco. He shall not lose in loving me. The Signor Giustinian Giustiniani is so stern —and one of the Chiefs—I would not vex him and bring down the displeasure of the Ten; I would bring my Marco happiness—not pain."

"Oh, the courage of young hearts!" the old man exclaimed with a thrill of pride and amazement. "Never had Giustinian a prouder bride. And already thou hast won my heart for this lover of thine, who hath hope of taking thee from thy old father, yet stays at thy bidding."

"He hath said that he would be here ere the fête began," she answered timidly, "since already, through the portrait, thou must know the truth; and it would seem unknightly, or as if he feared thy displeasure, if he came not this day to pay thee his duty. Father, methinks there is already a stir below——"

"Thou shouldst make thyself brave!" her father exclaimed, with a quick, anxious glance at her simple home toilette. "He will pass from thee to many noble ladies in the palazzo Giustiniani—all in bravery of festival."

"Nay, my father, so he found me; I would not hold him by devices, of which I know naught. There will be much to suffer, and these trifles cannot enter into anything so deep and real. I would rather he should change to-day—if he could be light enough to change. Besides," she faltered, with a quick, charming blush, "I think it is already his step without; and to-night he will have so few moments to spare me—Marco!"

Coming forward through the shadow of the doorway, the young noble—deferent, masterful, unrenouncing—was a suitor not easily to be baffled by any claims of Venice.

Girolamo turned quickly to his child, then looked away, for her face made a radiance in the room; he, her father, who had loved her through all the days of her maiden life with a great tenderness, had never known the fullness of her beauty until now; the soft folds of the simple robe flowing away from her into the surrounding shadow left the pure young charm of her head and face in luminous relief, as the brilliant young noble, in embroidered velvet and silken hose and jeweled clasps—a type of sumptuous modern day Venice—stepped forward into the little circle of light, bowing before her with courtly deference.

The vision of those youthful faces made it easy to forget the outward contrast—a mere accident of birth.

Girolamo Magagnati had promised himself that he would be a true knight to his beloved child; he would question and prove this bold young noble who claimed, with such presumption, so great a prize—not humbly suing, as he should have done; he would make him tremble and wait; he should learn that his daughter was not to be the more easily won because she was of the people! Then, with the fullness of his vow upon him, and with a heart loving indeed, but brave as proud, he had raised his eyes and beheld a vision in which neither nobles nor people held part—only a maiden, glorified by her love and trust; and a lover—prince or peasant it mattered not—for on his face it was luminously written that in all the world there was for him none other than she. And the vision, like an apprehension of Truth—rare and very beautiful— conquered Girolamo, because he was strong enough to yield.

"It is but a moment that I have for this dearest claim of the day," said Marcantonio Giustiniani, turning to the older man with winning courtesy; "and sooner should I have come to the father of

Marina to crave the grace I cannot do without, but that she bade me tarry. Yet, now—she herself hath spoken?"

He looked from one to the other questioningly.

"There are no secrets between us," Girolamo answered with dignity, while weighing some words that should welcome his daughter's suitor with discretion and reserve.

But the maiden broke in timidly: "And he is not angry, Marco mio!"

"Nay, my favor is for him who truly honors my daughter and proves himself worthy; for her happiness is dear to me. But the difficulties are great, as she herself hath told me."

"A little time and there shall be none!" cried Marcantonio, joyously. "For to-day, when first I have taken my seat in the Council, not more solemnly have I sworn allegiance to the Republic than I would pray Messer Magagnati to bear me witness that Marina—and none other—will I wed!"

"Give him thy hand, my daughter, for thy face confesseth thee; and to-day his lady should grant him so much grace."

"Yet, Marco—for thy sake—I make no vows to thee. Only this will I tell thee," she added, in a voice that was very soft and low, as he sealed his lover's vow on her fluttering hand. "For me, also, there is no other!"

"And I bring thee a '*boccolo*,' Marina, since thou art of the people and wouldst have me remember all thy traditions," he cried gaily. "Yet this one hath a fragrance like none other that hath ever blossomed on the festa of San Marco—my blessed patron!—for I culled it from the garland which my mother bade her maidens for a token make about the table where thy portrait is displayed."

He raised the rosebud to his lips before he placed it in her hand.

"And the Senator Giustinian Giustiniani?" Girolamo questioned, in his grave, deep voice, concealing his triumph.

But Marcantonio had already answered to the timid question of Marina's eyes, with a ringing tone of assurance.

"And for my father—we must have courage!"

XI

THE summons from the Ten had been presented with ceremony on the night of the fête at Ca' Giustiniani, and Marcantonio was grateful for the strong support of Paolo Cagliari's friendly presence, as they went together to the Sala di Collegio in the Ducal Palace; for this seemed to the young noble an opportunity, that might never come again, of presenting his petition to ears not all unfavorable; and there was a thrill of triumph in the thought that his maiden speech before this august body should be his plea for Marina's admission to the favor of the Signoria. Already fortune had been kind to him beyond his hopes, and, with the daring of youth, he was resolved to claim the possible. The Veronese alone knew of his intention, and as to his father—he could only put him out of his thoughts. If the Senate listened to his petition there would be no difficulties, but he would not weaken his courage by any previous contest, unavailing as it must be.

Meanwhile there was the remembrance of the roses of the Lady Laura—fragrant with her great renunciation.

The honor of this summons was reflected in the increased dignity of the elder Giustinian, and in a tinge of urbanity new to him, as he parted from

Paolo Cagliari and Marcantonio, who remained standing on the floor of the hall, to take his seat among the senators in the seats running around the chamber, as on the previous day, instead of the one rightfully his own àmong the higher Council who were to pronounce the laudatory words.

The industries of Murano had always been dear to the senatorial heart, but of late years the fostering care of the Republic had been increased to an unprecedented degree, and the stimulus thus given to the workmen of Murano had been evideuced in a series of brilliant discoveries, so that the marvel of their fabrics had become as much a source of jealousy to other nations as of revenue and pride to the Republic.

Thus the affair of this gift-piece of crystal was deemed of quite sufficient importance to occupy the attention of the senators, who prepared themselves to listen with every symptom of interest ˏto this report of the exhibit of Murano, which had been read on the previous day before the Ten.

It had chanced before that these reports had been followed by words of commendation, but it had rarely happened that a young noble had been summoned before the Collegio to receive such a testimonial, and the occasion lost none of its interest from the fact that many of those present had witnessed the presentation of the summons in the banquet hall of the palazzo Giustiniani.

The famous goblet, by order of the Senate, was also present, as a proof that the laudatory words pronounced by the Secretary of the Ten at the close of the repOrt were well deserved.

It was not often that a member won distinction on the day of his entrance to the Gran' Consiglio; the favor shown by the Senate was great; the position of the Ca' Giustiniani among the proud Venetian nobility was beyond question; and some of the fathers of the young and noble ladies who had graced the banquet watched the young Giustinian with a quite personal interest.

"It was time," they said, "that the handsome young patrician should choose a bride."

"And once before, in the history of the Republic, as now," suggested another, "there was but one of the Ca' Giustiniani.".

There was a sympathetic and ominous shaking of heads, for the story was well known.

"But to none of those golden-haired maidens who danced at his fête would he show favor, though upon his birthnight. And when the Lady Beata had asked him shyly why he wore a white rose in his doublet, he had told her saucily, 'The meaning of the flower is *silence.*'"

These and other trifles bearing upon the ceremony of the morning were discussed in pleasant asides, while the report had been read and the note of approval had been proclaimed to Marcantonio, who dropped the arm of his friend and came forward to receive it.

"My Lords of the Senate, the Collegio and most Illustrious Ten!" he responded, with a courtly movement of deference which included them all, "I thank you! In that it graciously pleaseth you to bestow upon me your favor for a trifle of designing which was the pastime of an hour, and made

o

for the pleasure of the giving in homage to the noble Lady Laura Giustiniani. But the praise of it should not be mine; it is rather to the stabilimento which hath shown perfection in its workmanship. But first to him, the master, who hath given it its crowning grace. I pray you, let me share the unmerited honor of this commendation with Paolo Cagliari, *detto Veronese*, without whom my little had been nothing!"

The chivalry and grace of the young noble elicited a murmur of approbation, as he courteously indicated his friend.

The Veronese, to whom this *dénouement* was unexpected, and who had long since been crowned with highest honors by the Republic, did not move forward, but, acknowledging the tribute of his pupil with a genial smile, he stood with folded arms, unembarrassed and commanding, scanning the faces of the assembly, well pleased with the effect produced by the words of Marcantonio, whom, at all hazards, he intended to befriend. He realized that the atmosphere might never be so favorable.

"The crowning grace of that goblet, my Lords of Venice," he said boldly, "is lent it by the face of the most beautiful maiden it hath ever been my fortune to paint—than whom Venice hath none more charming."

There was a murmur of surprise from the younger nobles, who were standing in groups about the hall of the Gran' Consiglio; they had supposed the face to be merely a dainty conceit of the artist's fancy, and those nearest gathered about the case with sudden interest.

But the face of Marcantonio betrayed him, while

he stood unabashed in the circle of the senators,
though with mounting color, his hand, under shel-
ter of his cloak, resting upon the jeweled hilt of
the sword upon which he had sworn his first
knightly vow.

Giustinian Giustiniani rose to his feet. "Her
name, Messer Paolo Cagliari!" he thundered.

But it was the young Giustinian who answered
to the challenge—"Marina Magagnati!" with an
unconscious reverence, as he confessed his lady's
name.

"Is no face found fair enough among all the
palaces on the Canal Grande to charm thy fastidious
fancy?" cried the angry father, losing all self-con-
trol. "It were fitter that the name of thine inamo-
rata were first declared elsewhere than in this
presence!"

"Not so, my father," Marcantonio replied, un-
daunted. "For I first would ask a grace of our
most illustrious Signoria,—the which may it indeed
please them to grant,—or never shall I bring a bride
to the Ca' Giustiniani. As I have sworn a noble's
oath of allegiance to Venice, so faithfully have I
vowed to wed none other than Marina Magagnati!
And it is my father who hath taught me to hold
sacred the faith of a Venetian and a Giustinian.
But my lady is not *called* of noble blood."

"She is daughter to Messer Girolamo Magag-
nati,"—it was the Veronese who spoke,—"than
whom, in all Murano, is none better reputed for the
fabrics of his stabilimento, nor more noble in his
bearing; albeit, he is of the people—as I also, Paolo
Cagliari, am of the people."

The words had a ring of scorn; the Veronese

folded his arms again and looked defiantly around him—a splendid figure, with the jeweled orders of France and Rome and the Republic flashing on his breast. His gaze slowly swept the faces of the assembly, then returned to rest upon the great votive picture which filled the wall from end to end above the Doge's throne—*his work*—like the glory of the ceiling, which declared the artist noble by genius, if not by birth. "I also am of the people!" he repeated, in a tone that seemed a challenge.

"Most Illustrious Signoria!" cried Marcantonio; "once, in the history of our Republic, hath it pleased this most gracious Senate to declare its favor to a daughter of a master-worker of Murano, in a decree whereby it was provided that the maid should wed a noble of most ancient house, and if there should be children of the marriage, each name should stand unprejudiced, with those of the nobles of Venice, in the 'Libro d'Oro.' If I have found favor in your sight—I beseech you—that which the Senate hath once decreed is again possible."

The senators looked at each other in consternation, awed at the boldness of the petition and the wit of its presentation.

The young patrician slowly ascended the steps of the dais, and closed his appeal with an obeisance to the Doge, full of dignity.

The Councillors who sat beside the Doge were holding grave discussion, for the few words of the young noble had touched upon weighty points; they had been presented with a simplicity which veiled their diplomatic force; he was a man of growing power who must be bound to the service of Venice, even were he not the last of a princely line which the Republic would fain see continued to her own latest generation. So unabashed in such a presence, he would be tenacious of his purpose and hold to his vow with unflinching knightliness.

Venice and his lady were included in his sworn allegiance, and to seek to make them rivals would be a danger for the Republic.

Never before had appeal been made to this decree; it was not fresh in the minds of the Savii and the six most venerated Councillors without whose acquiescence the mandate of the Doge was powerless, and they had listened to the bold declaration with a surprise not unmingled with resentment, that so young a man should make, in their presence, an assertion touching matters of State which they could neither affirm nor deny! At a sign from one of the chancellors, one of the three counsellors at law of the Avvogadori di Commun, who had the keeping of the Golden Book, had been immediately summoned from adjoining chambers in the Palace and had confirmed the statement. Such a marriage had indeed taken place in the latter half of the fourteenth century; the number of the decree authorizing the full nobility of the children had been noted in the Golden Book, the original decree could therefore be found, within the archives, upon demand of the Savii.

The case had changed from a matter of gracious policy to one of unquestioned importance in the minds of the gravest counsellors of the Republic—in spite of the glamor of romance which threatened to lessen its dignity by winning the enthusiastic support of the younger members of the assembly and the jealous opposition of the older senators, who were tenacious of the privileges and restrictions of the ancient nobility of Venice. The faces of many among them were dark and threatening. One of their number high in authority, whose seat was near the Savii on the dais, and who was known to be of the strictest oligarchical proclivities, risked the words, *"Remember the Serrata Consiglio,"* in a clear undertone, but was immediately repressed by a terrible glance from more than one of the commanding Savii.

Giustinian Giustiniani was alone kept silent by the force of conflicting emotions which left him only strength enough to realize that he was too angry to advise with dignity, though he was one of the Chiefs of the Ten. He had been outwitted in the presence of the Maggior Consiglio by a son who had shown an astuteness and courtliness of which any Venetian father might be proud, together with a knowledge of the point upon which he based his appeal, which required the summoning of the Avvogadori di Commun, though it was uttered in the presence of the six supreme Councillors of the Republic! He could not interpose to demean his ancient lineage by consenting to this unpatrician alliance; he would not accept the alternative for his only son—the last of the Giustiniani! Nor could he urge a Giustinian to break a vow of honor made before the highest tribunal of the realm. He was trembling with wrath and filled with admiration, while he sat speechless, awaiting the issue of a question which so deeply concerned the interests of the Ca' Giustiniani.

The impression was profound, and a silence fell upon that magnificent assembly through which the rulers of the ship of state seemed to hear the throbbings of a threatened storm. They were men of power, and they realized that it was a moment when action should be prompt and positive.

A yellowed parchment, with the great seal of the Republic appended, was brought in state from the adjoining chambers of the Avvogadori and laid before the Doge, who passed it, in turn, to each of his Councillors.

The silence was breathless. All eyes turned instinctively upon the young noble, who had withdrawn to the side of his friend, and stood, unconscious of their gaze, radiant with his hope of Marina.

"Nobles of the Gran' Consiglio of our Most Serene Republic," said the Doge at last with deep impressiveness, "this record is the original decree of this Senate, of the fourteenth century, given under the Great Seal of the Republic in 1357. It hath been duly laid before our Councillors in your presence and unanimously confirmed by them. And they do unanimously consent to this our ruling in favor of the petition which hath this day been presented before this Council by the noble Marcantonio, of the ancient and princely house of Giustinian. Since in this sixteenth century our Republic, by grace of God and favor of her Rulers, is not less enlightened than in those earlier days to perceive when graciousness may promote her welfare, in granting favor to a noble house which hath ever shown to Venice its valor, its discretion, its unfailing loyalty."

A cry of exaltation rang through the house like an electric thrill; the senators started to their feet.

"My life, my faith, my strength—the might of all my house for Venice!" shouted the young Giustinian, with his sword held high above his head, like an inspired leader.

XII

THE permission of the Maggior Consiglio, under favor of this imperious government, was equivalent to a command and a public betrothal, and for a few ecstatic days the heir of the Ca' Giustiniani went about in a state of exaltation too great to be aware of any home shadows—the slumbering anger of the Capo of the Ten and an inharmonious atmosphere wherein each was intensely conscious of an individual estimate of the great event which touched them all so nearly.

For suddenly the betrothal of this only son of an old patrician family had assumed almost the proportions of a State marriage; and a young fellow for whom time-honored observances of the realm could be set aside, and who had won so extreme a proof of favor by his own wit and grace, was surely a figure that might well occupy public attention.

But the decree would soon be a state paper; it was already an accepted fact in the halls of the Council and in the *salons* of the nobility, and the disappointed great ladies from the neighboring palaces were calling, with curious questions decorously dressed in congratulatory form.

"When should they have the pleasure of welcoming the *new* Lady of the Giustiniani?"

137

"Was it not true that the Lady Marina—that was to be," there was always some little stinging emphasis in the gracious speech, "had given a votive offering to the convent of the Servi? She was a devote then—quite unworldly—this beautiful maiden of Murano?"

"What a joy for the Lady Laura that so soon there would be a bride in the Ca' Giustiniani!"

"The Lady Laura had never been more stately," they told each other when they entered their gondolas again, "nor more undisturbed. There were no signs of displeasure; it must be that the lowly maid was very beautiful."

"Was it a thing to make one sad, to have a son who could twist the rulers round his little finger, and break the very laws of the Republic? Nay, but cause for much stateliness!" said a matron with two sons in the Consiglio.

"The bridal must be soon," said the Lady Laura to herself, as she sat alone in her boudoir, "for the ceasing of this endless gossip." And, because she could think of nothing else, she was already weary with the planning of a pageant which made her heart sick.

But Giustinian Giustiniani had no words, for the case was hopeless—only a face of gloom, and much that was imperative to keep him in the Council Chamber.

For these few blissful days the lovers had heaven to themselves, floating about at twilight on the shores of the Lido, where there were none to trouble the clear serenity of their joy by the chilling breath of criticism. "That white rose which I brought thee was in sign of my mother's favor," Marcantonio reminded Marina more than once; "and for the rest—all will be well; and for a little, we can wait."

"Ah, yes, they could wait—in such a smiling world, under a sky so exquisite, gliding over the opal of the still lagoons at twilight.

But old Girolamo, sure now of the decree which should number his daughter among the patricians of this Republic where, through long generations, his family had made their boast that they represented the people, was in a feverish mood—grave, elated, sad by turns, unwilling to confess to the loneliness which was beginning to gnaw at his heart, for Marina was his life; he did not think he could live without her; he *knew* he could not live and see her unhappy beside him; and he was old to learn the new, pathetic part he must play—the waiting for death, quite alone in the old home.

And those others,—in the sumptuous palace on the Canal Grande,—would they prize the ·treasure which was the very light of his life, that he should break his heart to yield her up?

He could have cried aloud in his anguish, as he sat waiting for the happy plash of the returning gondola, the princely gondola of the Ca' Giustiniani, bringing those two before whom life was opening in a golden vista; but as the slow ripples breaking over the water brought them nearer, his heart girded itself again with all his chivalrous strength, lest he should dim the glad light in his beloved one's eyes— lest he should seem ungenerous to the brave young knight who had dared the displeasure of his house and of the Republic for the love he bore his daughter.

And the shadows in that other home, the palazzo on the Canal Grande, in these days of waiting, were colder, hasher,—born of selfishness rather than love, of disappointed ambition perhaps,—but they were very real shadows nevertheless, obscuring the clear-cut traditions of centuries, out of which one should struggle through increase of pride, the other through the broadening of a more generous love.

Meanwhile the gondola floated in light—between shadow and shadow—so slight is the realization of the throes by which joy is sometimes born; and the pathos of the change which made their gladness possible was for the two young people still an unrecognized note.

But waiting was now over; more positive steps must be taken. Two Secretaries had been sent from the Senate to bring the news of the filing of the decree.

"Madre mia!" cried Marcantonio eagerly, when they were gone; "it has come even before our hope!"

"Even sooner than thy hope," she echoed, feeling dreary, though he was sitting with his arm around her, as if for a confidential talk.

But he was too happy to interpret her tone.

"The token!" he pleaded; "for Marina—and thou wilt come to see how beautiful she is!"

She looked at him searchingly. He did not mean to urge her; he seemed too happy to understand.

She rose and going slowly to her cabinet brought him her token—a string of great Oriental pearls.

140

"These," she said, sitting down beside her son and opening the case, "have I made ready for thy bride, since thou wert a little lad—at one time one pearl, at another more, as I have found the rarest lustre. Some of these, they say, have been hidden in Venice since the time of John of Constantinople, who left them for his ransom; it may be but a tale, yet they are rare in tint; and I have gleaned them, Marco, since thou wert a little lad, not knowing who should wear them—not knowing, Marco——"

She broke off suddenly, touching the gems wistfully, endearingly, with trembling, tapering fingers.

He laid his firm young hand upon hers lovingly. "How good thou art, my mother; how good to think of thy boy through all these years! But thy pearls are superb—they will almost frighten Marina. Later thou wilt give them to her. Mother, dearest, let me take this rose which thou hast worn, with thy little word of love—sweet mother——"

"They are fit for a princess, Marco," she said, still toying with the pearls, apparently unheeding his request; "I chose them with that thought—since they are for thy bride."

"And she will wear them worthily," Marcantonio answered, flushing, "and like a queen, for none hath greater dignity, else could I not have chosen her—I, who have learned a lady's grace by thee, my mother!"

She drew him to her with sudden emotion, for these days had been very hard for her. "My boy—my boy! Does she love thee well for all thy faith and devotion—for all that we are yielding her?"

"Madre mia, thou shalt see, if thou wilt let me take thee to her!"

"I had not thought—" she said, and stopped. "Would she not come with thee?"

Marcantonio walked suddenly away to a window and stepped out on the balcony for a breath of air; he was beginning to comprehend the under side of his great joy, and it had come with a shock, on this very day which he had thought would have been filled with a rush of gladness. He grasped the cool marble of the parapet and tried to reason with himself; he suddenly foresaw that many days of reasoning had entered into his life, and always he must be ready to meet them with cool wisdom, since enthusiasm was one-visioned. It was like taking a vow against youth, but he himself had chosen it for his lot in life; his love was not less to him, but the sudden realization had come that it *was* hard to fight against the traditions of centuries. Yet how bravely she, his mother, was trying to surrender her social creed for his happiness; it was not a little thing that he had asked of her, but it seemed to him that her soul had been nearer to her eyes than ever before during these days when she had been suffering. At all costs these women—his dearest in the world—must love each other, must bless each other's lives.

He went back with some comprehension of the barrier he had thought so lightly to remove, with a vow in his soul to be more to each; because of it neither should lose aught for his sake. He seemed suddenly older, though his face was very tender.

"That which seemeth best to thee, my mother, in the matter of the meeting, Marina would surely do; for it is thou who must guard for us these little matters of custom, which none knoweth better. But her father—never have I known one more courtly, nor more proud——"

"Marco, it is much to ask that we should think of him!"

"Ay, mother, it is much. Yet if thou knewest him thou wouldst understand. For Marina is all the world to him, and I would take her from him. Yet so he loveth her that never hath he said me nay. Naught hath he asked for her of gold nor jewels, but only this—that she shall not come unbidden to our home."

He spoke the last words very low and with an effort, as if they held a prayer.

"And so—?"

"And so, sweet mother, none knoweth half so well as thou how best to greet her whom I long to bring to thee, that she may know and love thee as she doth love her father—with a great love, very beautiful and tender."

She looked up as if she would have answered him, but she could not speak.

"More than ever I think I love thee, now that I am grieving thee," he added after a pause, in a tone so full of comprehension that it smote her.

"Nay, Marco—nay," she said, and drew him closer, clasping her hand in his. But they sat quite silent, while the mother's love intensified, displacing selfishness.

He raised her hand to his lips with a new reverence. "In all this have I asked so much of thee I think thou never canst forgive me, madre mia, until —until thou knowest Marina!"

She touched his hair with her beautiful white hand caressingly, as she had often done when he was a little child; but now, in this sudden deepening of her nature, with a new yearning.

"Marco, when thou wert a babe," she said, "there was little I would not give for thine asking. And now, when my soul is bound up in thine, I seem not to care for the things I once sought for thee— but more for happiness and love. Yet, if I go with thee— I seem to know thou wilt not change to me—?" She paused, wistfully.

"Save but to prove a truer knight!" he cried radiantly. "So more than gracious hast thou been!"

"Nay, it will be sweet to have part in thy happiness," she cried bravely. "To-night, at sunset, will I go with thee, quite simply, in thy gondola, to bid my daughter welcome—as our custom is. I will not fail in honor to my Marco's bride! And since it is love that her father asketh, I will give her this rose, for thy dear sake. But the bridal must be soon, to make this endless talking cease. And before we leave her—for she will learn to love me, Marco mio, and she will not take thee from me?— I will give her the token that is fitting for a daughter of our house."

. . . .

Among the members of the Senate, meeting by twos and threes in the Broglio, Marcantonio's name was often heard. "It would be well when this marriage was over, for verily it was likely to turn the heads of Venice—the pageant, and the beauty of the maid, and the favor of the Collegio——"

144

"Nay, not that," said an older senator, resentfully; "those are but trifles. But the young fellow himself is the danger; too positive and outspoken, revolutionary and of overturning methods, withal persuasive——"

"He would be a power in an ambassade," suggested another, "for he hath a gift in diplomacy and law which, verily, did astound the old Giustinian. The eloquence of his great-uncle Sebastiano hath fallen upon him.—If he were not so young—! Here in Venice he is rolling up influence, and the charm of his inamorata. is also a danger; and already in the Consiglio all eyes are upon him."

"For a secretary to an ambassade is the age not set," answered the other warily, "and the office hath space for diplomacy, which, it were better for our privileges, were used elsewhere than in Venice. And the honor of it would blind the eyes of his partizans—for the boy is young."

The winds, wandering through the Piazza, sometimes blew lightest whispers from the Broglio into the Council Chambers of the Republic; and so it was decreed that when the beautiful wedding pageant should be over, just as the whole of Venice would have laid itself at the feet of the charming bride—would have made the young nobles of the palazzo Giustiniani the idols of the hour—these dangers to Venice should be honorably removed by the appointment of Marcantonio Giustiniani, di Maggior Consiglio, as Secretary to the Venetian Resident in Rome, with the gracious permission of the Senate for the Lady Marina to bear him company.

"It is well," answered Giustinian Giustiniani, as

the Lady Laura made her little moan on hearing of the appointment which the Senator reported with such pride. "Marcantonio hath the head of a diplomat and the bearing of a courtier. It is the way of distinction for such a man."

"That is justly spoken," said the mother; "and nobly hath our boy fulfilled our hope. In Venice, or elsewhere, must he ever win distinction. But to keep them in their palazzo near us—of this and of their happiness was I thinking—the sight of it is so beautiful."

The filing of the decree of the Senate had acted like a charm upon our Capo of the Ten: the importance thus accorded to the Ca' Giustiniani soothed every vestige of wounded pride, while the beauty and grace of his prospective daughter-in-law had filled him with a triumph which only the frigid stateliness of his habitual demeanor enabled him to conceal, so great was the revulsion from his former state of feeling.

"I tell thee, Lady Laura," said her husband, coming nearer and speaking low, "we may well be proud. All this trifling in art and knickknacks in which it hath pleased the boy to spend himself, like so many of his hose,[1] hath fluttered off from him like silken ribbons hanging harmless in the wind, and hath left him with a head quite clear of nonsense for the Senate's work. *That day*"—he had referred to it so often that it had become an acknowledged division of time—"*that* day when he made his speech not one arose to answer him; for the cunning of it was so simple one listened, fearing naught, until the end was reached; and the words of

[1] The young nobles were called "the gay company of the hose."

1 6

it were so few that the end was a surprise; and, lo!
the Counsellors were confounded by the weight of
his demand, and the reason for the justice of it,
and the wit of its presentation—lying folded in a
sentence scarce long enough for a preamble! And
the boy! Holding himself like a prince and win-
ning them all by his grace, as if he were a child!
Nay, but I do forget he is a man, wearing honors
from his country!"

"Giustinian, I fain would keep them here!"

"That is the woman's side of it," said the Chief
of the Ten, easily dismissing her plea. "But for
Marcantonio the appointment is good. When the
late-returned Ambassador to His Most Christian
Majesty did render his report before our Maggior
Consiglio—an oration diplomatic and of weight—
I noted many of our graver men with eyes observ-
ing Marcantonio closely, as they would mark how
he weighed the speech of the old diplomatist."

"And Marco?"

"He seemed not to take note of them. Or it may
be a grace that he hath, that he seemeth not to see;
for he weareth the 'pensieri stretti e viso sciolto'[1]
meet for a Venetian councillor—age could not
teach him better to guard his thought, but it would
make the wearing of his careless face less easy. Or
it may be that his mind hath space for the speech
only—one knows not! Save that all things come
easily to him—even the most beautiful bride in
Venice, raised from the ranks of the people to suit
his whim!"

"Giustinian! She will be our daughter, and none
need question her dignity and grace."

[1] Close-locked thoughts and open countenance.

"My Lady Laura, none knoweth better of her beauty and none so proud of her as I, who had thought to hide my head for the disgrace of it! But the daring of this son of ours doth make me gay! I am ready to give thee a compliment on thy bringing up, which often I had feared was over frivolous. And now, he hath the Republic before him, where to choose."

"Giustinian?"

She rested both hands on his shoulders and looked full in his eyes with the gravity of her question which was the dream of his life, and was often tacitly touched, when they conferred together in confidence.

"Ay," he answered, "even that, the highest—by favor of San Marco—he may win. For the grace of him maketh his head seem less."

But the shadow of the coveted Lion's paw had suddenly overclouded him and changed his mood.

XIII

WHEN the first faint flush of dawn was waking in the east, the fair, sweet face of Marina of Murano was outlined for the last time, vague as some dream memory, against the deep shadows of the interior, between the quaint columns that framed her window.

Birds were twittering in the vines of the pergola not far away; honeysuckles were pouring forth their fragrant morning oblations; and the salt sea-breeze wafted her its invigorating breath as the early tide, with slow, increasing motion, brimmed the channels that wound through the marshes on the borders of Murano and overflowed till the lagoon was a broad, unbroken vista of silver-gray, in whose shimmer and radiance, when the tide was at its full, the morning stars died out. But still they glistened dimly in the twilight of the sky to which she raised her questioning, believing eyes. Life was always beautiful to her loving soul; for when the shadows held a meaning deeper than she could solve, her answer was faith; and now, that her new joy was to grow out of a deep solitariness for the father so tenderly beloved, it was he who upheld her courage.

"Life may not be," he said, "without some shadow; this is the shade of thine, which, without it, were too bright. Heaven hath some purpose in its sending, but not that it should darken our eyes to miss the joy."

"The day will be o'er-lonely in this home, my father."

"Nay, Marina, let love suffice; so shall we be always together! Shall I not go to thee? And thou wilt come to me, bringing thy new interests and holding thy dear heart ever pure and loyal to Venice, and thy home, and thy God—not forgetting. For thou hast chosen with thy whole heart, my daughter?" since she had not answered. "Thou dost not fear thyself?'

"Dearest father," she had said, hiding her face in his tender embrace, "all of my heart which is not thine is wholly his—only my happiness is too great."

"Nay, daughter, since it is of God's own sending; take all the joy and grieve not."

"Only at leaving thee."

"I would not keep thee here, to leave thee mourning and alone when my days are closed."

"Father!"

"Not to sadden thee, my child, but to show thee that life is linked to life—God wills it so. Thou and I are bound to that which has been and to that which is to be. We do not stand alone to choose. The sweetness of our life together should make it easier for me to yield thee to the fuller life which calleth thee. We must each bear our part in the beauty of the whole. For perfect love, there must be sacrifice."

She was thinking of these things as she stood in the gray dawn waiting for the beauty of the oncoming day, quite alone with her thoughts and with her God, the giver of this beauty; and often as she had stood there with her morning offering of trust and adoration, never before had the day-dawn seemed so full of mystery and promise, nor the new life which the morning held within its keeping so full of hope and beauty. The very tide, flowing round her island home, brought thoughts of her home that was to be, as it swept through the channels of the City of the Sea, past the palace where her lover was waiting, bringing murmurs and messages of liquid harmony. The marsh grasses swayed and yielded to its flow, lending new depths of color to the water-bed, as they bowed beneath the masterful current—so the difficulties which had seemed to beset their hopes had been vanquished by the resistless' tide of his love and constancy.

The stars were lost in the deep gray-blue of the sky; a solemn stillness, like the presage of some divine event, seemed for a moment to hold the pulses of the universe; then a soft rose crept into the shimmer of the water and crested the snows on the distant Euganean Hills, the transient, many-tinted glory of the east reflected itself in opal lights upon the silver sea, then suddenly swept the landscape in one dazzling glow of gold—and the joy-bells rang out. For to-day a festa had been granted in Murano.

Then, wrapping herself closely in the soft folds of her gray mantle, falling Madonna-wise from her head and shrouding her figure, she glided for the last time over the *ponte* and down past the sleeping homes of Murano; for it was yet early for matins, and she would have the Madonna all to herself as she knelt with her heart full of tenderness for the dear life this day should merge in that other which beckoned her with joyous anticipation—yet stilled to serenity by the golden glory and promise of the dawn, and the beautiful, self-sacrificing, upholding faith of the great-hearted Girolamo.

He had followed her and folded her passionately to his heart, as she crossed the threshold of their home on her way to San Donato. "I must be first," he said, "to bless thee on thy bridal day. Fret thee not, for thou art bidden to a mission, since thou goest forth from the people to the highest circle of the nobles. And love alone hath bidden and drawn thee. Forget it not, Marina! So shall a blessing go with thee and rest upon thee!"

She had brought a gift to the Madonna of San Donato—an exquisite altar lamp of ivory and silver —and from the flowers which she had laid upon the altar while she knelt in prayer, she gathered some to scatter over the grave of the tiny Zuane.

When Marina returned slowly through the little square, Murano was awake; the painted sails of the fishing-boats were tacking in the breeze, the activities of the simple homes had commenced, women with their water-jugs were chatting round the well, detaining little ones clinging to the fringes of the tawny mantles which hung below their waists; a few stopped her with greetings; here and there a child ran to her shyly—their mothers, from the low cottage doorways, calling to them that "the donzel Marina had given them festa."

Yes, there was to be festa in Murano. Giro-
lamo had obtained from the Senate the grace of pro-
viding it. For now, since his daughter would have
no need of the gold which his industry had brought
him, he might spend it lavishly on her wedding day
to gladden the hearts of the people whom she was
leaving; for to him this bridal had a deeply conse-
crated meaning which divested it of half its sadness.

The workmen of Murano were to have holiday,
and a great feast was spread for them by Girolamo in
the long exhibition hall of the stabilimenti, for which
it had been needful to procure permission of the
Senate; but for once it suited well the humor of this
august and autocratic body that one of the people
should, for a day, make himself great among them.
Thus for the inhabitants of Murano—men, women,
and children—there was a welcome waiting the day
long in the house of the bride, where they should
come to take her bounty and shower their bless-
ings; for this time only Murano had no voice for
critica—it was too busy in congratulation.

When Marina reached her home she found it
garlanded from column to column with festal
wreaths of green, while the maidens from the vil-
lage still lingered, veiling the walls between the
windows with delicate frosts of fruit-bloom from
the gardens of Mazzorbo. And closely following
this village tribute came a priest from San Donato
with the band of white-robed nuns who formed the
choir of the Matrice, bearing perfumes of incense
and benediction for the home of the bride, that all
who passed beneath its portal, going out or coming
in, might carry blessing with their steps.

In Venice also there were joy-bells ringing; and

to overflowing tables, spread in the water-storey of the Ca' Giustiniani, the people of Venice were freely bidden by silken banners floating legends of welcome above the open doorway. But now the expectant people were thronging the Piazza; the *fondamenta* along the Riva was alive with color, balconies were brilliant with draperies, windows were glowing with vivid shawls, rugs, brocades— tossed out to lean upon in the splendor that became a fête; above them the spaces were crowded with enthusiastic spectators in holiday dress; the children of the populace, shouting, ecstatic, ubiquitous, swarmed on the quay below.

The splendor of the pageant which brought a bride from Murano to the highest patrician circle of the Republic—to that house which held its patent of nobility from those days of the seventh century when an ancestor had ruled as tribune over one of the twelve Venetian isles—was long remembered, almost as a royal wedding fête, and for days before and after it was the talk of Venice.

They were coming over the water to the sound of the people's native songs and the echo of their laughter, the young men and maidens of Murano, in barks that were wreathed with garlands and brilliant with the play of color that the Venetians love.

"Marìdite, marìdite, donzela,
  Che dona maridada è sempre bela;
 Maridìte finchè la fogia è verde,
  Perché la zoventù presto se perde."[1]

[1] Marry, maiden, marry,
  For she that is wedded is ever fair:
 Marry then, in thy tender bloom,
 Since youth passeth swiftly.

154

By the port of the Lido many a royal pageant had entered into Venice, but never before had such a procession started from the shores of Murano; it made one feel fête-like only to see the *bissoni*, those great boats with twelve oars, each from a stabilimento of Murano, wreathed for the fête, each merchant master at its head, robed in his long, black, fur-trimmed gown and wearing his heavy golden chain, the workmen tossing blossoms back over the water to greet the bride, the rowers chanting in cadence to their motion:

"Belina sei, e'l ciel te benedissa,
Che in dove che ti passi l'erba nasse!"[1]

A cry rang down the Canal Grande from the gondoliers of the Ca' Giustiniani, who were waiting this sign to start their own train from the palazzo; for the bridal gondolas were coming in sight, with *felzi* of damask, rose, and blue, embroidered with emblems of the Giustiniani, bearing the noble maidens who had been chosen for the household of the Lady Marina, each flower-like and charming under her gauzy veil of tenderest coloring. It was indeed a rare vision to the populace, these young patrician beauties whose faces never, save in most exceptional fêtes, had been seen unveiled beyond their mother's drawing-rooms, floating toward them in a diaphanous mist which turned their living loveliness into a dream.

The shout of the Giustiniani was echoed from gondola to gondola of the waiting throng, from

[1] Beautiful thou art, and may Heaven bless thee,
So that in thy footprints the grass shall spring.

the gondoliers of all the nobles who followed in their wake, from the housetops, the balconies, the fondamenta, mingled with the words of the favorite folk-song:

"Belo zè el mare, e belà la marina!"[1]

It was like a fairy dream as the bridal procession came floating toward San Marco, in the brilliant golden sunshine, between the blue of the cloudless sky and the blue of the mirroring sea, each gondola garlanded with roses, its silver dolphins flashing in the light, and in the midst of them the bark that bore the bride. The stately pall of snowy damask, fringed with silver, swept almost to the water's breast, behind the felze of azure velvet, where, beside her father, sat the bride, in robe of brocaded silver shimmering like the sea—a subtle perfume of orange blossoms heralding her advance.

Once more the shout went up—the quaint love-song of the people—

"Belo zé el mare, e belà la marina!"

and then a breathless silence fell, for the bark of the ministering priest of San Donato had taken the lead, the white-robed nuns of the Matrice grouped about him, chanting as they approached some ancient wedding canticles of benediction. The bissoni parted and came no further, having brought their maiden from Murano with every sign of love and honor; the barges of the people fell back be-

[1] Beautiful is the sea, and beautiful the marsh.

hind them, and through their ranks the bridal gon-
dolas followed the bark of the priest of San Donato
to the steps of the Piazzetta, where the train of the
Giustiniani, in a magnificence that was well-nigh
royal, had just disembarked, and Marcantonio stood
bareheaded among the nobles to receive his bride.

But it was only for a moment of recognition in
the sight of the thronging people, for messengers
were arriving with greetings from the Doge, which
this bride, whom the Senate had taken from the peo-
ple to bestow upon a noble, must receive from the
lips of the Prince himself before the wedding cere-
mony should take place; so the train of Giustiniani,
with all the nobles of Venice—who, from immemo-
rial custom, had come together to witness and re-
joice over this great event in the life of one of their
number—entered San Marco by the great doors of
the Piazza; while the bride, obeying the gracious
summons of the Doge, passed through the gate of
the Ducal Palace on the seaside, into the great court
where the Signoria were descending the Giant's
Stairway on their passage to the ducal chapel.

The ceremony of presentation to the Serenissimo
was quickly over, and the bride and her maidens,
with Girolamo Magagnati, in sign of the Prince's
favor, followed the Doge and suite into the golden
glooms and shifting twilights of this place of sym-
holism and wonder, where the vast throng waited
in a solemn hush.

The gloom was broken by countless tongues of
flame from lamps of silver and alabaster burning in
the farther chapels, while wandering lights stream-
ing through the openings of the dome filled it with

wonderful waves of color—only half-revealing the treasures of ivory and jewels and precious marbles and mosaics, wrought with texts and symbols, but wholly making felt the mystery and beauty. The vague perfume of those faint mists of floating incense, crossing and recrossing the scattered rays of sunshine, mingled with the fragrance of the orange blossoms from which the light tread of the bridemaidens seemed to crush a breath of benediction.

Coming out of the sunlight into this still, beautiful, holy place—the chant sweet and sacred aecompanying her steps, with the Cross repeated again and again in the heights of the domes, with the dear familiar form of the Mother Mary on every side lifting adoring eyes to the crowning figure of the Christ, while the saints who graciously leaned to her from their golden backgrounds in the great vaulted spàces above recalled the legends inseparably linked with their intimate friendly faces and brought back the atmosphere of her own Matrice—her mother church—this maiden of Murano felt suddenly at home.

The Patriarch with his pomp, the Signoria and Senate in their robes of state, the nobles and the pageant were all forgotten. In the sacramental lights of the ceremonial candles of the great altar, flashing back from the marvelous *Pala d'Oro*, she saw only Marco waiting for her—to whom her father, beloved and trusted, was leading her with her heart's consent.

How should she falter on the path from love to love!

XIV

BUT even in Venice—the magic city—there were days of mists, silvery and gray, when life took on the indistinctness and indecision of a dream; as there were days less lucent, when sea and sky melted in an indistinguishable line and the chameleon tints of the marshes mellowed into a monotonous gray surface—when the wonted brilliancy of the sunset clouds, and the glittering domes and campaniles were only faint gray shadows on the gray whiteness of the waters. And gondoliers came suddenly into vision, parting the mists with thin, black, swaying outlines, as quickly fading in the near, gray distance when they passed, while the shipping loomed like phantoms on an immediate horizon, vanishing, vision-like; and even the sounds of life came muffled over the still lagoon, like ghostly echoes from a city wrapped in dreams.

These were days of dim forebodings, too, for the anxious men of action who ruled the Republic. In the Broglio there was more often silence than speech, as the older senators gathered in knots, with faces the more expressive because of much reticence in words; the sense of approaching contest increased their mental restlessness and made them outwardly more stern. Each looked into another's stormy, resolute face, so passing many a

159

counsel whose echoes he feared to start under the rambling porticoes of the Piazza, where friars of every order mingled freely with the crowd, and idlers carried tales into dark, basement recesses, and one knew not which was friend or foe. Meanwhile the Winged Lion, with those terrible, jeweled, glaring eyes, and the primitive patron San Teodoro— each high on his column, in a Nirvana of quiescence —kept solemn semblance of vigil over that dread space where sometimes a horror of which one dared not speak scattered the sunshine high in air between those silent wardens of San Marco. Yet the horror of those figures swinging lifeless, with veiled faces, was met in silence by a people trained to suffer this secret meting out of penalty for transgressions in which justice and vengeance stood confused.

The ceaseless chains of elections had begotten bribery, corruption, and strife; the over-weening luxury had fostered unworthy ambitions—it was a time of much lawlessness. Under the shadow of the embassies infamous intrigues were planned by bands of idle men, who shrank from no deed of evil which held its promise of gold; the water-storey of some splendid palace might be a lurking-place for unprincipled men—spies and informers by profession—who wore the liveries of noble families whose secrets they would unhesitatingly consign to that merciless *Bocca del Leone*, for favor or vengeance of those they secretly served. For underneath the glitter and the pomp of these latter days of Venice—its presage of decay—a turbulent mass of malcontents, foreigners disappointed in intrigue,

Venetians shut out from power, grasped and plotted for its semblance,—sold murder for gold, treason for gold,—escaping justice by the wiles they so deftly unveiled, or by the importance of the deposition it was in their power to make. Secret, swift, relentless, absolute—Venice had work for men who did not court the sunlight; and such a nucleus drew to its dark centre intriguers from other courts, and gathered in and strengthened the worthless within its own borders, until the evil was growing heavy to deal with.

Causes of discontent between Church and State were alarmingly on the increase; and while in no other dominion, save that of Rome alone, were ecclesiastical possessions so rich, or their establishments more splendid than at Venice, nowhere were the lines of power so jealously defined and guarded as in the government of this Republic from which ecclesiastics were rigorously excluded,—although no least ceremonial was held complete without the presence of the Patriarch and priests who evidenced the devotion of Venice to the Holy Mother Church,— though every parish kept its festa, and the religion of Venice was an essential part of the life of its people. But if the priests had no visible seat in the splendid Council Chambers of the Republic, they boasted at Rome that their sway over the consciences of these lordly senators was well established by virtue of the confessional and that, in the event of contest, there would be many votes for Rome.

The *ridotti*, the informal clubs of Venice in those days, were important centres of influence—political, legislative, and literary; and there was a certain palazzo Morosini, well known to many of the senators who gathered in the Broglio, where questions of vital interest to the thinkers and rulers of Venice were discussed with the degree of knowledge that might have been expected from so eminent a company as that which made the home of the distinguished senator Andrea Morosini the scene of its ridotto, and where freedom of speech was much greater than seemed wise in the candid sunshine of the Piazza.

Of its present numbers all, at some period of their lives, held high office under the Republic—they were senators, secretaries of state, ambassadors—and three among that little group of thirty lived to wear the beretta. It represented essentially the patrician culture of Venice, and Morosini himself was already eminent as an historian; but the chief literary centre was still acknowledged to be that quaint house in Campo Agostino, of Aldo Manuzio, *il vecchio*, bearing, as in his day, shield-wise, its forbidding inscription, "Whoever you are, Aldo requesteth you, if you want anything, to ask it in few words and depart; unless, like Hercules, you come to lend the aid of your shoulders to the weary Atlas. There will always be found, in that case, something for you to do, however many you may be." But in this Aldine mansion only the most learned men of letters gathered, and Greek was the sole language permitted in its discussions.

One of the *habitues* of the Aldine Club was chief among this noble company of the Morosini. He was a grave, scholarly man who listened and questioned much out of a seemingly inexhaustible fund of historic, legal, and ecclesiastical knowledge—a man who had the power of stimulating others, and whose rare word, when uttered, was of value. He had opinions gathered at first hand from influential minds of every land and creed to contribute to the talk when it flowed in narrowing channels; and he himself came thither for refreshment from abstruse studies, out of a quiet cell in the convent of the Servi, while seemingly unaware that many a stranger begged for an invitation to the palazzo Morosini in the hope of an introduction to this "miracle of Venice."

Perhaps this grave friar, apparently so careless of his distinction, was the unsuspected intellectual thread which bound, as it were, together the various influential circles of Venice; for in every centre, plebeian or patrician, where there was anything new to be mooted or anything of value to be discussed, he was a visitor so welcome and so frequent that he might well have exerted a steady, unifying influence upon Venetian thought.

At the sign of the "Nave d'oro," in the Merceria, where the vast commercial interests of Venice were the absorbing theme, and strangers from every clime and merchants just returned from distant ports were eager now, as in the days when Marco Polo had so valiantly entertained the goodly company, to rehearse the tale of their adventures—it was neither merchant nor noble who stood forth on the bizarre background of brilliant baubles and gold-woven tissues as the centre of this ridotto, but a friar, learned in languages and sciences, of whom it was pleasantly affirmed that "he was the only man

163

in Venice who could discuss any subject in any tongue!"

As this friar, unattended and on foot, turned out of the narrow calle from San Samuele into the Campo San Stefano, the Giustiniani, father and son, were just landing from their gondolas in the midst of a gay retinue, on the steps of the palazzo Morosini; other gondolas of other nobles were floating in full moonlight before the quay; and to Fra Paolo, who did not share the Venetian love of color and of art, the elaborately frescoed façade of an opposite palace—an extravagant freak of the Veronese's which the Venetians were already beginning to cherish as the work of their great artist who would paint no more—seemed an impertinence unworthy of that dazzling illumination.

Marcantonio Giustiniani had but lately returned from Rome, where, during his residence as Secretary to the Venetian Ambassador, the affair of the Venetian Patriarch Zani, which had roused such indignation in Venice, had taken place. The matter was still of interest in official quarters, because the death of Zani had caused a new vacancy, to which Venice, according to her ancient right, had appointed the successor; and this new Patriarch Vendramin should never go, as Zani had done at the request of the Holy Father, to receive his benediction and be met with that perfidious announcement that he had "examined and approved the Venetian candidate," whom he now confirmed as Patriarch to the Most Serene Republic!

At the thought of the manner in which they had been entrapped and outwitted—denuded, as it were, before the Roman Court of some semblance of their ancient privilege of appointing their own Patriarch —there was fresh indignation among these proud patricians. The secretary Marcantonio Giustiniani had been present at the audience granted by Clement to the Venetian Patriarch. "He would know if it had been possible—even with the most favorable intentions toward Rome,"—they were crowding round him and questioning with jealous eagerness, —"even with the feeling which loyal sons should possess for their Mother Church—to interpret that rude cross-questioning of his Holiness, so unexpected and unexampled and contradicting his own explicit promise—otherwise than as an examination—*an examination which prejudiced the ancient right of Venice?*"

A scarcely perceptible smile flitted over the young secretary's handsome face—they were so venerable and eager, so careful of shadows of form!—and in a sudden side-light a hint of a question obtruded itself on his consciousness, as to whether there could be a slightly farcical aspect to such an episode between two most Catholic and Christian governments? He saw them both fired with feelings of very human strength, both dealing only with shadows of reality—the Sovereign Pontiff grasping at a semblance of power in insisting that this candidate, named by Venice to a see within her gift, to which he, the Pope, would dare present no other, was invested by *his* examination and approval; and the Republic, receiving back its own appointee, confirmed with the papal benediction, jealously aroused to unappeasable indignation by the empty form of questioning which had preceded this singular ceremony.

But the dignified company were pressing the young secretary for his answer, and one of them anxiously repeated the keynote, *"An examination which prejudiced the ancient right of Venice?"*

"Courtesy and wisdom would render any other opinion inadmissible," Marcantonio replied,—"in Venice."

The elder Giustinian had detected the slight pause which preceded the last two words. "Wherefore 'in Venice'?" he questioned, with some heat. "It is a question not of locality, but of justice and judgment."

"It is a question of judgment," Marcantonio echoed suavely, "upon which, it hath been told me, the Senate hath already passed a law that shall keep our Most Reverend Signor Vendramin from such a fate."

"Ay, never again may our Patriarch leave the Republiç for confirmation of the see which she alone may grant. The law is just," said the Senator Leonardo Donato.

"In the days when his Holiness was but an Eminence, it hath been said, he gave our ambassador a chance to prove his temper?" Morosini questioned of Donato, who had been ambassador in Rome while Paul V, who had but just ascended the throne, was still Cardinal Borghese.

"It was in the matter of the Uscocks," Donato answered, after a moment's hesitation, seeing that some were waiting for the story. "And it was the second time that half-civilized tribe hath provoked disputes between two most Christian nations. 'If

I were Pope,' said the cardinal, 'I would excommunicate both Doge and Senate!'"

Fra Paolo scrutinized the faces of the listeners, and fixed his gaze searchingly on the speaker. There was an uneasy movement among the company, but Leonardo Donato did not flinch.

"May they not know your answer, most noble Signor?" Morosini urged. "For, verily, it was of a quality to illumine a page of history."

"The words were few," said Leonardo, with dignity. "*If I were Doge, I would trample your edict under foot.*'"

There was a sudden hush, in which those who had not been listening became intensely conscious of the words just uttered by the aged and illustrious Cavalière Leonardo Donato, for there had been of late an abiding undercurrent of suppressed excitement ready to awake at any mention of Papal supremacy. The Republic had always jealously guarded against any transference of temporal power from prince to prelate, and many events which seemed linked in a chain that might lead to the most deplorable results had succeeded to the election of Camillo Borghese as Paul V; the desire evidently manifested by Clement during his latter days to encroach on the perquisites and possessions of the minor Italian States was crystallizing into a fixed purpose of ecclesiastical aggrandizement on the part of the new Pope.

"He was brandishing Saint Peter's sword before he had been knighted," remarked the Signor Antonio Querini, who was deeply interested in all disputes between Church and State.

"But not before he had received strenuous train-

ing," responded the grave, clear voice of the friar.
"For five years he hath held office as Auditor of
the Apostolical Chamber, the style of which is writ-
ten thus, '*Universal Executor of censures and sen-
tences recorded both in Rome and abroad*'—a duty
which he may be said to have discharged more
faithfully than any of his predecessors, as one can-
not recall in any previous fifty years as many thun-
derbolts and monitions as were launched during
those five years of his office!"

Some romance could but attach to the unswerving
judicial attitude of a friar who had friends in high
favor at the Court of Rome—who had known a
Bellarmino and a Navarro, and yet pursued, un-
changing, the calm tenor of his critical way. It
was rumored that Sixtus V had been known to
leave his coach to converse with him, and would
have given him, at his mere request, a cardinal's
hat; that Urban VII, as cardinal and pope, had
been his devoted friend; that Cardinal Borromeo—
the saintly San Carlo—had wished to attach him to
his cathedral; and many were the instances reported
when marks of special appreciation had been granted
him from Rome, in lieu of denunciations which
those jealous of his rapid advance had sought to
bring upon him. Even the late Pope Clement had
expressed admiration for his learning, while it was,
nevertheless, well known that Fra Paolo's counsels
to the Senate, in certain troubles arising out of
Clement's attitude at Ferrara, had brought him the
refusal of the bishoprics of Candia and Caorle; but,
whatever the occasion, he was invariably discreet
and fearless.

However pungent the tone, the words of this man could no more be attributed to personal bitterness than they might be influenced by personal interest; and although the opinion which they indicated was a surprise to some of the company, instinctively they felt the situation to be graver than they had feared, and the evening's talk drifted as wholly into the current of Church and State as if this ridotto were a commission appointed by the Ten to prepare resolutions upon the situation. And the list of grievances now reviewed, which had occupied the Senate during the closing years of Clement's reign, was, in truth, long. Vast differences of opinion concerning the Turks and the piratical tribes who infested the shores of Italy and the uses their villainy might be made to serve; troubles at Ferrara, teasing and undignified, temporarily brought to a close by the sending of the galleys of the Republic to prevent the seizure of their fishing-boats by agents of his Holiness; questions of boundaries and taxes; attempts to divert the trade of Venice, to arrest improvements redounding not only to the advantage of the Republic but to that of the neighboring country; to forbid, under pain of excommunication, all commerce with countries tainted with heresy. These were matters meet for discussion by temporal sovereigns touching the balance of power—so viewed and strenuously resisted by the clear-headed Venetians, with much deference of form, whenever practicable—as became loyal sons of the Church; but occasionally, when nothing might be expected from temporizing, with a quiet disregard which proved their consciousness of strength.

169

From time to time, as the informal summary progressed, there was an outburst of indignation.

"Could an aggression be more palpable than that *Index Expurgatorius* demanded by Rome in 1596, when the ruling doctrine of exclusion involved no question of morality or irreligion, but solely concerned books upholding rights of consciences and rulers!"

"It was a contest honorable to Venice, and one which Italy will remember," responded a secretary of the Senate, who was a regular member of this ridotto. "I am proud that it was my privilege to transcribe for the records of the Republic the papers relating to that Concordat which secured so great a measure of freedom for our press."

There had been a short truce between Rome and Venice since the accession of Paul V, who had been so immediately concerned with a certain prophecy foretelling the death of a Leo and a Paul that his fears were only set at rest by a further astrological announcement, judiciously arranged in the palace of his eminence the brother of the Pope, to the effect that "the evil influences were now conquered." Whereupon Paul had undertaken in earnest the work which he conscientiously believed to be the highest duty of a sovereign pontiff, had recalled all nuncios not in full sympathy with his views of aggrandizement, and had replaced them with envoys whose notions of authority were echoes of his own; and, as an opening move, had made the demand, so resented by Venice, that the new Patriarch Vendramin should be sent to Rome for examination before he could be allowed to take possession of his prelacy.

"But what hath Venice to fear from a Pope who is paralyzed for the first two months of his reign by a reading of a horoscope!" exclaimed one of the company scornfully.

"Nay, then," said Donato, who had seen much of the world; "it is a petty superstition of the age; it is not the fault of the man, who hath sterling qualities. And by that same potency of credulity have his fears been set at rest. It is a proof of weakness to undervalue the strength of an adversary —for so at least he hath recently declared himself on this question of temporal power, by his petty aggressions and triumphs in Malta, Parma, Lucca, and Genoa."

"I crave pardon of the Cavalière Donato," Antonio Querini responded hotly. "May one call the action at Genoa *petty?*—the compulsion of the entire vote of a free city, the placing of the election of the whole body of governing officials in the power of the Society of Jesus?"

"And it was under threat of excommunication, which made resistance a duty from the side of the government," Giustinian Giustiniani asserted uncompromisingly.

"But impossible from the Church's point of view. It is the eternal question," Leonardo Donato answered gravely.

"*The solution is only possible by precisely ascertaining the limits within which each power is absolute,*" the friar announced, with quiet decision.

A momentary hush fell upon the company, for the words were weighty and a surprise.

"It is well to know the qualities we have to fear," said Andrea Morosini, "and we have listened in the

Senate to letters from our ambassador at Rome which bespeak his Holiness of a presence and a dignity—save for over-quickness of temper—which befit a Pope; and that he hath reserved himself from promises, to the displeasure and surprise of some of those who created him."

"It was rumored in Rome," said the younger Giustinian, "that the learned Bishop Baronious, in the last conclave, by his persistence found means to save the Consistory from the election by 'adoration' of another candidate whose life would bear no scrutiny and who never darkened the doors of his own cathedral! By this election the Church hath verily been spared a scandal."

"Therefore, let it be known," said Fra Paolo, with deep gravity, "lest the nearness of such a scandal should breed confusion—and I speak from knowledge, having been much in Rome—we have now a Pope blameless in life; in duty to his Church most faithful and exemplary and concerned with her welfare, as to himself it seemeth; of an unbending conscience and a will most absolute; moreover, of marvelous reading in certain doctrinal writings which seem to him the only books of worth, and with the training of a lawyer wherewith to assert them. This is the man with whom we have to contend."

"Are there no faults?" thundered Giustinian Giustiniani, while the others listened disconcerted. "A soldier seeks for weak spots in the armor."

"I know him," said Leonardo Donato, "and there *is* one fault. It limits his power to achieve; it increases his absolutism. It is near-sightedness— smallness of vision."

"Draw him strongly," said Giustinian, in a tone of concentrated wrath. "Let us measure our foe before we meet."

"There are no books Borghese hath not read; there is no point of view but that which he doth teach, no appeal from the law as he interpreteth it. *It is a fault of unity.* One power—the Church; one duty—its aggrandizement; one prince—temporal and spiritual alike; one unvarying obedience. All is adjusted to one centre; it is the simplification of life!"

There was an ominous silence and an evident wish to change the theme, and the company readjusted itself by twos and threes. The Senator Morosini turned graciously to Marcantonio. "It hath been told in Venice," he said, "that the Lady Marina was received in Rome with marks of very special favor."

"The introduction of our Reverend Father Paolo had preceded her," the young secretary answered lightly, bowing in the direction of the friar, who sat apparently lost in thought. But Morosini repeated Marcantonio's speech with some amusement, for the scholarly friar had never been known to have a friend among the women—old or young.

"I do not understand," he said, with no perception of any humor in the situation.

"It was the gift of the Reverend Father Paolo to the chapel of the Servi," Marcantonio explained. "The Madonna del Sorriso was well known in Rome."

"Ah, I recall now the face of your lady, though I have not known her," the friar responded courteously, yet he hesitated a moment before accepting

173

the seat which the secretary rose to offer him. "If it is the face which the Veronese hath painted, her spirit must be fair. It should make a home holy," he added, after a moment's pause.

Marcantonio's face flushed with pleasure. The friar was still regarding him with a gaze so penetrating, yet apparently so guiltless of intentional rudeness that it ceased to be an impertinence, and amused the young Venetian by its unconventionality. "Is there anything it would please Fra Paolo to ask of me?" he inquired affably.

"If there are children—" the friar pursued quite simply.

"Our little son was baptized in Saint Peter's in Rome; he had sponsors among the cardinals and a private audience and benediction from his Holiness, Pope Clement," the young nobleman replied, trying to repress a pleasurable sense of importance. "It was a pleasure to the Lady Marina—she is devoted to the Church, and his Holiness was always most gracious to her."

"As was fitting for the lady of a Venetian representative, and due to Venice," the elder Giustinian hastened to explain, "his late Holiness was ever courtly and a gracious diplomat."

He had been aware from his little distance how the talk had turned, and he was alert to give it the coloring he liked best. For while the young people were still in Rome, Signor Agostino Nani, watchful as an ambassador well might be of the interests of so princely a house, had confided to the "Illustrissimo Giustiniani," in a private and friendly letter, that courtesies so unusual had been extended

174

to this noble young Venetian lady—so devoted to the Church, so gentle and unsuspicious, so incapable of counter-plotting—that it would be wise to guard against undue influence by a too prolonged stay at the Roman court; and the honorable recall of the Secretary Giustiniani had soon thereafter been managed.

The friar's face had grown stern, but he did not resume the conversation until the elder Giustinian had strolled away with his host. Then he turned to Marcantonio, speaking earnestly. "Simplicity is no match for subtlety," he said, "and much favor hath been shown to her. You will pardon me, Signore, not because you are young and I am old, but because the face of your lady hath moved me with a rare sense of unworldliness. There should be no flattery in an act our Lord himself hath taught by his example, and an old man like Pope Clement might well bestow his blessing on your little child. But the times are not free from danger; the home is best for the little ones—do not send him from his mother to the schools."

"He is but learning to speak," the young man answered, smiling at the friar's earnestness; "only his baby word for his mother's name."

"There are schools for the sons of noblemen in which he will forget it," said the friar bitterly; "where they teach disloyalty to princes and unmake men to make machines—and the mainspring is at Rome. Gentle women are won to believe in them by the subtle polish of those who uphold them, and the marvelous learning by which their teachers fit themselves for office. And among them are men

noble of character and true of conscience—but
bound, soul and body, by their oath; the system of
the Jesuit schools in Venice is for nothing else but
the building up of their order—at all costs of char-
acter or happiness. Let her keep her little son, for
her face seemed wise and tender; the favor which
hath been shown her may have a meaning."

"Will not my father some time come to the pa-
lazzo Giustiniani? The Lady Marina would make
him welcome."

"Nay, I thank you," the friar answered, instantly
resuming his habitual reserve. "Such gentle friend-
ships form no part of my duty. I spake but in
friendly counsel. We, from without, see how the
home should be more. The orders are many to
maintain the Church—they need no urging—but the
home hath also its privileged domain of childhood
to be defended."

XV

WITH the return of the young people from Rome, gala days had once more dawned for the Ca' Giustiniani, and the two sumptuous palaces which met at the bend of the Canal Grande were scenes of perpetual fête. The palazzo Giustinian Giustiniani had been chosen from all the princely homes of Venice as best fitted, from its magnificence, to be offered as a residence to Henry the Third of France, when that monarch had deigned to honor the Republic by accepting its prodigal hospitality. In the banquet halls, which had been prepared with lavish luxury for his reception, the few years that had passed had but mellowed the elaborate carvings and frescoes, while the costly hangings —of crimson velvet with bullion fringes, of azure silk embroidered with fleurs-de-lis, of brocades interwoven with threads of gold—had gained in grace of fold and fusion of tints.

If there were no halls of equal splendor in the palace which had been prepared for Marcantonio and his bride, it displayed in all its appointments an elegance and fitness which the stately Lady Laura was eager to exhibit to the critical appreciation of the fastidious upper circle of Venice.

Marina had had no share in its decorations, and when consulted before her marriage had expressed but one wish. "These cares of rank are new to me," she had said, with gentle dignity; "but thou wilt best know how to choose the elegance befitting Marco's home; for my father hath warned me that in these matters there is a custom which I, more than others, may not break. Dear Lady Laura, for Marco's sake forget that I am of the people, yet, remembering it, to choose but so much of splendor as seemeth needful, lest the palazzo be too costly for a mistress not noble by birth, and so"—she hesitated—"and so win Marco's friends to love me less."

"Marina, Marco hath told me, with a very lover's face, that some are noble by birth who are not so by name."

"Dear Lady," the girl answered, with a charming flush, "had Marco not so plead with me there could have been no question of this home."

The eyes of the great lady beamed with a new and tender pride; in nothing that her boy had ever done for her had he offered her so much as in this love of his which had threatened to part them, but had stirred instead the mother depths of her soul, which had become clouded by years of luxury and artificial life and the knowledge of the ceaseless ambitions and selfish scheming which her husband —for the intellectual stimulus she gave him—had been accustomed to confide to her. And now Marco was not less to her, but more, as he had promised; and if the uncertain hope of that dim, distant, ducal coronet moved her less, it was not that she would not still do her possible to help Giustinian to his ambition—but it had become a smaller peak in the distance since the home life had grown broad enough to bear her calmly when the proud Senator rehearsed some failure or disappointment, with disproportioned bitterness.

Thinking of these things she smiled at Marina with new appreciation; the girl's gentle face seemed to her more lovely and her rare calm and grace of spirit more truly noble than the Venetian vivacity of charm in which at first she had found her lacking.

"Thou hast a way of winning," she said, "which many might envy thee; and in seeming not to ask, thou shalt be served for love. It is the grace of one born to rule. But hast thou *no* wish? Is there no one place I may make all beautiful at thine asking, within thy palace, to prove, sweet Marina, how thy Marco's mother loves thee?"

She parted her soft hair and kissed her forehead, but neither of them noticed that it was a first caress.

"I should like the oratory to be beautiful!" Marina cried, clasping her hands with sudden enthusiasm; "*very* beautiful—like a gift to the Holy Mother!"

"And it shall bring a blessing on thy marriage," the Lady Laura answered her.

So when the secretary and his young wife had returned to Venice and their palace was thrown open to guests, the private chapel of the Lady Marina was discovered to be a marvel of decoration —with superb Venetian frescoes set in marvelous scrollwork by Vittoria, with carvings of mother-of-pearl from Constantinople, with every sumptuous detail that could be devised; for, during the three years of their absence, the Lady Laura had not wearied of her gracious task nor stayed her hand. And into this incongruous setting—costly, overloaded, composite, and destitute of true religious feeling, a very type of the time in Venice—Marina brought the redeeming note of consecration, a priceless altar—ancient, earth-stained, and rude, almost grotesque in symbolism—as a great prize and by special dispensation, from an underground chapel in Rome. Also the rare and beautiful ivory crucifix had its history; the malachite basin for holy water had been a gift to the infant Giustinian from his eminence the cardinal-sponsor on the day of his baptism; there were other treasures, more rare and sacred still, within the shrine of the oratory, and there was a gift from his Holiness Pope Clement VIII.

There was no banquet hall in the palazzo Marcantonio Giustiniani, but it was not needed, for the two palaces were like one.

The Lady Laura was radiant. If there had ever been a question of the place that Marcantonio's bride should occupy in that patrician circle, the distinction conferred upon her by the Senate had sufficed to establish it. There could be no jealousy of one who occupied the highest place, of one so gracious and equal to her honors, only of those who should win her favor. So all came in the hope of it, and all were won; but there were no partialities, no intimacies; for all ambitions of the young and newly created patrician, the fullness of the home life sufficed to her.

Marina had grown more beautiful out of the joy of loving and the increased satisfaction of her religions life, to which she was more than ever devoted; her passion for beauty expressed itself by delight in sumptuous ceremonial, while her love of romance and her unquestioning faith were alike nourished on the legends of the saints which had become far more to her during her stay in Rome, where every hour had been happiness.   These three years of absence had made some subtle difference in the Lady Marina; there was more mystery about her with less reserve, and a certain calm acceptance of the position all conceded had given her courage to discuss religious history and opinions in a serious way that was quite charming to the older prelates who mingled in Venetian social circles, where simple earnestness of soul was a quality so rare that it might have been mistaken for a depth of subtlety; but the Lady Marina talked or listened only because the themes were of vital interest for her.   Besides, she had now her child to guide and she must know; and the learned men who gave their lives to the study of higher things were those, above all others, from whom she could learn the most; and with this unconscious flattery a little court, of a character somewhat unusual in Venice, had gathered in her salons. Her husband, coming in late from the Council Chamber one evening, rallied her upon it, saying that her receptions might be mistaken for those of a lady abbess—there were so many friars and grave ecclesiastics among her guests.   His light tone concealed a little uneasiness, for the friar's warning had more than once recurred to him.

But it was impossible to convey anything to Marina by a half-concealed thrust, her nature was so essentially ingenuous, incapable of imagining intrigues of any sort.

181

"Yes, it is indeed an honor!" she answered, with her ready, trusting smile. "It is good of them, they are so much more interesting than the others; and to-night the talk was quite delightful! I would thou hadst been here, my Marco! Life is so much more beautiful since we have been to Rome! *Everything* that was delightful came with our marriage," she added, turning her radiant face toward him.

He smiled, too, quite disarmed by her beauty and candor, and a little amused that this life of a Venetian princess should be so lightly included in this "everything" which marriage had brought to this maiden of Murano; but he could not help thinking how easily she wore her honors, and how she graced them; all Venice was at her feet, and she preferred the dull talk of a few ecclesiastics to the vivacious gallantry of the brilliant young nobles who thronged her salons—the more anxious to please this queen of the day, that their efforts won only the dignified and gracious, yet reserved, recognition that was extended to all her guests alike. She was the very reverse of Venetian in character and manner, but since she had been so honored by the Republic that difference was recognized as her distinction and charm.

"I doubt not," Marcantonio said, laughingly, "that if nuns might take part in our social functions thou wouldst prefer them also to thine own maidens and all the noble ladies of the Canal Grande. But who held part in this interesting ridotto to-night?"

"Truly, Marco, I think some day perchance I may get a dispensation and have all the nuns of San

Donato for baby's festa in the oratory—would it not be beautiful to hear them chanting in our own palazzo! But that is only a dream; I know not if it may ever be."

She came toward him, in her shimmering festal robes, with the unconscious, happy grace of a child, dropping into a low seat close beside him, leaning back and letting her hands fall in an attitude of complete repose, while she gave him, without effort, the detail of the evening's talk. He was a little surprised at the way in which she made this graphic recital of a discussion he would have supposed beyond her comprehension—or at least beyond her concern—and he was not wholly pleased. He had quite forgotten that one of the charms of Marina upon which he had insisted in the days when he had made much of this maiden to his patrician mother was that in capacity for thought and in force of character she was far above the maidens of ancient lineage, from whom the Lady Laura would have had him choose his bride.

Marina had named, among others, Fra Francesco, her own spiritual director, a Servite friar of gentle and winning demeanor, who was much beloved both in his convent and in other circles where his duties called him. He was a man of simple habits and the most exemplary life, whose whole force lay in his extreme devotion to duty and his passionate love for the Church; his sole anxiety was for her glory, and he would have been supremely happy in the life he had chosen, were it not for his growing anxiety lest from her own sons she should receive dishonor. He was always a welcome visitor at the palazzo Giustiniani, and already the little prince of the household had a special smile for him.

"Ah, Fra Francesco, of course!" said Marcantonio, in an indulgent tone; "our own friars and ecclesiastics are welcome. But, carina, these foreign priests are often of a different way of thinking; and Don Fernanzo Lillo, that fluent Spaniard—verily I would have thee don thy most freezing dignity when he comes again."

"But, Marco mio, thou doest him injusice; he is most interesting; he was telling about the frescoes of the Michelangelo in the Sistine Chapel; he knoweth them well, yet I think he liketh them little."

"It matters not," said Marcantonio, a little disdainfully; "thou hast already seen them; thou canst have thine own opinion of their merit."

"But to hear all the allegories explained and all the illusions to the history of our Holy Church is *most* interesting," Marina pursued calmly; "for the dear padre of San Donato had but little instruction; I must know about all these things for baby's sake —he is growing so fast."

"He is not going to be an artist,' his father answered shortly; "and if he were, we could find a better person to instruct him than a Spanish member of the Jesuit College."

"*Marco!*" exclaimed his wife, with a long note of surprise; "is not our Holy Church one? and are not her sons scattered over the whole world? I knew not he displeased thee," she continued, in a changed tone, after a little pause. "Of course I will not see him again. But is it Don Fernanzo Lillo himself, or—or—Marco—it cannot be the order! Thou canst not be so narrow!"

"At this time, Marina, with matters thus between Venice and Rome, I do not care to entertain any of their order or any foreign priests in our home; they do not place things in the proper light, and we have always held a special position of loyalty toward Venice. When she is in difficulties all the Ca' Giustiniani should seem to remember it; it could make no other difference."

"I do not understand," she answered, looking at him with perplexed brows.

"Why shouldst thou!" he exclaimed, glad to change a distasteful topic; "such weariness is not needful for thee. I will not bring the worries of the Council Chamber into thy boudoir."

"Nay, Marco, it would please me," she answered eagerly, rising instantly from her languid attitude to come and stand over him, laying one hand on his shoulder, half in caress and half in command. "Thy father tells these matters to the Lady Laura; and for baby's sake I should understand these troubles which touch our Republic. He will ask me questions very soon."

"Well, then," he consented ungraciously, "what is it thou wouldst ask?"

She laughed at his reluctance, pressing her hand with a firmer and yet more loving touch on his shoulder. "Because I am a Giustinian," she began, with a plea which invariably won him, "tell me about this question of Vicenza which occupies them all so much—I could not understand. Who is this Abbott of Nervessa?"

At her first words he had folded her caressing hand in his, but he dropped it in immediate displeasure and walked quickly away from her, speaking indignantly. "They talked of this in thy presence?"

"They said an abbé was imprisoned in the Piombi; they said it was against the law to imprison ecclesiastics except by the authority of the Pope. Oh, Marco mio, I am afraid he will be very angry!"

"What else did they tell thee?" he questioned doggedly.

"They said there was a Canon Saraceni also—both imprisoned in Venice. Marco mio, it is an insult to our Holy Father!"

"What else?"

"Nothing more—but only about some law of Venice that I did not understand; I wished to ask thee."

"And Fra Francesco was here and heard them talk?"

"Nay, Fra Francesco stays never long; and this was but a few moments before thy coming. I left the Sala Tiziana to see if all were going well in this little salon, and they were speaking of Vicenza, and I asked them. Wherefore art thou angry, Marco? What kept thee so late to-night?"

She had never seen him in such a mood; he had persistently refused to meet her beseeching glance; but now he drew a quick breath of relief, and came back to her side.

"It was this miserable matter of Vicenza that detained the Council in such lengthy session," he said, "and it was not fit to have been mentioned in thy presence, my sweet wife; I might well be angry. But since thou wert not there, I can pardon them."

"Yes, it was I who questioned them," she repeated eagerly, anxious to shield her guests from her husband's indignation, though she did not understand it. "They were talking of the Abbot of Nervessa and of his Holiness, and when I came they rose to do me honor; and I also, to be not lacking in courtesy, said, 'Le prego, Signori—I beg of you,' and bade them continue the talk in which they had seemed full of interest. Marco, in the Senate—do they know that the Pope is angry about the Abbot of Nervessa?"

Her eyes were full of the eagerness of her question. If they but · knew all would be well, she thought; she had so wished for Marco to be there and hear them talk!

"Marina, this whole matter is a question for the government to decide; it is not for ecclesiastics to discuss—they know nothing of any laws but their own. This is a civil case."

"Would they not understand things better if they were allowed representation in the Senate?" she persisted. "And what is this law? And why is the subject not fit for Venetian nobles to discuss, since it touches them so nearly?" She was growing disturbed, for she feared some injustice, since Marco had not been indignant at the strange condition she had unfolded to him, and she had thought it must suffice only to name it to him.

The young patrician looked at her in amazement. Fra Paolo was indeed right, yet he had been almost indignant at the suggestion.

"The subject cannot be discussed," he said, in quick, hard tones, "because the Abbot of Nervessa

187

hath committed crimes so atrocious that thou would'st shrink at the bare naming of them. And for Saraceni—the Canon of Vicenza—there came one day to the Senate a noble lady of Vicenza, young, and very beautiful, and in great trouble, casting herself at the feet of the Serenissimo, imploring protection from disgrace that the canon would bring upon her—a scandal I had never thought to name to thee. And there are other charges."

"It cannot be true!" she cried, flushed and trembling. "Dear Marco, they are priests!"

"The truth will be decided by the integrity of the law," he answered, severely; "they shall have justice at our courts; but it is a question for the civil courts, since the people also cry for justice, and the ecclesiastical law is not to deal with heinous civil offenses—though committed by one in priestly robes. It is a just law of Venice—ancient, and only now reaffirmed."

"This is the law they spake of, Marco?"

Now that she dimly understood there was some great trouble coming on the people, she must know the right at any cost—even that of her husband's displeasure; it was her duty to him, and she had put her question firmly.

"This—and another," he answered, unwillingly. "Listen, Marina, for I am weary of thy questions. The law to forbid new foundations of church or monastery, or the introduction of new religious orders without the sanction of the government— also an ancient law, and but now reaffirmed—is doubtless that of which they· spake."

Marina stood confounded, with flashing eyes;

how could the Republic dare to question the liberties of the Church! "Thou meanest, Marco, that the Church, which is the head, must ask the Doge what she may do when she would increase her own religious institutions—when she hath need of buildings for her holy work!"

"Thou hast an understanding quicker than I had believed," he answered, with irritation; " and listen further, Marina—'since a Giustinian should know the reason for the matters which concern the government,' that was thy word, if I remember—the half of the territory of Venice hath already passed into the hands of the clergy. Is that not ground enough to hold their establishments, that thou wouldst grant them more? And for the value of these possessions—for nowhere is a government more generous to the ecclesiastics than the Republic hath been—it hath been rated that a fourth part of the entire realty of the dominion—nay, some count it a third part—is already the property of the Church. Shall we nobles of Venice turn paupers and humbly beg of the clergy a pittance for our children?"

He laughed and kissed her hand as he rose. "Since thou hast asked it," he said lightly, "I have given thee the law—and there is an end of it. But let it not fret thee; Venice will know how to care for her own."

But Marina had suddenly grown very pale. "Marco," she gasped, detaining him, "will it be a war?—a war between Venice and—and——"

She. broke off; she could not speak the word which seemed a sacrilege.

"Think of our child!" she whispered, as he gath-

189

ered her in his arms, and tried to soothe her. "Marco, are we not a Christian nation? And our Patriarch—does he know about the displeasure of the Holy Father? What will become of us?"

"There will be no war," Marcantonio declared, with assurance. "Thou see'st, carina, these matters are not for women to discuss; they cannot understand; they are questions for the government alone; and well it is for us that the clergy are out of it, or we might have the spectacle of a Senate drowned in tears! There will be no war," he declared again, mistaking the self-control for which she had bravely struggled as an outcome of his attempts at consolation. "And now, since thou art thy sweet self again, hath the boy not made the day richer for thee with some tale of wonder thou wouldst unfold?"

XVI

THERE was no longer any doubt as to the intention of his Holiness toward the rebellious spirit of the Most Serene Republic; the Ambassade Extraordinary which had been appointed to convey to the Holy See the dutiful congratulations of her devoted Venetian sons, on the accession of Paul V, had few amenities to report in those lengthy dispatches to which the Senate listened with a dignity which disdained to show the least outward trace of irritation or forgetfulness, in a presence so exasperating as that of the Papal Nuncio, Orazio Mattei.

Day after day the Senate sat, in solemn state, to hear its delinquencies rehearsed in the words of Paul V, by the graphic pen of his Excellency Agostino Nani, Ambassador from the Republic to the Holy See, with ceaseless repetitions of demand on the part of the Sovereign Pontiff; with ceaseless repetitions of refusal, most deferently couched, from the courtly representative of the offending power; with threats of that most dread compeller of obedience which none but a sovereign pontiff may wield; and very clearly phrased, that all might understand, the declaration in the words of his Holiness himself, that he had determined to "mortify the over-weening audacity of the secular rulers of the world."

With a patience which bore its fruit in a more rigid determination to conquer, they listened, also, to many violent speeches from the Nuncio, explanatory of papal authority, founded upon the dicta of a Gregory, *"That none may judge the Pope. That all princes should kiss the feet of the Pope,"* and invariably sustained by this axiom of Mattei, delivered as. a refrain—so sure were the college of its repetition, "I am Pope here; I want no replies, only obedience," and the reiterated assertion that "Christianity depends upon the acceptance in its entirety of the doctrine of papal supremacy, and that he has heard much of the vaunted piety of the Venetian Republic, of which he fails to find evidence."

In vain the Senate pleaded that on such a point there might be differing views, and that men should be known for Christians by their faithfulness in duty, by their practice of almsgiving and of the sacraments and of all other good and Christian works; but the answer came swiftly, "Naught else availeth."

It was a relief to the stately and grim Giustinian to lose his temper in the sanctity of his home, since that freedom was beneath the dignity of a Venetian ruler in the company of others who were chafing like himself from insults they would have rejoiced to hurl back in the face of the speaker; and he was the less inclined to view favorably the efforts toward conciliation of the embassy to the Holy See, because it would have pleased him to have been named among those six of this Ambassade Extraordinary, on a mission so important, as an honor due to his ancient house.

"It is repetition *ad nauseam*," he insisted hotly, "of demands for abrogation of those laws, for yielding up of those two reverend criminals to the ecclesiastical courts, of Nani's soft replies to the quick speeches of his Holiness—an unending farce!"

"Giustinian," said the Lady Laura quietly, "the difficulties are great. How can the Holy Father yield a point which touches the honor of the Church?"

"Verily, my lady, I believe thou art not responsible for thine own foolishness!" her husband exclaimed angrily. "If that prelate cousin of Saraceni comes again to thy salon, let him be refused! He shall not prate to thee of 'law' and 'supremacy,' who hath sought for this occasion to embroil us with the Holy See. For the Senate hath learned to-day, through the trustworthy open mouth of our watchful Lion, with evidence irrefragable, that it is this reverend father who hath carried.the tale to Rome."

"Tell me the right of it," she said again. "How may the honor of the Church be saved, yet the dignity of Venice be maintained? If there be a way, we women should speak for it."

"Is the honor of the Church maintained by standing as a shield to crime? It is Venice who would save the Church; the civil ruler shall purge her sacred courts of such iniquities and leave her the purer for her sons to love. Such is the law—ancient and just—and a right Venice cannot yield. And more than this," he continued impressively, "all Europe is waiting on the issue, for the real contest is on the rights of civil rulers, and these imprisoned ecclesiastics are but the pretext for a quarrel; and ill-judged, verily, on the part of the Holy Father, since if the cases were less heinous there might have been occasion for confusion of judgment. But now, who will dare assert that the honor of the Church is concerned in protecting men who disgrace mankind!"

"The Republic is then sure of her ground?"

"So sure we are of right that letters are already sent to every Christian court of Europe, announcing the causes of this quarrel and the stand of Venice."

"Marina is greatly troubled," said the Lady Laura, with a sigh.

"Let her go often to San Marco and pray for us—the child is good for nothing else since this trouble came."

"She hath more comfort at San Donato; and the mother superior is a noble woman and beloved by her."

"Ay, it is all one—so that she wear not out the patience of Marcantonio by her importunities. The Senate will stand firm on the issue, and not one of the Ca' Giustiniani shall flinch."

"Is there no possible doubt of the ending?" the Lady Laura questioned, after a little troubled silence. Her heart was very sore for Marina, who slept but little, and was constantly fasting.

"Only of that which lieth between; the end is triumph for Venice," Giustinian declared. "Tell that to Marina, and calm her fears. Also, let it not be known that she is so weak in courage; it would be held against Marcantonio, to whom the suspicion of being wife-ridden would do an infinite injustice. And bid Marcantonio himself tell her of the vote that hath passed the Senate, without dissent of a single voice, for letters to be sent to the imperious Paul to make an end of his demands, declaring that Venice recognizeth for the temporal government of her states no superior, save God alone."

Meanwhile in Rome, to the Ambassador Agostino Nani, Paul had already superbly made answer, "We are above all men, and God hath given us power over all men; we can depose kings and do yet more than that. Especially our power is 'quæ tendunt ad finem supranaturalem.' (Over those things which tend to a supernatural end.)"

All thoughts of festivity in the City of the Sea were over; the strength of her patricians—men and women—was concentrated on this momentous quarrel with the Holy See, which they would indeed have put off were it possible, but which, having come upon them, they would bear with conquering pride. All through those dark December days the pressure tightened; there were mutterings of the coming storm, against which the rulers of Venice were planning defense; there was an oppression, like a sense of mental sirocco, in the air—a vague terror of the unknown among the people, gathering like the blighting breath which precedes some fierce tornado—while in the palace of San Marco, the Doge, Marino Grimani, Chief of the Republic in revolt against the Holy See, lay dying!

The Lady Marina Giustiniani had forgotten how to smile. When her little one lifted his rosy baby face to hers she smothered him in caresses, that he might not see her tears; and her husband failed to note the change, for the Senate sat in unbroken session and the permitted absences from the Council Chambers of the Republic barely sufficed for sleep. Daily in the oratory of her palace Mass was said, and Marina passed long hours there on her knees alone, tracing the coming horror to its most dread issue, trying to understand it wholly, that she might pray with all her soul against it—this *Curse* which was to blight the lives of all she loved, and of which her dearest seemed to feel no dread! She scarcely ate nor slept—watching, for the morning, when a new intercession for mercy should rise from the oratory in her palace; waiting for the evening, when she might go with her maidens to vespers in San Marco. And still the days darkened in threats— had God forgotten to be gracious?

And on this Christmas morning, when the Doge of Venice lay dying in his halls of state, the nuns of San Donato, won by the prayers and gifts of the Lady Marina, were making a procession to all the shrines of Murano, praying, if by any means, God would stay this curse from falling upon Venice.

No joy-bells rang to usher in the sunrise Mass of this memorable Christmas day. The royal standards of the mighty Lion drooped at half-mast before the dimmed magnificence of San Marco, their glowing gold and scarlet deadened to shades of mourning steel; and low, muffled tones, like the throbbings of the heart of a people, dropped down from the campanile through an atmosphere still and cold as a breath of dread; while from the embassies, the homes of the senators and Signoria, the

Patriarch and bishops of Venice, gondolas by twos and threes loomed black against the gray-dark of the winter dawn, hurrying noiselessly to the steps of the Piazzetta; and dark, stately figures, each heralded by its torch-bearer, glided like phantoms under the arcades of the Ducal Palace, up between the grim, giant guardians of the stairway, and on to the galleries adjoining the apartments of the Doge, to await the hour of Mass.

An edict, more unanswerable than any ever issued by Republic or Curia, had gone forth, and in solemn state Venice awaited its fulfilment.

In that hush of reverent waiting, before the first faint saffron streak had glimmered in the east, up through the flaring torches of the lower court, unbidden and unwelcome, came the single figure in all that throng which seemed to have no part in the solemn drama. To-day was like other days for the nuncio, who was no member of the court of Venice, but a figure without discretionary privilege, sent to keep in perpetual mind a higher power. By his peremptory instructions he requested at once a formal audience to deliver a message from his Holiness Paul V, which could brook no delay.

"Behold!" said he, after due grace of apology, when the senators had withdrawn to the Sala di Collegio and taken their accustomed places, "here are two briefs which, by the imperative instructions of our Sovereign Lord the Pope, I must at once deliver to your Serene Highnesses."

They were sealed with the sacred seal of the Curia, and each bore the inscription:

"A Marino Grimani, Duce; e alla Republica Veneta."

There was but a moment's consultation among the Signoria.

"The Serenissimo is *in extremis*," the most venerable of the Ducal Councillors announced, "therefore these briefs which, in the name of the Serene Republic of Venice, we receive, cannot be opened until the solemn ceremonials of the death and the election shall have been concluded," and so dismissed the bearer of the Papal message to return to the audience of the greater king.

Meanwhile there was no arresting of that other message, which came swiftly, and the placid old Grimani—wise, beloved, and regretted—laid down his sceptre of state in the moment of the greatest need of Venice, and passed on to a Court of Inquiry whose findings are inalterably just.

Calmly, as if they knew not the contents of the unopened briefs, or like men never to be surprised into forgetfulness, the Signoria and councillors assisted at the crowded ceremonials of the days that followed, when the Serenissimo lay in state in the *chapelle ardente*, which was prepared in one of the great chambers of the Palace, with twenty nobles in ceaseless attendance, the people thronging silently to pay their duty to their Prince—when, by night, in solemn procession, with torches and chanting of requiems, they carried him to the church of San Zanipolo, their gondolas draped in mourning, their banners furled in crêpe, the imposing insignia of the state he had put off forever borne before him to the giant baldichino before the high altar, where, surrounded by innumerable candles, he lay until the morning should bring the closing pomp of the last solemn Mass.

Not one honor had been omitted, not one ceremonial abridged because of those briefs upon which the seal of the Vatican was still unbroken; and when the imposing obsequies were over, and there was no longer a prince to lift the weight of the gold-wrought mantle and the ducal beretta in the sight of the people, the ship of state yet bore herself superbly, steering as serenely through the troubled sea as if each man still read his signal in the face of a beloved commander.

And now the singular strength of the Republic and the perfection of the machine of government was evidenced, as, without a moment of indecision, the officers proceeded to discharge the duty allotted to the hour, according to the forms prescribed in those endless volumes of the "Libri Ceremoniali," which provided for every function of life or death of the punctilious Venetian court.

No leader, however loved and revered, was individually great, but only as he contributed to the greatness of Venice—the one deathless entity; her noblest were content to give of their greatness and be themselves nameless; and against the less great, for whom self-effacement was impossible—men strong in gifts and eager for power—the jealous Republic had provided a system of efficient checks, based upon an astute understanding of the fears and claims of self-interest. Venice knew no hiatus in rule; all were leaders to point the way of that inviolable constitution when the supreme voice was temporarily silent, for it was the voice of an impersonal prince, and not of the man—who had absolutely put off individuality when he assumed the insignia of royalty.

199

In this hour of adversity the men of Venice rose to their greatest, forgetting their rivalries and standing breast to breast in phalanx around their vacant throne, that Venice might meet trouble with increased strength when the eyes of the world were curiously turned upon her.

Inexorably, though no voice had been raised against Grimani, they appointed that commission of inquisitors to review every official act of the last wearer of this crown which now lay idly waiting on the golden cushion; as sternly elected, those five "correctors" of the coronation oath so soon to be administered to a new wearer of the ermine, and without pause for praise or strife, proceeded to the cumbersome choice of the ducal electors whose word should suffice to create a new Venetian prince.

Meanwhile, against the barred doors of the Council Chambers, where those grave Signori were balloting and re-balloting with exemplary patience for the golden balls, the nuncio knocked again, breathless with his latest message sent in haste from the Holy See: *"The election of a new prince would be void, being made by a people under censure."*

But the law of Venice was ready with its decorous shield, and the message could not pass beyond. The punctilious Signoria might give no audience in the days that intervened between Doge and Doge, except to receive that message of condolence which it had not entered the heart of his Holiness to frame, and the nuncio appealed in vain to other authorities in Venice to win him audience for the delivery of his sovereign's mandate.

With whatever burnings of heart and secret

hopes and ambitions those forty-one elected nobles, after days of weary, patient tossings of gold and silver balls—a mere intricate child's play had it not been for the greatness of the prize—saw themselves closed within the chamber from which they might not issue forth until there was again a prince in Venice; with what vividness a Giustinian foresaw his own stern visage stamped on the coin of Venice in that moment when his name appeared on the first folded paper drawn from the fateful urn; with what dignity he concealed his baffled hope and watched, from under frowning eyebrows, a Morosini and a Ziani pass, in turn, through the fierce ordeal of relegation to obscurity—the annals of that secret council do not reveal.

. But in this stress of Venice the electors quitted themselves like true men, and when the noble Cavalière Leonardo Donato—full of dignity, of wisdom, and of honors, skilled in diplomacy and experience, and bold as wise—came forth to scatter his coronation gift of coin in the Piazza, and after solemn religious ceremonial was shown from the pulpit of San Marco as Prince of Venice, well might the people shout in acclamation, *"Provato! Provato!"* ("Approved!") and the watching courts of Europe hasten to express, through their resident ambassadors, eager congratulations that one so fitted to fill the position with distinction had taken his place among the rulers.

But Orazio Mattei brought no message of congratulation from Rome.

XVII

GIUSTINIAN GIUSTINIANI had been among
the electors and had listened to that strict can-
vassing of acts, both private and official, which pre-
ceded the final vote for the Prince of Venetia.

"Venice hath taken stand before the courts of
Europe with a leader who feareth naught—save not
to do the right," he magnanimously assured the
Lady Laura one evening when, according to their
wont, they were discussing the theme which never
failed in interest. "Nay, not even that; for Donato
hath courage in himself, and in his own rulings
faith, and more a man needs not."

"Then wherefore hath the Signoria created this
office of *Teologo Consultore*, and appointed thereto
this friar of the Servi, of whom they tell such mar-
vels—as if the Collegio, with all our learned chan-
cellors, were not enough!"

"Leave thou these matters to the Signoria, who,
verily, know how to rule—ay, and how to choose;
for the man is like none other."

"What uses hath the Senate for this cloistered
scholar, skilled in many sciences and master of
tongues," the Lady Laura persisted, "that it should
create an office—which since the *serrata* it hath not
been known to do—and appoint a friar over the
heads of our nobles who have loyally served the Re-

public since our ancestors first sat in the Consiglio? There are the halls of Padua for our scholars, where already his friend, the master Galileo, holdeth high honors, by favor of the Senate; and if Fra Paolo were named Rector Magnifico, and put at its head——"

"Nay, nay, the Senate is wise," her husband interrupted, not ill pleased at her vehemence and the patrician pride which prompted it. "And if the Republic hath no present need of the Consultore's mastery of sciences, the fame thereof hath made a hearing for any speech of his. But he hath no mind to any social pleasures—how, then, my lady, hast seen him, or knowest thou the quality of his learning?"

"Fra Francesco is never weary of telling of his wisdom; they have been friends since boyhood in the Servi. The master Galileo, if one may believe him, can do naught without consulting Fra Paolo, and together they are building some strange tunnel that shall bring the stars nearer! It is like a fable to listen to these marvels of his friend, who for his discoveries might well hold all the chairs in Padua if Fra Francesco might decree his deserts! But Fra Francesco is simple-minded. Tell me, Giustinian, how doth the Consultore appear to thee?"

"To me and to all men like one who betrays no secret and speaks no idle word."

"Once," pursued the lady meditatively, "I had sight of him, going with Marco to the convent to see our Madonna of the Veronese, and Fra Paolo ministered in the chapel of the Consolation; very quiet and simple he seemed, like the other frati. I

203

had not thought him great, nor a leader of men. Are there no statesmen in Venice who might better fit the dignity of so great an office?"

"Think not to teach subtlety to the Signoria, my Lady Laura! Is not every noble a statesman trained, and every one at the service of the Republic? But there is no greater theologian at the Court of Paul V, nor any ecclesiastic among them all more familiar with the writings of their authorities; and he hath a memory so astounding that he beareth the meaning of all their codes on the end of his tongue wherewith to confute the fallacious arguments of Rome."

"Giustinian!"

"It is like a woman to ask a thing and cry out if the answer be not smothered in sweets!" the old Senator retorted irritably, resenting her accent of reproof. "It is small marvel if the Consultore seemeth not great to thee; the power of the man is in the clarity of his vision and the brevity of his speech."

"Who named him to the Signoria?"

"Donato knew him well, and Morosini and all our ablest men; and his knowledge of the ways of Rome, where he hath been much in legislation at the Vatican, is a power in the Senate—which hath no mind to be taken in argument, nor to fail in courtesy, nor to show ignorance in its demands. It is much to have a judge whose opinion our adversary must respect."

"The Senate will be cautious—will not forget the reverence owed to the Holy Church?" she asked, in warning, troubled at his bold use of words.

"Nay, but the Republic will first remember the duty owed to our prince, since it is a matter that toucheth the State," he answered, uncompromisingly, "and for our duty to the Church—leave that to our frate, than whom none is more devout."

She was too keenly interested not to put the further question:

"Is it safe for Fra Paolo to lead this controversy? Is it pleasing to his order?"

Giustinian gave a contemptuous laugh.

"Thou mayest well ask! Fra Paolo also would not hear of it at first, foreseeing where it might lead. But from urgency of the Senate he yielded—if the consent of the general of the Servi were first won. Wherefore it was granted one knows not; but the purple robe had, perchance, some weight in the argument,—being a pleasing honor,—though one may dare assert that Fra Paolo himself gave it not a thought, having gathered honors all his life with no care for any greatness they might bring."

"Nay, it was not this that won them," said the Lady Laura, with decision, "but their hope that Fra Paolo would support the claims of the Holy Father; it could have been nothing else."

"A hope most reasonable, were he a man of less remarkable force," Giustinian answered confidently. "But, as if he held a divining-rod, he findeth at once the heart of a matter, and Venice hath no fears."

No, Venice had no fears. If there had been heartburnings, they were all forgotten; her rulers were one in determination while they calmly weighed the balance between Church and State, and confidently awaited the issue. The briefs had been opened and the chief Counsellor, the new Teologo Consultore, had given an opinion which filled the Senate with admiration.

"Two remedies might be found: one, material, by forbidding the publication of the censures and preventing the execution of them, thus resisting illegitimate force by force clearly legitimate, so long as it doth not overpass the bounds of natural right of defense; and the other moral, which consisteth in an appeal to a future council. But," continued this sagacious Counsellor, after a word explanatory of the "future council," "it were better to avoid this appeal in order not to irritate the Pope more than ever; and also because he who appealeth admiteth that the goodness of his cause is doubtful, whereas that of the Republic is indubitable."

Such was the opinion, brief as positive, to which the senators listened in undisguised satisfaction on that memorable day in January, 1606; and although those briefs, "Given in Saint Peter's, in Rome, under the Ring of the Fisherman, on the 10th of December, 1605," darkly threatened excommunication unless these dearly beloved sons of Venice withdrew from the stand they had taken, yet with a Doge who "would laugh at an excommunication," and a learned Counsellor who assured them that the cause of the Republic was indubitable, well might the shadows lessen in the Senate Chamber; while in calm assurance the Savii[1] prepared the reply to these communications from his Holiness, which the

1 These Savii, or *wise men*, had charge of the diplomatic despatches of the Republic.

Signor Agostino Nani presently delivered in an audience at Rome.

But the task of the courtly Nani was not an enviable one, deferent as was the form of the epistle in which these devoted sons declared that nothing could have been further from the thoughts of Venice than to prejudice the rights of the Church—humbly as they implored the Holy Father to recall the many acts of loyalty by which Venice had shown her love and reverence. Had she not been foremost in the Crusade? Was the Church anywhere more magnificently supported in temporal weal? Earnestly as they assured him of the harmlessness of those laws which he condemned as hurtful to their souls, quietly announcing that the Republic had transgressed no right in making laws for her own independent civil government,—and gracious and diplomatic as were the ways of Nani,—his Holiness declared the letter to be "frivolous and vain," and dismissed the ambassador with temper, assuring him that unless the Republic found means to retract those laws "the gates of hell should not prevail" to deter him from inflicting the utmost threatened penalty.

It was a frank contest of wills, in which each opponent conscientiously believed himself in the right; but it was, nevertheless, not an equal contest; for Paul, conceiving that his duty in the exalted position of head of the Church which had been so unexpectedly thrust upon him, lay in its mere temporal aggrandizement, while consciously turning all his powers in that direction, misnamed the struggle a *spiritual* one. But Venice not only believed but confessed it to be merely a question of civil rights of rulers, and, strong in the sense of the justice of her cause, used every grace of trained diplomacy in asserting it—upon an understanding of civil law which was beyond the attainment of the lawyer Camillo Borghese, and with the aid of specialists whose knowledge of canon law equaled that of his Holiness.

Among the important matters touched upon in those days in the Senate the question had been broached, not without anxiety, as to whether Rome would have recourse to force of a less spiritual nature, and a secret commission had been appointed to examine and report from the frontiers any accession of papal troops, while envoys were sent to Ferrara on the same furtive errand; and the more serious Venetians were already discussing the possibility of war as one of the aspects of this quarrel with the Holy See.

One day, through the swift and secret mouth of the Lion, an unusual message reached the Ten, standing strangely out amid a mass of darker matter—denunciations, sinister information, hints of intrigues; the reason for the choice of this mysterious messenger was stated in the preamble: "To the end that this may, without circumlocution, immediately reach your noble body and be acted upon in your discretion—being secretly dismissed, if this seemeth wisest in the interests of the State." It was a brief offer on the part of Girolamo Magagnati to equip and maintain, at his expense, in the event of war with the Holy See, a war-galley of the largest size, as a gift to the Republic in the name of his little grandson, the infant Giustinian.

Venice, being more munificent in expenditure than her unassisted treasury would warrant, was at all times ready to receive and encourage private bounties from her wealthy citizens; and the promptness and generosity of Magagnati's gift, the first which had been offered in this emergency, seemed in the interests of the government to demand some adequate public recognition, modestly as it had been proffered. Haughty as was the attitude of Venice in the face of the threatened excommunication, the occasion was one of peril to which she was not blind, and the danger was greatest among the people—the *popolo*—who were more under the influence of the priests, and who still included in their beliefs many superstitions which were not likely to deter the disciplined body of nobles from acquiescence in the decisions of their chiefs.

It was therefore a moment for diplomacy, when Venice might fitly show magnanimity in her acceptance of so princely a gift from one of the people, as this master-worker of Murano was still esteemed; and Girolamo Magagnati was invited to appear before the Senate and receive the acknowledgment of the Serenissimo, who had already been informed by the Councillors that while the spontaneous offer of a galley so maintained had no precedent in the annals of Venice, the reward which the Senate proposed to bestow had, in fact, in early historic days been offered by the Republic as a stimulus to such a gift.

Girolamo Magagnati, a grave and venerable figure,—with white locks falling from under his round black cap, and a full gray beard flowing over the long merchant's robe of stiff silk, and wearing the insignia of his calling, a golden chain which by its weight and numerous links was also an indication of his wealth,—might have been one of the Signoria, as he stood among them to receive their thanks— unabashed, as became one of his dignity of character and age, unattended, as befitted one of the people.

The Doge himself made a gracious speech of acceptance on behalf of the Republic, to which Girolamo briefly answered: "Most Serene Prince and Noble Lords of the Council, in the name of my grandson Giustinian, I thank you," and with a grave obeisance he would have retired; but it was signified to him that he might not yet withdraw.

"Yet one thing remaineth, most esteemed Messer Magagnati, by which this Republic would testify her appreciation of such loyalty and forethought, by reason of which—as for the esteem in which this Republic hath ever held the ancient house of Magagnati, which from the earliest times hath been foremost in our industry of Murano—we propose to confer nobility upon thine house, and to give thee an immediate seat of right in the Maggior Consiglio."

The honor was so unexpected that the body of grave Councillors had risen in congratulation before Girolamo Magagnati could frame other response than his profound and grave obeisance.

But there was no hint of indecision in the deep, measured tones with which he made reply:

"Most Serene Prince and Lords of the Council, I beg you to believe in my deep appreciation of the honor you would bestow. But let it rather be said of me that I—being still of the people, as all of my house from the commencement of this Republic have ever been—have yet received such favor of my Prince that he accepts from one of the people this token of loyal service to the government. And more I ask not."

"Also," he proceeded calmly, taking no note of the consternation on the faces of his auditors, "is it not fitting for old men to receive favors from children, rather for them to bestow—as I, this galley, in the name of the boy; the which—were I to accept in return the munificence of the Senate—would be the offering of my galley as so much base coin, wherewith to purchase an honor not mine by birth. Let it not be said in scorn that Girolamo Magagnati hath bought the nobility with which his birth hath failed to endow him!"

"Is it better, Messer Magagnati, that some should now say 'it is for arrogance that this noble son of the people refuses a seat among the nobles of Venice'?" the Doge questioned coldly.

"Not so, Most Serene Prince; each man is rather noble if, in that place which God hath assigned him, he doeth nobly the duty belonging thereto; as ye, my Lords, Nobles, and Councillors of the Republic, each in the seat appointed you by birth, serve, without wearying, the interests of Venice. I am already old and the last of my race, for those of my blood who come after me, by the favor of Venice, are inscribed in the 'Libro d'Oro.' If I have deserved aught of your bounty, be gracious when some right of the people is in danger of being forgotten; and let my grandson, among the nobles, ever serve nobles and people alike—as Venetians—

without distinction of interests. But let me die as I have lived, among the workmen of Murano—Magagnati, of the Venetian people."

"Never before, in the annals of the Republic, was one known to refuse the gift of nobility," Giustinian explained, as he described the scene to the Lady Laura. "And, verily, one saw that the displeasure of the Ten was great; the more so that in the interests of the government the return they would have made may not be kept from the knowledge of the people. Yet our senior master of Murano was suffered to depart with a gracious word of regret from this consummate Donato, 'that a new noble, so loyal in sentiment, should not be numbered among the councillors of Venice.' Truly this grandsire of our little one lacketh not pride, and his bearing became him well, though the Senate would have had it otherwise. His gift was generous; but verily he needeth little for the maintenance of the state he keepeth!"

"Giustinian, it was a noble act! And already the Republic is more beholden to our baby than to any child in Venice; it will bring gladness to the face of our sad Marina."

"Nay, guard thee from speech of it; perchance she may not hear thereof, being thus concerned with grief for this quarrel—womanlike; and she hath not strength to bear the thought of war. Verily, the reverend father confessors in Venice have much to answer for; I would thou couldst find means to keep Fra Francesco from his ministrations in her palace."

"Fra Francesco—so holy and gentle—a man to trust!"

"Ay, I have naught against him, save that he is trained in the school of Rome, having a conscience to uphold their claims, and with no thought or care for anything but the Church—no wisdom to discover any right of princes. Such confessors make trouble among the people. I doubt not our daughter trusteth the word of Fra Francesco beyond thine or mine. Do thy possible to keep him from her; there is no knowing what Marcantonio may do at her bidding, and in this crisis there shall be no stain upon our house."

"Thou, then, Giustinian, speak with Marco."

"Nay, I dare not name Marina to him under such suspicion; it might be the forcing of the very thing we fear. He hath a way with him of hearing all and saying naught, save some gay, facile word, courteous to the point one can find no fault; and underneath he hath perhaps some scheme, and never can one get a promise from him."

XVIII

THE Lady Marina was wan from fear and fasting but very resolute, though her face showed traces of tears, as her husband entered the oratory of the palace, whither she had implored him to come to her before he went to the Senate Chamber—a dignity to which he had but just been elected.

"Why hast thou summoned me hither?" he asked somewhat coldly; for, like most light-hearted people, he disliked scenes, and differences between himself and his wife were the more intolerable to him because he truly loved her.

"Oh, Marco, my beloved!" she exclaimed imploringly, "thou lovest Venice as much as I, and thy little word can save her from this great horror, for thou art in the councils of thy people."

"Nay, Marina, thou dost not understand," he answered deprecatingly, softening at the sight of her trouble. "I have but one vote; it is as nothing in the Senate—it would but draw indignation against our house. It is not possible to fail in loyalty to the Republic on this first occasion of moment."

"Thy father might be won, if thou hast but courage. Thou art a Giustinian; it is thy duty to speak in time of peril, and thy words would make others brave to follow thee. Thus shalt thou save Venice."

"If thou didst but know, carina, how the Senate and the Ten are set against this wish of thine! I

214

should not speak of this matter to thee, for it is secret—but to calm thee and help thee understand."

"How shall it calm me to know that the people and the city are rushing under the ban? If this terrible resolution passes, if our child—our tender child—were to die to-morrow he would go without burial—a little wandering soul! Marco, thou lovest our child?"

Her pauses and her desperate struggle for control were full of inexpressible horror.

"Calm thyself, my darling; it shall not be," he answered, reassuringly.

"Oh, Marco mio! And thou wilt give thy vote against it? And thou wilt use thine influence in the Council? Promise me!"

She clung to him, sobbing and exhausted.

He soothed her for a moment silently; should he leave her under such a misunderstanding? It would be easier for them both, but he had intended no untruth. How was it possible to make such a woman understand? She was quiet now, and he was stealing away from her with a kiss on her forehead.

"Promise me!" she insisted, following him and clasping his arm with sudden strength.

"Marina, they are very set; and the Ten—thou dost not know their power."

"And shall all Venice brave the wrath of our most Holy Church because the Senate is afraid of the Ten? Are the Ten more powerful than the Holy Father and all the priesthood and sacraments of the Church? Marco, my beloved, how shall I save thee?"

"Carina, these things are not coming upon Venice; thou dost not understand the law of Church and State."

"No, Marco," she answered boldly, "it is rather thou who dost not understand. There will be no services, no marriage for our people, no burial, no consolations of our holy religion, no sacraments—if this excommunication should come upon us."

"If we had sinned, Marina, and laid ourselves open to interdict, then these things should come—not otherwise."

"Ay, but we *have* sinned—by rebellion against the Holy Church. Marco, it is not easy for men to submit; but Father Francesco says the women shall save Venice."

"The women of Venice are priest-ridden!" the young Senator cried angrily, breaking away from her. "If there is trouble, it is the priests who have brought it. They cannot be a separate power within Venice!"

"Not a separate power, Marco, only the representative of the Church, which is the supreme power."

"These things are not for women to discuss," he exclaimed in astonishment that she should attempt to reason on such a subject.

"Not for women, and not for men," she answered quietly. "The power of the Holy Father is by *divine* right."

"Marina, if thou canst say so much, thou *shalt* understand the rest!" he cried desperately. "So also is the power of temporal princes by divine right—if not even more, as some of the authorities would have it. But the temporal prince hath right only to that within his own jurisdiction. Granting the divine right to the spiritual prince, it lieth only within his own province. Paul V hath exceeded his rights. Leonardo Donato, Serenissimo of the Republic, is not guilty in self-defense."

She quivered as if a knife had been thrust through her; then, controlling herself by force, she dipped her fingers in the basin of holy water. that stood upon the little altar. "It is sacrilegious to speak against the Holy Father," she said in a low, grieved tone, as she made the sign of the cross upon his breast. "May God forgive thee, my dear one—it is not thy fault. But in the Senate they are misleading thee!"

"My sweet wife," he answered, much troubled, and folding her closely. "Do not grieve. All will be well for Venice. We shall not bring harm upon her."

But she detected no yielding in his tone. She lifted her head from his breast, and moved slightly away from him.

"Marco," she asked firmly, "when is the vote to be cast?"

"To-day, before sunset, and I must not linger. It would bring misfortune upon our house if I were to be absent in an affair of such moment. Else would I not leave thee."

She did not seek to detain him.

"Promise me that thou wilt be reasonable," he said, looking back, as he parted the draperies of the doorway; "thou wilt not grieve."

"A promise for a promise, Marco; thou hast given me none, and may the Madonna have mercy upon us!"

After a long, lingering look at the drooping figure of his wife he dropped the curtain and descended to his gondola, sombre in spirit because of the work that awaited him in the Senate Chamber; his footsteps lagged wearily upon the stone floor of the long, dark passage, and the brilliant outer sunshine flooded him with a sense of desperately needed relief.

When Marina moved it was to throw herself before the altar, resting her head upon her clasped hands, in an agony of supplication.

. . . .

In the midst of an excited debate, immediately preceding the final vote, the door of the Senate Chamber was suddenly thrown open by the keeper, who announced in an awestruck tone:

"A citizen claims the right of the humblest Venetian to bring before Messer the Doge a message of vital import in the question under discussion."

He uttered the words tremblingly, as if he had been taught them, and the interruption at such an hour, though not unprecedented, was at least unusual enough to cause consternation. The flood of words ceased; there was an uneasy movement among the senators, then a hush of suspense.

Without waiting for the customary consent of the Doge, a procession of white-robed, white-veiled women passed through the open doorway, moving slowly and solemnly to the Doge's throne. The leader stepped forth from her group of maidens and knelt at the foot of the dais.

This sudden arrest of action by these white-robed gliding figures, at a moment when the Senate was about to defy the authority of the Church, brought a superstitious thrill to many hearts within that chamber.

Among the younger senators it was whispered, in unsteady tones, that a message delayed for the death of a prince was likely to bring trouble—messengers, perchance, from another world—when forced again to discussion. They listened breathlessly for the message; but the figure still knelt in silence.

The group of Councillors on the dais swayed and parted against that wonderful background of Tintoret, the dead Christ and the two Doges reverently kneeling in proof of the devotion of this Most Serene Republic. Around the vast and sumptuous chamber, where the proud Signoria assembled, like a council of kings, Venice had chronicled her triumphs and her religious humility in endless repetition and intimately blended, as became her faith; the Doges Priuli, kneeling in prayer; Venice, mounted defiantly on the Lion of Saint Mark; other portraits of other doges, in attitudes of devotion; other pictures of the Christ, of the saints, always symbolic; but over all,—triumphant, beautiful,—with its irresistible sea-tones, cool and strong, Venice, Queen of the Sea, compelling the homage of her rulers, from the ceiling's height.

Twice the Doge essayed to speak, but the faces of the younger men warned him of the danger of such an interruption at a moment when the entire vote had seemed sure, and so filled him with wrath that he dared not speak until he could control his voice, lest its tremor be mistaken for fear. The moment seemed an hour.

"Reveal thyself!" Leonardo Donato commanded at last; "and rise!"

The supplicant slowly rose, throwing back her veil, and revealing a face that was spirit-like in its pallor and beauty, with deep eyes, unfathomably sad. Her maidens gathered close about her, as if to support her, for she trembled as she stood.

A low murmur arose. "The Lady of the Giustiniani!"

In all that vast Council Chamber there was no movement, save the slight commotion among a group of red-robed senators farthest from the throne, who were forcibly detaining the Senator Marcantonio Giustiniani, and the imperative gesture from the dais which had waved him back and hushed his involuntary exclamation of horror. Among the Savil, Giustinian Giustiniani sat livid with anger, close under the eyes of that one calm, terrible Counsellor whose gaze, fastened upon him, rendered speech impossible.

"My daughter," said the Doge, in a tone full of consideration, "this is not fitting. At another moment we will listen to thy request. Thou mayest withdraw."

"Serenissimo, Prince of Venice!" Marina cried, stretching forth her hands, "be gracious to me! *Now* must I speak my message, or it will be too late —and it hath been granted me in a vision, for the welfare of the people of Venice. *If the Ruler of this Republic will win the consent of the Senate and the Council to comply with the admonitions of the Most Holy Father, the day shall be happy for Venice.*"

"Take her away—she is distraught," commanded one of the Chiefs of the Ten, starting forward.

There was a movement of irresolution among those immediately surrounding the Doge; but the Lady Marina, like one commissioned for a holy emprise, had no fear.

"Nay, for I claim my right, as citizen of Venice, to bring my grievance to the Doge's throne!" she answered proudly. "I am mother to a son who shall one day take his seat among the nobles of this Council; I am daughter to a man of the people,—beloved by his own class and honorably known, in the records of the Ten, among the industries of Venice,—who hath but now refused the seat of honor they would have granted him, that he might more truly serve the interests of the people; I am wife to a noble whose ancient name hath been written again and again in records of highest service most honorable to the Republic. My grievance is the grievance of Venice—of the nobles and the people!"

She spoke with the exaltation of inspiration, and there was a hush in the chamber, as if she had wrought some spell they could not break.

Presently into this silence a voice—low, clear, emotionless—dropped the consenting words, "Speak on, that justice be not defrauded by the half-told tale."

Instinctively the eyes of the senators turned to the face of the Chief Counsellor, whose opinions had ruled the debate for many days past; but he sat serene and unmoved among his violet-robed colleagues, with no trace of sympathy nor speech upon his placid and inscrutable countenance. If the words were his they were simply an impartial reminder of duty—they concealed no opinion; the senators were to be the judges of the scene, and justice required them to listen.

They gave a quickened interest.

"I plead for the people, who have no representatives here—for the people, who are faithful to the Church and dutiful to the Holy Father; let not this undeserved horror come upon them. Leave them their heaven, who have no earthly paradise!"

The lady's strength seemed failing, for the last words had come more painfully, though with a ring of passionate indignation.

Again Marcantonio Giustiniani broke from his detaining colleagues in an attempt to reach his wife; and a second time the hands of the Councillors waved him back.

"Spare us this anathema, most gracious Prince!" she cried. "I speak for the mothers of all the babes of Venice. And oh, my Lords,"—and now the words came in a low, intense wail, as she turned instinctively and included them all in the beseeching motion of her hands,—"if you have no mercy on yourselves, at least have mercy on your tender little ones! Do not bring damnation on these innocent, helpless children by your own act. Be great enough to submit to a greater power!"

"It is unseemly," murmured another of the Councillors, yet low, as if afraid of his own judgment in a case so strange.

Leonardo Donato had been in possession of the supreme ducal authority but a few weeks, not long enough to unlearn the tone of command and the quick power of decision which had distinguished him as ambassador, when he had been chosen with the unanimous approval of this august assembly, to conciliate the court of Rome in the hour of the Republic's great emergency. His presence of mind returned to him; the scene had lasted long enough, and the situation was critical. The noble Lady Marina must be retired without disgrace, for the honor of the Ca' Giustiniani; but, above all, that she might not heighten the impression which her presence had already created. And she must be placed where she could exercise no further influence, yet in a way that should awaken no commiseration; for she was beautiful and terribly in earnest, and in her deep eyes there was the light of a prophet, and all Venice was at her feet.

The Doge spoke a word low to his Councillors, who sat nearest him on either side, and they, with decorous signs of approval, passed it on to the others. Thus fortified he rose, descended the steps of the ducal throne, and addressed her with grave courtesy; the whole house, as in custom bound, rising also while their prince was standing.

"We do not forget, most noble Lady Marina Giustiniani, that more than many others thou art a daughter of the Republic, being especially adopted by the Act of the Signoria; and thy love for Venice wins forgiveness for the strangeness of thy fear that we, her loyal rulers, could work her harm. But thou art distressed and needing rest, from the pain of the vision which thou hast confided to us. We will care for thee, as a father should.

223

"Let the noble Senator Marcantonio Giustiniani approach and conduct his lady to private apartments within our palace, where she may rest, with her maidens, until she shall be refreshed. One of our secretaries shall show the way and remain to see that every aid is bestowed."

The secretary whom the Doge had designated by a glance had approached and received a rapid order, spoken in an undertone; Marina hàd fallen, almost fainting, upon her husband's arm, as he reached her after the permission so intolerably delayed, yet he dared not move in that imperious presence without further bidding. His hand stole over hers to comfort her. She had suffered so much that he could not be angry.

Leonardo Donato's eyes quickly scanned the faces of the senators, seeking the two least sympathetic.

"The Senators Morosini and Sagredo will escort them," he said, "and will return in haste with the Senator Giustiniani to do their duty to the Republic."

At the door Marina turned again, rallying her failing strength with a last desperate effort, but the words came in a broken, agonized whisper: "O Santissima Maria Vergine! Mater Dolorosa! because thou art the special guardian of this Virgin City—and here, in her councils, none of thy reverend fathers may plead for thee—be merciful, Madre Beatissima! Save us from our doom!"

XIX

A S the door closed upon the retreating cortège the attitude of the Doge grew stern. He turned as if about to address the still standing Senate, when, remembering that he had already assumed the initiative to an unusual degree, and having so recent a recollection of that formidable coronation oath whose slightest infraction would be visited upon his nearest of kin, he mounted in silence to his seat and consulted with his Councillors until the senators were in their places. Then, in a tone of authority, he proclaimed:

"That which hath just occurred within this hall of the Senate shall be for those who have witnessed it as if it had not been, and the secretaries of the day shall not transcribe it upon their records, since it hath already more than sufficiently consumed our time. This vision of the lady was doubtless wrought by unwise tampering, being a vision of a nature that may gain credence with women—dependent and timid and unversed in law—but with which men and rulers have nothing to do."

An expression of relief slowly grew upon the faces before him while the Doge was speaking; noting which his words were allowed to produce their full effect during the few moments of relaxation and informal talk, which, as was immediately announced by a secretary, would occupy the time until the return of the three senators—all meanwhile keeping their seats that no moment might be lost in resuming the important interrupted debate.

The strain had been so great, both during the discussion and the visit of the Lady Marina, that there was a willingness among the senators to unbend, to throw aside serious impressions and make light of all dread, as womanish and weak, accepting the Doge's words as leaders. For in those days the faith of many of the gravest walked only a little way from the borderland of superstition; and it was long since any of their princes had held so great a reputation for judgment and diplomacy as Leonardo Donato.

"The Senate now being complete," the Doge solemnly announced, immediately upon the return of the three senators, "the interrupted speech will be concluded, and before the final vote is taken there will be presented once more before this august body that argument of our most learned and venerated Counsellor, Padre Maestro Paolo, upon which the decision of the Ten hath been based, and upon which the College, the Senate, and the Great Council will presently be called to vote."

This marshaling of the entire ruling body of the Republic could not fail to exercise a steadying power, and neither fear nor irresolution were revealed to the impressive, penetrating, and commanding gaze of Leonardo, when the Senator Contarini resumed the speech which had been so strangely interrupted. The enthusiasm and determination of the morning had returned; the words fell upon a receptive and positive atmosphere. The opinions of the distinguished Senator carried great weight, so loyal and catholic was he known to be; and above the portal of the Contarini many times the Lion of St. Mark had proudly rested.

"We are loyal sons of the Church," he said, "but no highest ecclesiastical court—though with authority from Rome itself—may rule that any decree of this imperial Senate of Venice, bearing upon Church and State alike, can be set aside by Church alone."

"We have not subjected ourselves to being put out of the body of this Church, which we revere, by any failure of duty on our part—duty being a rendering of that which is owed.

"As citizens of this Republic, our duty in things temporal is owed to our Prince—by right divine; as men, our duty to our Church, by right divine, is in things spiritual alone—which we render; but in things temporal God gave not the Church rule over us. If, at any point, these two dominions may seem to touch and intersect it is our Prince who disentangles, by his decree, the twisted thread. For he is Lord over us, who are Venetians and not Romans."

The words had a ring of victory; enthusiasm spread from face to face, and the house rose in a tumult of approval to express its loyalty, unchecked by any sign of dissent from the dais at a demonstration so unusual.

But the Contarini saw his advantage and broke in upon the wave of feeling, while an imperative motion from the Chief Counsellor restored order for the hearing of an important legal point upon which it was desired that action should be based.

"These laws—whose abrogation the Holy Father doth demand—are ancient rights of Venice, acknowledged by many previous popes, and reaffirmed, in these our own days, after wise and learned scrutiny of our chancellors, in the light of modern, civic requirements, as needful to the healthful administration of this realm; as binding upon our Prince, who hath ever in mind the welfare of Venice; and to be upheld by our people who believe in the divine right of princes. They are by these reverend Councillors also declared non-prejudicial to the spiritual authority of our Most Holy Church, which this Serene Republic of Venice doth ever reverently acknowledge. The question is of civil and not of spiritual rights."

An enthusiastic senator made a motion for the casting of the final vote, as an expression of the sense of the chamber. The speech of the Contarini and the manner of its reception gave pleasing assurance of the general temper of the Senate; the faces of the Doge and of his Savii recorded the sense of security with which it was needful to impress the assembly, and wore, if possible, a more dignified calm. Nevertheless Leonardo, with his statesman's eye, detected here and there a face that was set in an opposite opinion or likely to yield from fear, and his pride decreed that the vote, when cast, should be unanimous.

Again the Doge consulted his Councillors.

"The nations will owe us much," he said, "if our unanimous vote shall record the sentiments expressed in this speech of the noble Senator Contarini as the faith and will of this Republic. Never hath there been a greater opportunity to win a triumph for the liberty of princes.

"Therefore, because the question is weighty, we will request our most learned Counsellor and Theologian to the Republic to give us an exposition of the law as it doth appear at this latest moment of our discussion to his judicial mind."

All Venice knew that Fra Paolo's nerve and knowledge were the central forces of the resistance of the Republic in this crisis.

As he moved slowly forward and stood before this magnificent assembly with the same simple dignity that had characterized him among the friars of the Servi,—after the splendors of the ducal costume, the scarlet, the ermine, the beretta, the gold-brocaded mantle,—the plain folds of the violet robe of the Counsellor seemed almost austere. His lineless face was so fresh in color that it looked youthful, though of singular gravity and refined asceticism. Yet men of force were drawn to him because of his strength, his broad grasp of duty, and his absolute fearlessness.

As he stood for a moment perfectly still before them, his eyes—blue, penetrating, and unrevealing —swept the faces of the assembly with a magnetic glance which compelled their entire attention. The hush was *felt* among them, and in the silence his voice—clear, passionless, low, and far-reaching— seemed not so much a voice as a suggestion within the inner consciousnes of his hearers of the thoughts he uttered. The strange sense of impersonality which was one of his distinguishing attributes prevented the usual desire for contest with which most thinking men meet other strong minds, and was, perhaps, a secret of his triumphs.

"Most Serene Prince, Counsellors, and Nobles of the Council, if you ask me of the law as it hath declared itself to my understanding, the matter is simple and quickly to be uttered.

"The dominion of the Church marches in the paths of heaven; it cannot therefore clash with the dominion of princes, which marches on the paths of earth. But the Roman court—calling itself the Church—is no longer satisfied with that spiritual dominion to which it hath right, having become aggressive and seeking to impose doctrines far removed from the primitive law of the Church."

There was a slight pause, while the quiet eyes held his audience with a challenge of assent; the faces of those who were unqualifiedly with him in doctrine grew eager; here and there a dignified head bowed, unaware, as if surrendering some belief.

"Christ himself hath said, 'My kingdom is not of this world,' and the power of the Sovereign Pontiff over Christians is not limitless, but is restricted to spiritual matters and hath for rule the Divine Law.

"If the Pope, to enforce his commands—unlawful when they exceed the authority given him by Christ —fulminates his interdict, it is unjust and null; in spite of the reverence owed to the Holy See, it should not be obeyed.

"Seven times before hath Venice been so banned —and *never* for anything that had to do with religion!"

230

Again that strange, slight, emphatic pause, as if he need wait but a moment for his reasoning to dissipate any conscious unwillingness.

The Contarini quoted low to his neighbor a recent *bon mot* of the Senate, "Everybody hath a window in his breast to Fra Paolo;" for several senators of families closely allied to Rome started at the boldness of the thought, and exchanged furtive glances of disapproval, and the fearless eye of the friar immediately fixed upon them, holding and quieting them as they moved restlessly to evade his glance. It was as if he assured them silently, "I speak that I do know; cease to oppose truth; let yourselves believe." And resistance lessened before the impersonality of the pleader.

"One of the fathers tells us that an excommunication is null when it would usurp over citizens the right of their prince. *'By me kings reign and princes decree justice'*—it is the word of God."

There was on need of further pauses in the quiet flow of words, for there was no longer any resistance; the Senate and Council hung breathless upon his speech, which answered every misgiving; they knew that his reading of canon law had never been questioned in Rome itself; the man spoke with immense authority. But there was no triumph in his bearing as he tuned the atmosphere of that august assembly into absolute harmony, conquering every discordant note—only a further lowering of the quiet voice, which seemed to utter, unchallenged, the conclusions of each listener.

"The Sacred Canons agree that a Pope is liable to error and fallible in cases of special judgment.

231

"Isaiah denounces such legislation, 'Woe unto them that decree unrighteous decrees.'

"Wherefore I declare the justice of the cause of the Republic, and the nullity of any judgment that may be pronounced against her in this matter.

"Nor shall evil befall one for a sin not committed, nor can there be disobedience to a mandate which hath been issued, without lawful authority, by him who proclaims it; and authority, transcended, is no longer lawful."

XX

WHEN Marcantonio, finally released from his long day of service in the Senate Chamber, sought the private apartments of the Doge, where Marina with her maidens was waiting for him, he found her lying back, wan and spiritless, in one of the great gold and crimson arm-chairs of the state salon; her eyes were closed, her lips were moving in prayer, but her rosary had dropped from her weak clasp. Some of her maidens, as thus doing their lady truest service, were still kneeling with hopeless petitions to the Holy Mother to avert the doom from Venice; but one, the Lady Beata, who was tenderly devoted to her, had not ceased from efforts to rouse her with nameless little gracious cares. She was watching for Marcantonio, to whom she signed eagerly to hasten, as the guard of the Doge permitted him to pass the doorway.

"Thus hath our lady been, and naught hath moved her," she said low, and in distress, "since the Secretary of the Serenissimo, who with much futile reasoning hath sought to change her, hath taken his leave, save that ever and anon she hath opened her eyes to watch the door and bid us pray for Venice."

Her husband had reached her side and taken her listless hand before Marina had noticed his ap-

233

proach; but there was no smile in her eyes as she raised them to his—only a look of unutterable misery.

"Is there no hope?" she questioned. Her fingers, weakly folded about his, were burning.

He controlled himself with a great effort.

"Yes, carina, every hope. All is well; and the Serenissimo hath been most gracious. To-morrow, when thou hast had thy rest, he will send to thee the Reverend Counsellor Padre Maestro Paolo, that he may quiet all thy fears. For all is well."

She tried to draw him nearer, but her hand dropped powerless. "The vote?" she questioned, with her eager eyes; and, more falteringly, with that hoarse, broken whisper which pierced his heart.

"It is well," he answered her tenderly. "Carinissima, all is well."

She fixed him with terror-stricken eyes, in which her soul seemed burning and her lips moved with a question he could not hear. He bent closer, touching her cheek caressingly.

"The vote?" she had asked again.

"Tell her the count," said the Lady Beata, with an imperious touch on his wrist; "it is killing her."

The Senate had adjourned in triumph; without a dissenting voice Venice had rallied to the support of her prince. Marcantonio had thought he should be proud to tell her of this unanimous action of their august body, which could not fail to restore her confidence and quiet her fears. But now he could not find the words he sought, for never had he looked into eyes so full of a comprehending woe.

"Marina," he began. "Carinissima—" help-

234

lessly repeating his powerless assurance: "It is
well."

Still her deep eyes seemed to question him relent-
lessly, though she did not speak; her gaze fasci-
nated him, and he could not withdraw his eyes
until he had read in hers the great agony he had
so lightly estimated—the agony of a soul deeply
religious, of unquestioning faith in the strictest doc-
trine and dogma of the Church of Rome; the grief
of such a soul, tenderly compassionate for the suf-
fering brought upon an innocent people by no re-
bellion of its own; the terror of this soul—passion-
ately loving—measuring the horrors of an unblessed
life and death for all its dearest ones.

"All?" she had seemed to question him, leaning
nearer, and Marcantonio could not answer; but he
saw, from the deepening horror in her eyes, that she
understood. She knew that *he* had helped to bring
the doom. Oh, if he could but have told her that
he had not voted—that he had withheld his one
little vote from Venice to comfort her! If, for this
once, he had failed to give what Venice expected
of him, only for Marina's sake!

He bent over her passionately, a thousand rea-
sons rushing to his rescue, clamoring to be told her.
"Marina, beloved, there is nothing to fear!" he cried
desperately, eager for his own defense, resolute to
make her comprehend the perfect safety of Venice,
to calm the beseeching horror in her eyes; "Fra
Paolo will come!"

Her gaze relaxed, her eyelids quivered and closed;
she had fainted.

—Or was it death?

He folded her to his heart with a cry of deso-
lation.

The Lady Beata hastily thrust him aside and
opened the white robe at the throat, and Marcan-
tonio started back; there were stripes of half-healed
laceration on the tender flesh—some fresh, as if
but just raised by the lash.

"Ay, my lord," Beata answered very low, to his
quick, grieved question; "all that a daughter of
the Church may do hath our lady added to her
prayers for Venice. She hath been rigorous in fast-
ing and in penance until her strength is gone; but
the pain of it she feeleth not, because of the greater
pain of her soul, which is lost in supplication that
availeth naught."

.   .

Leonardo Donato would be very gracious to the
Lady of the Giustiniani, though she had come so
near to costing the city a divided vote, because he
had seen the misery in her eyes with her great love
for Venice, and because the Council had so declared
its vote for the State that he could afford to be mag-
nanimous. Nay, since even the Senator Marcan-
tonio had not flinched before that wonderful agon-
ized white face, he need not confine her, as he had
intended, in a convent for decorous keeping; he was
glad of the change in her favor which would pre-
vent the harshness that might have increased her
influence to the degree of danger. He sent, instead,
a gracious message by his secretary—"Might the
father pay a visit to his daughter of the Republic

to inquire of her welfare and assure her of his favor, before she returned to her palace?"

But the message of courtesy, sent by the Doge himself, had been stayed on the threshold of his own state salon.

The Republic had, indeed, quitted herself nobly in her vote; so valiant a blow had she struck for the rights of princes that this consciousness rang out in the bold tones of her announcement to the courts of Europe—"Which things we have thought best to tell you for your sole information, so that if mention be made of them to you, and not else, you may be able to answer to the purpose and to justify this our most righteous cause."

And from the moment that the Senate had been unofficially apprised by Nani that the terrible Interdict was already printed and would presently be fulminated, every possible precaution of self-defense had been put in operation throughout the dominions of Venice, with an ingenuity, a foresight, and a celerity which the watching courts of Europe not only viewed with amazement, but accepted as an evidence of the conscious power and justice of the Republic. Overtures came fast from England, from Spain, from France—every monarch wished some share in the pacification between these courts of Rome and Venice.

Meanwhile, in Venice life went on superbly. There was no question of any spiritual disfranchisement; these sons of the Church were not under interdict, having committed no sin which laid them open to that charge. Moreover, no ban had been *published* throughout the wide extent of their domain. Hence, for the Venetians, there was no interdict, whatever awful anathema might be affixed to those distant doors of Saint Peter's in Rome; with whatever voice of anger its terrors might be thundered at the Holy See, against rulers, people, priests, and sacraments within the doomed city—the wide waters of the lagoon laved its shores in benediction, like a baptismal charm upon the fair front of Venice, against which the Curse threatened impotently.

At the centre of this superb and daring court sat a friar, trained from his childhood up in the customs, traditions, and beliefs of his Church and of his order—a reverent practitioner in her fasts and sacraments, simple in his habits as a hermit-monk, faithful in his religious duties as the most punctilions priest in Rome, sure in his faith that God would uphold the right, and asserting, without compromise, that right was on the side of Venice.

What a stay for rulers who fortified their every position by some appeal to precedent—who would punctiliously know the source and interpretation of every law upon which they rested!

Above all, what a stay for the simple people who, in these days of bewildering conflict, knew not what to believe!

Would Masses go on, and the church doors be open and the sacraments continue? Might they still take their. brides and baptize their little ones, and follow their dead to burial, and sign the sign of the cross, in token of the favor of heaven—as loyal sons of the Church?

And would the Madre Beata—blessed guardian of this Virgin City—still smile upon them from all the separate shrines of Venice?

Should the labor and the imprecation of this simple people go on until the evening in their wonted flow, and should nothing fail them of the benedictions they had known?

It was a mystery; but threatening Rome was far and unfamiliar, and Venice they knew—present, protecting, peremptory—impossible to disobey.

Before the commands of the angry Pontiff could reach the heads of the orders in Venice, people, priests, and prelates throughout the dominions were forewarned; they must continue in every accustomed practice of their religion; they might neither receive nor publish any minatory papers—these must be instantly brought to the government, under severest penalties.

Offending prelates were brought from distant sees to meet the displeasure of the Republic; hesitating priests were silently hastened to decision by scaffolds, looming suddenly within their precincts. While leaflets—expressly prepared to disaffect the Venetians—proclaiming that no obedience was due from a people to its prince *under censure;* that all vows, contracts, and duties between man and man, husband and wife, children and parents were nullified for those who remained faithful to the Church in acknowledging the censure, as against those who disclaimed it— these leaflets, introduced by secret agents of the Pontiff and interdicted by the Republic, flowed in vast numbers, but silently, into the hands of the Ten, and were seen no more.

Meanwhile that terrible thing which the people had vaguely feared had *not* come upon them; though at first they paused, half-hearted, when they passed the house of the Tintoret, where the quaint figure of "Ser-Robia," the Pasquino of Venice, had often a bit of news that the people cared to hear, grotesquely placarded over his broad mouth. He was a good friend to the people, Ser-Robia, and gave them many a pleasant bit of gossip to cheer their evening stroll; but it was wise not to laugh until one had heard the words, and there was often a priest or a scholar near to tell the meaning to those who could not spell it out for themselves. Always, in these days, there was some one who could read to the people, for this was that solemn "protest" of "Leonardo Donato, by the Grace of God Doge of Venice," etc., wherewith the most Christian Republic defied the interdict. Here, along the Rialto, in all the public squares of Venice, on the doors of the churches,—wherever proclamation was wont to be made,—the people might pause and read this consoling word of Venice, instead, perchance, of some copy of the interdict which had been smuggled into the city and pasted, surreptitiously, over the Doge's "protest," but which those faithful *Signori di Notte*—the night-watch of Venice—were sure to destroy before the morning dawned.

"To the Most Reverend the Patriarchs, Archbishops, and Bishops of our Venetian Dominions," said this "Protest," "and to the Vicars, Abbots, Priors, Rectors of Parochial Churches, and other Ecclesiastical Prelates, greeting:" forthwith proceeding to declare that "the Interdict which his

Holiness was 'said' to have published was null and void, and forbidden to be observed—not having been incurred by any fault of Venice."

But even those who could not read soon recognized the features of that message, which met them everywhere, hiding the scars of other messages which they must not see.

"No, no," they said, with laughing thanks to some friendly interpreter who stood near; "it is enough; *va bene*—we know it like our Ave Maria!"

But sometimes a family group came back for a word, when the others had scattered.

"Thou, Gigio, tell the good padre!" says the bright-eyed young contadina, pulling the gray sleeve of her fisherman who stands stolidly beside her.

"*Si, si,*" he answers indifferently, shrugging his shoulders and relapsing into silence, as he pushes his wife and mother before him for a refuge; for the men of the islands were less at home in argument with the priests than were the women of their households.

"It is thus, your Reverence," the young woman explains cheerily. "It is the grandmother who is afraid. Santa Maria! *how* she is afraid!" She touches her forehead significantly.

The simple old woman, comprehending only that they speak of her, drops a courtesy, looking furtively about her with troubled eyes, and fumbling over her beads; the "protest" has no meaning for her, although it is written in good Venetian.

But a few words suffice for such as these who have caught only some vague hint of the Holy

Father's displeasure, and are reassured by the open church and the promise of Mass and benediction.

It is those others who make trouble; they come, from time to time,—by twos and threes, never alone, —and read for themselves, with lowering brows, but ask no questions. And sometimes, if they watch too silently, the courteous friar who has graciously interpreted the message which is above the heads of the crowd, exchanges a glance of intelligence with some gay young signor who belongs to the great army of secret service—as revealed to the friar on guard by the password of the day; and the sullen-browed group is courteously accosted by the young noble—"Excuse me, signori, you are strangers in Venice; a gondola is waiting to conduct you to the palace."

They will be tried as secret agents of the enemy. But resistance is rare, for an escort of guards pours out from the doorways and calles, if a stiletto but gleam in the sunlight; and no secret agent may cope with Venice in promptness of self-defense and ingenuity of prevention.

It is interesting in the campo in these early days, before the effect of the government's measures for coercing the opinions of the populace is fully declared.

"I am a good Catholic, most reverend father; I keep the mariegole; every year I go to confession," protests some sturdy gondolier, who has been made anxious by his womenfolk. "And many a fare I pay to light the traghetto of San Nicolò; with an ave for the favor of the Blessed Mother to confound the scoundrel Castellani, who threw a good Nicolotto over the *Ponte Senza Parapetti*, in the last fight; and it cost us oil enough to light Venice for a year—faith of San Nicolò!—to keep them from winning at our regatta—*maledetti!*"

For even those gondoliers who kept the mariegole were not precisely angels, and the part of their creed which they religiously upheld was a deathless antagonism to the rival faction which won more lamps and pretty gifts for the patron madonnas of the various traghetti than any other article of their faith.

To a few, chiefly women with devout, sad faces—watchers, perchance, beside beds over which the shadow of death is creeping—the padre tells compassionately of consoling, helpful words that are preached daily in the great deserted church of *I Gesuiti;* for in this parish, more than others, there are difficulties, since it had been the centre of the disaffection. But now its doors are ceaselessly open for a refuge; no service is omitted, no sacrament denied; and daily, before vespers, the people may listen to a few simple words from Fra Paolo. Thither, in these early days of the struggle, the crowd flocks, drawn partly by curiosity to hear a man of whom it is whispered that he has just been individually put under the greater excommunication by the Holy Inquisition, because of his attitude in this quarrel.

There is much talk of Fra· Paolo sifting about the church and square, where the gathering of the people shows a sprinkling of red-robed senators; for the Padre Maestro Paolo, which is his title since he has been Consultore to the Republic, is a great man now, with a greatness that means something to the

243

populace, to whom letters and sciences are nothings. But the Consultore is the friend of Venice; he is *their* friend—coming each day to talk to the people. "It is not true that great trouble has come upon Venice, for Fra Paolo makes it all quite plain, and he knows everything," they say; "our padre in San Marcuolo is like a bimbo to him! The Jesuit Fathers went too soon, and might have spared themselves the burning of their papers and their treasure. Santa Maria!—what is it they are saying about Fra Paolo finding the die for making money that the *padri* left behind? What is a 'die,' Luigi? If thou hadst had the sense to bring thy boat to clear away the rubbish, instead of thinking there are only fish in the world, thou mightest have had the luck to find it; it must be better than working lace bobbins all the week for a handful of *soldi* that would n't buy one macaroni!"

"Peace, then, with thy babble!"

"See, then, the holy water is quite safe; I saw our padre cross himself by that first basin. Thou hast done well,—*hein* Luigi,—to bring me from Burano, if there are *no* fish to-morrow at the Ave Maria; for now we can sleep in peace! They told such tales of I Gesuiti, one thought the devils were having a holiday—Santa Maria!"

"The women are worse for chattering," Luigi retorts, with a forcible imprecation. "Here cometh the Consultore—hold thy tongue."

"No, no, Luigi; it is only a frate from the Servi; Fra Paolo is a great man, with a robe like the Serenissimo; he might wear a crown if he liked! Ah, to be great like that!"

But Fra Paolo and his secretary wore the grave garb of their order, to the great disappointment of the younger women, who had been attracted by the expectation of some pomp.

"Word hath reached the Contarini secretly from Rome," said one senator to another, as the Consultore passed them, "that they have found themselves a new diversion before the palace of the Vatican, and that some of our great ones here are burned in effigy to instruct the populace. A pile of Fra Paolo's writings doth light the funeral pyre; and all that he hath written or *may hereafter write* is placed upon the Index."

"*Davvero!* his words would make me wrathful if I held the views of his Holiness, who may well fear the incontrovertibility of his wit. But our Consultore looketh a simple man to have been shown such honor!"

"He beareth honors bravely," the other answered, with due appreciation of the humor; "but lately, when the master Galileo was before the Senate with his telescope, he had a pretty tale of Gian Penelli and Ghetaldo, wherewith in Padua Fra Paolo hath won the title of 'the miracle of the century.'"

"I heard it not; some commission held me at the arsenal; San Marco be thanked that it is over!"

"Ebbene, old Penelli—gouty so that he can scarce move—hath a visit from our great mathematician Ghetaldo, who findeth with our magnificent patron of letters a friar to whom Penelli showeth such honor—limping to the door with him, as if he were a prince—that Ghetaldo, wrathful at this foolish waste over a friar, asketh his name with scorn.

245

And is not better pleased when Penelli telleth that Fra Paolo is the 'miracle of the age in every science.' 'So, I will prove it,' saith Penelli, 'for verily the world knoweth the great Ghetaldo for a mathematician! Come, then, with problems the most difficult thou canst prepare, on a day it may please thee to name, and meet Fra Paolo at my table, without warning to him.' *Ecco!* Penelli is subtle; great satisfaction and much labor on the part of our mathematician. Enter Fra Paolo,—simple, unadvised,—solves the propositions at a hearing. 'Miraculous!' cries the superb Ghetaldo, gentle as a lamb! A friendship for life, and Fra Paolo is the teacher! But it is more wonderful to hear the tales of how he preacheth to the people here, in the Gesuiti. Let us follow, for he giveth them not many minutes, for fear of wearying them. We need lift our mantles high, for the pavement is like a market garden of Mazzorbo, with broken bits from the women's baskets—Faugh!"

The splendid senators seldom mingled in such a crowd, except at guarded distances, to make a pageant for it; it was picturesque, shabby, malodorous, composed chiefly of young women with bright-eyed babies and baskets emitting unctuous savors of *frittola* and garlic; now and then an old peasant who could not be tranquil until she had heard Fra Paolo speak was escorted by a rebellious grandson, bribed to quiet by the promise of a *soldo* for his little game of chance; occasionally a man, impatient to have done with it all and get out on the canal again, moved restlessly from place to place; only here and there the dim light showed a face pathetic in its

246

questioning, to whom the answer meant life or death.

"What hath a man of such rare powers and learning to do with these simple ones—a man whose time is precious to the State?"

The noble senators withdrew a little from the crowd to watch the scene, as they put the question to each other; their servants brought them chairs within the shadow of a column.

They did not know that few are great enough in an age of superstition to hold a conscience uncontrolled by traditions, and a primitive faith simple as a child's, with the tenacity of a strong man; there had been nothing in his labors at the Senate to call forth this most sacred side of his reserved nature, and they did not understand that it was to this he owed much of the marvelous poise of will and judgment which kept him unspoiled in spite of intellectual gifts that would have ruined him without his absolute dependence on the One Supreme. But on this sacred side alone was there any entrance to his emotions.

Fra Paolo was not speaking from the pulpit; he stood beside a table that had been placed in the nave, and the people gathered close about him, as children near a father, while he opened a great vellum-bound volume with massive golden clasps, which his secretary had brought from the library of the Servi.

"Come nearer," he called to them simply, beckoning with his hand, "so that all may hear; put the old people and the little ones nearest."

He looked around him, not smiling, but very quiet

and patient, as if he were waiting for the slight confusion to subside; for at first they pushed each other rudely to get closer.

"There is room for all," he said, "in God's house;" and as he looked into their faces each felt that it was a word to him, and held his breath to listen—which suddenly seemed quite easy! The smaller children nestled contentedly on their mothers' arms, munching some dainty brought to keep them quiet, and fascinated by the low, clear voice, watched with round, solemn eyes to see if he would smile; while two or three who were tall enough to reach just over the edge of the table steadied themselves by clutching it with their chubby hands, dropping their hold of their mothers' mantles —for the pages were full of pretty colors, and the voice of the padre was like a lullaby to keep them still, and they were not afraid—at all.

Fra Paolo never gave the people many words, but sometimes they were strong and beautiful, like an old poem, and in their own Venetian—not in the Latin which had been made for the great ones.

"It was a wonderful book, written long ago," he told them; "before the Bishop of Altinum fled with his people to Torcello and built the old Duomo; before Venice began to be."

Many of them did not know there was *anything* so old as that! They looked at each other and began to think.

"And it was written for the comfort of every one who loveth God, our Father, whatever his troubles may be. See what is written here for any who fear that the consolations of our holy religion shall be taken away. For that is what you fear?"

They looked at each other, hesitating. "Si, si—yes—" timidly. "No, no," more bravely.

Fra Paolo smiled.

"No!" they said, distinctly.

"If any of you are afraid," Fra Paolo said, looking full into their faces as they pressed nearer, "because the fathers of this church have gone away and left you, there are words in this old book—written long ago, before there was any Venice—to condemn those who would close the churches. 'Woe be unto the pastors that destroy and scatter the sheep of my pasture,' saith the Lord. 'Behold, I will visit upon them the evil of their doings, saith the Lord.' 'Where is the flock that was given thee, thy beautiful flock?' "

"And here are some words that are written for you—whom they have deserted. 'Thus saith the Lord: again there shall be heard in this place, *which ye say shall be desolate*, the voice of joy and the voice of gladness; the voice of the bridegroom and the voice of the bride; and of them that shall bring the sacrifice of praise into the house of the Lord.' It is all very simple. Love God and pray to him, and be faithful in your duty. And he will keep you happy and safe from harm."

The ringing treble of children's voices sounded through the open door of the sacristy and distracted the attention of the congregation, who turned to watch the choristers as they came in sight, by twos and twos, chanting the canticle, "Praise the Lord of Hosts; for the Lord is good; for His mercy endureth forever!"

While Fra Paolo slipped away unnoticed.

XXI

SO life went on, and those who looked to see the people fail and falter under this burden which the rebellion of their rulers had brought upon them saw them, with unshaken confidence, still loyally upholding the banner of Saint Mark. Preparations for war—marshaling of soldiers, building of galleys, increased activities at the arsenal—enlarged the industries and added a judicious vivacity to the life of the people.

There was no war declared; but it was a time when border-lands should be looked to and bravery encouraged and the martial spirit developed; and the ever politic Senate tickled the fancy of its pleasure-loving people with the pomp of a fête, on the day when the newly created general-in-chief of the armies of the Republic assembled, with fanfare of trumpets and roaring of cannon, his splendidly appointed corps in the Piazza, the people thronging the arcades, crowding the windows and balconies, waving and shouting, as the stately escort of three hundred nobles, in crimson robes, led the way to San Marco for solemn dedication. And here, like a knight vowed to holiest service, the general knelt before the altar, while the Patriarch blessed his sword. "In defense of Venice and the right," with a memory of the old battle-cry of the Republic.

"Non nobis, Domine—sed tibi gloria!"

And the people, accepting as a favor the pageant which had been cunningly devised to impress them, followed, thronging, up the giant stairway, into the halls of the Council Chamber, into the stately presence of the Serenissimo and the Signoria, to hear their latest magnate profess his gratitude for the honor of his investiture and the magnificence of his outfit, with solemn oaths of loyalty.

There was no war, though talk of it had little truce in those days; but the cardinal nephews were busy in Ferrara and Ancona with the marshaling of troops, and four of the princes of the Church had been appointed by the Holy Father—vice-regent of the Prince of Peace—to superintend his military operations and prepare his army of forty thousand infantry and four thousand cavalry! Thus, in Venice, the spectacle of a general-in-chief, with his splendid accoutrements, was timely and inspiriting.

Meanwhile, in the palazzo Giustiniani the days dragged wearily, and knew no sunshine; the Senator Marcantonio had been by special favor excused from attendance in the Council Chamber; in his mind Venice was no longer regnant; one thought absorbed him wholly through all that miserable time —he had but one hope—everything centred in Marina.

When they had undressed her to apply restoratives a small, rough crucifix had been taken from the folds of her robe near her heart; it had belonged to Santa Beata Tagliapietra,—that devoted daughter of the Church,—and the Lady Beata herself had given the precious heirloom out of the treasures of the chapel of their house to her beloved Lady Marina. Possibly she reflected, with a shudder, as she laid the relic on the altar of the oratory of the palazzo Giustiniani, that the remembrance of the constant dangers of Santa Beata had incited the Lady Marina thus to peril her life. Of the long nights of vigil on the floor of the oratory and of many other austerities which had filled those last sad days since the quarrel with Rome had begun, the Lady Beata was forced to give faithful account to the physicians who were summoned in immediate consultation to the bedchamber of the Lady Marina. These practices and the horror upon which she had dwelt ceaselessly would sufficiently account for her condition, said the learned Professor Santorio; and if she could but forget it there might be hope; meanwhile, let her memory lie dormant—at present nothing must be done to rouse her.

Perhaps already she had forgotten it; for the shock had been great and life was at a very low ebb; had all memory gone from her of her life and love? They thought she knew them, but she expressed no wish; she scarcely spoke, lying listless and white under the heavy canopy of the great carved bedstead, which had become the centre of every hope in those two palaces on the Canal Grande, while the absorbing life of the Ducal Palace, so little distant, was for Marcantonio as though it did not exist. In that time of waiting—he knew not how long it was nor what was passing—life was a great void to him, echoing with one agonized hope; time had no existence, except as an indefinite point when Marina should come back to him with her soul and heart in her eyes once more.

He had gathered the few books from her oratory and boudoir, and at intervals when he could control his thought he pored over them, treasuring every faint pencil-line, every sentence blotted by tears, as an indication of having specially occupied her. Now that he could no longer discuss these moods, how eagerly he sought for the light she would so gladly have given him in those past, happier days!

In vain he asked of the Lady Beata whether they had discussed these thoughts together—whether Fra Francesco had brought her the little worn volumes.

"My lord, I know not," she answered coldly, resolved in her own heart to tell him nothing that he did not already know, since only now it had pleased him to concern himself with that religious attitude which was costing Marina so dearly. For the whole strength of the love she would once have yielded him for the asking, the Lady Beata now lavished upon Marina, in jealous devotion.

But he could not be angry with Fra Francesco, who had only been faithful in sharing his belief with her, while he, her husband, had refused to help her. "My God!" he groaned; "why are we blind until the anguish comes!"

As he drearily paced the stately chambers—so empty without Marina—what would he not have given to hear her voice again repeat those eager questions he had been so willing to repress! How

253

could it ever have vexed him that she should wish
to understand the question that was occupying Ven-
ice! But now he remembered having grown less
and less patient with her as she had returned to
this theme, until, in self-defense, she had said with
gentle dignity, yet half-surprised at his irritation:

"Marco, have a little patience with me. Remem-
ber that our young nobles are trained in knowledge
of these laws of Venice from quite early boyhood."

"It is part training, if thou wilt," he had answered
lightly; "or in these questions women are stupid—
I know not. But these matters concern them not."
And after that, he remembered now with shame,
she had troubled him no more, and he had felt it
a relief; for during the few discussions they had had
together he had been aware that they approached
the question from a radically different point of view.
He had never taken the trouble to comprehend her
ground nor to give her reasons for his own; he
had simply made assertions, with a sense of irrita-
tion that any repetition should be called for in a
matter quite out of a woman's province; for the
women of Venice had no part in that salon influ-
ence on politics which was ascribed to their sisters
of France, and her attempts to gain understanding
for a personal judgment had chafed him like an in-
terference in his own special field. He, with his
subtly trained intellect and legal knowledge, could
so easily have convinced her, he told himself re-
morsefully; but he had not taken the trouble even to
look through her lens, while she had been so eager
to understand his point of view—and only that she
might reach the truth!

Now he had much time to understand it all! He recalled a strange, hurt look when her questions had ceased, but it had not troubled him then; she would forget it,—would understand that he preferred to talk about other things,—he had said to himself, and he had been careful in gracious little ways to show her that he was not displeased. And she had been wise and had vexed him no more; there had been no arguments on this or any other theme. And then the days of strain had come and the labors of the Council had absorbed him. Now he saw that she had been too proud and strong to subject herself to repeated insinuations of inferiority of understanding, as she had been too loving and dutiful to prolong the contest. And so—he groaned aloud as his mistake revealed itself to him in those long, unhappy hours—he had lost the dear opportunity of leading her aright; for he contemplated but one possible issue of such an attempt on his part; he had scorned her entreaty when she came to him for understanding of a mystery that was killing her, and he had driven her to take up the study alone, with the help of her father confessor, who knew but one side of the vexed question, and that *not* the side of Venice!

He was sure that it was a matter of conscience and not of contest with Marina, therefore she *must* know; he should have realized that! How had Fra Francesco met her questions? Had he told her it was a matter beyond the comprehension of women? Or had he been patient with her difficulties and solved them with terrible positiveness? Was it he who had brought her these manuals on "Fasts and

255

Penances," "The Use and Nature of the Interdict," "The Duty of the Believer," which completed for her the pictures of horror her faith had already outlined? Marcantonio had taken in all their dread meaning in rapid glances. How could she believe those terrible things he had seen in her eyes—those terrible, terrible things!

"Nay, how should she not believe them? And how implicitly she must have believed them to have endured so much in hope of averting this doom!

"Marina! Carina!" his heart went out to her in a great wail of pity; a woman—so tender, so young —kneeling at night in her chapel, alone with the vision of the horror she was praying to avert; bearing the fasting and the penance and the weakness, all alone, in the hope that God would be merciful; gathering up her failing strength so bravely for that thankless scene in the Senate. And he, her husband, who had never meant that his love should fail her, could have spared her all this pain by a little comprehension! Could she ever forgive him? And would she understand some day? Might he reason it all out lovingly with her when her strength came back to her—"For baby's sake!" that sweet, womanly, natural plea which he had disregarded?

"Signor Santorio," he moaned, "if I might but reason with her, I might cure her!"

"Nay," said Santorio, "not yet; the shadow hath not left her eyes. Let her forget."

She had been growing stronger, they said, doing quite passively the things they asked of her toward her restoration; she recognized them all, but she expressed neither wish nor emotion, lying chiefly with closed eyes in the cavernous depths of the great invalid chair where they laid her each day, yet responding by some movement if they called her name—rarely with any words; nothing roused her from that mood of unbroken brooding.

"She will not forget," the great Santorio said in despair. "We must try to rouse her. Let her child be brought."

The ghost of a smile flitted for an instant about her pale lips and over the shadowy horror in her eyes, as Marcantonio leaned over her with their boy in his arms. "Carina," he cried imploringly, "our little one needeth thee!"

She half-opened her arms, but this wraith of the mother, he remembered, frightened the child, who clung sobbing to his father.

Marina fell back with a cry of grief, struggling for the words which came slowly—her first connected speech since her illness. "It is the curse! It parts even mothers and children!"

A strange strength seemed to have come to her; a sudden light gleamed in her eyes; she turned from one to the other, as if seeking some one in authority to answer her question, and fixed upon Santorio's as the strongest face.

"The official acts of a Pope are infallible?" she questioned, with feverish insistence, after the first futile attempt to speak. "The Holy Father who succeeds him may not undo his acts of mercy?"

"Yes, yes, it is true," Santorio assented, waiting eagerly for the sequence.

A little color had crept into her cheeks; her hands were burning; they grasped the physician's arm like a vise; the change was alarming.

"The edict cannot hurt my baby! Santissima Maria, thou hast saved him!" she cried. "For he hath the special blessing of his Holiness Pope Clement, and our Holy Father cannot reach him with this curse of Venice!"

"We cannot keep her mind from it," said Santorio, aside to Marcantonio; "it is essential to calm it with the right view—no argument, it might induce the most dangerous excitement. Send for some bishop or theologian who takes the right view; let him present it as a fact, and with authority; her life depends upon it."

He leaned down to his patient in deep commiseration to tell her that all was well—that Venice was under no ban, that God's blessing still shielded her churches and her children; but she raised her eyes steadily to his, and the strength of the belief, which he saw clearly written within them, filled him with awe and hushed his speech. How was it possible to make her understand!

"Nay," said Marina faintly, still holding him with her sad, solemn eyes, "do not speak. Since Fra Francesco comes no more there is but one who speaketh truth to me. It is the vision of my beautiful Mater Dolorosa of San Donato, which leaveth me not."

There was a stir in the depths of the streets below—a noise of the populace coming nearer, following along the banks of the Canal Grande, as if the cause of their excitement were in some hurried movement on its placid waters; the shouts and jeers of the strident voices were broken by authoritative commands of the Signori della Notte—the officers of police—and the tramp of their guards failing to create order; and above the hubbub rose the cry, distinctly repeated again and again—the cry of an angry populace, "Andè in malora! Andè in malora!" ("Curses go with you!")

XXII

EVEN Giustinian Giustiniani came and went heavily, asking for the latest change before he returned to the Senate Chamber, and carrying with him always a vision of that white, pleading face which had so wrought upon his anger when he had seen it luminous with her hope for Venice. But now his anger was transferred to her confessor who had bewitched her, to all those Roman prelates who had paid her court—a mere child, not able to defend herself nor to understand, killing herself for a question beyond her! And Marcantonio, for love of her, useless and unmanned! It was more than his senatorial pride could endure to find himself powerless under such complications. To appease his wrath he denounced Fra Francesco through the Bocca di Leone, but when the friar was sought for, by order of the Ten, he was not found. Fra Paolo was appealed to, for he was the friend of the gentle confessor; but he had not known his plans. "If his conscience held him not, it was well for him to flee," he said, "and best for Venice."

But when Fra Paolo was alone in his cell, which, in those days of greatness, he would not exchange for quarters at the Ducal Palace though the Senate pleaded, the memory of a confidential talk held since this quarrel with Rome began brought a hint of the reason for this sudden flight.

He was tender of conscience and strong of faith, this good Fra Francesco; always sad, but never stern toward Fra Paolo's failure to hold a belief implicit as his own in some doctrines of his beloved Church which he held to be vital. Yet his reverence for Fra Paolo's great knowledge and holy life made him unwilling to criticize where he unconsciously questioned. It was the severest test of friendship to keep his faith and affectionate devotion in one who was taking so prominent a part in a movement opposing papal authority; but sometimes, when Fra Paolo had uttered many things he would not have tolerated in any other priest, Fra Francesco said only to himself, in great sadness, "It is God who maketh men different; we do not know the why!"

The gentle friar sometimes wondered in himself that he could not openly say to Fra Paolo when they met, after matins, the many things which had lain hot in his heart through the night—for how *could* it be right to oppose the supreme authority? But when the placid face of his friend met his, bathed in the fresh benediction of his altar service—new each morning and never omitted—he forgot the horror with which he had been reasoning that Fra Paolo was hastening the curse upon Venice.

But if Fra Paolo derived no added *finesse* for his masterful thought from the confidences he so often unconsciously invited from this lifelong friend, his faith in the sincerity and spiritual depth of this brother friar who, out of love for him, listened to much that pained him, taught him to value at its highest this opportunity of the closest scrutiny of his own motives, as he noted the impression of their talk on a nature as sincere and spiritual as it was transparent.

But that night, when they had passed from the cloister into Fra Paolo's study-cell, continuing as they walked the train of thought they had been discussing, his listener soon became so distrait that Fra Paolo, who was singularly conscious of unspoken moods, dropped the problem he was unfolding and laid his hand upon his shoulder with the rare tenderness expressed only where he hoped that he might serve.

"We were speaking of weighty matter and thy thoughts are not with me. Tell me thy trouble."

"It is a question of responsibility—the burden of the confessional," Fra Francesco answered simply.

Fra Paolo drew back his hand, and his tone was a shade less tender.

"Of all that hath been reposed in thee under that sacred seal thou must bear the burden alone."

"My brother, dost thou think I can forget my vow?" Fra Francesco exclaimed, reproachfully. "I spake not of that which hath been reposed in me, but of my duty growing out of that sacred office. It was for this I wanted counsel, and I had sought thee before to pray thee to confess me; but I know thy views and I ask thee not."

"Yet as brothers of one holy order thou mayest confide in me, if perchance it may bring thee comfort. For us of the Servi it is our duty of service."

Fra Francesco sat for a moment in silence. "Life

is heavy," he said slowly, "and hard to interpret. Yet I seem to feel that thou wilt understand, though it be in the very matter of our difference. There is one—highly placed and noble in spirit, and to the Church a most devoted daughter—who cometh to me for teaching in this matter of the interdict. She asketh of me all its meaning—what it shall bring to Venice?"

"Thou tell her, then, it shall bring naught. For if it be pronounced it will be unjustly, and without due cause."

"Nay, Paolo, my brother; it is written in the nineteenth maxim of the 'Dictatus Papæ' 'That none may judge the Pope.'"

"My brother, who gave thee thy conscience and thine intellect?" Fra Paolo questioned sternly. "And hath He who gave them thee so taught thee to yield them that it should be as if thou had'st not these gifts which, verily, distinguish man from the animals—to whom instinct sufficeth? Yet, if thou would'st have answer from one of our own casuists in whom thou dost place thy trust, the Cardinal Bellarmino, in his second book on the Roman Pontiffs, will teach thee that without prejudice to this maxim of Gregory thou mayest refuse obedience to a command extending beyond the jurisdiction of him who commands; as Gaetano in his first treatise on the 'Power of the Pope,' will also tell thee. For the peace of thine own mind, my brother, I would I might make thee understand!"

"Nay," answered Fra Francesco, not less earnestly. "Peace for him who hath faith cometh not with one intellectual solution, nor another; but with calm purpose to do the right, however it may be revealed."

"Which, as thou knowest, Francesco, Venice seeketh—and naught else. It is a matter of law in which thou hast made no studies, and therefore hard for thee. Now must I to the Council Chamber, but later I would willingly show thee all the argument. But of this be sure. The Republic will not offend against the liberty of the Holy Church; but she will protect her own."

"Fearest thou not, dear friend," Fra Francesco questioned, greatly troubled, "that thou mayest lead Venice o'erlightly to esteem this vow of obedience which every loyal son of the Church oweth to the Holy Father? My heart is sore for thee. I see not the matter as thou would'st have me."

"Nay," said Fra Paolo quietly, "to each one his burden! If thy conscience bears not out my teaching, thou art free from it. I interpret the law by the grace which God hath given me; I, also, being free from sin therein, if my understanding be not equal to the tasks wherein I seem to feel God's guidance."

"Yet tell me, I pray thee, Paolo mio, and be not displeased by mine insistence,—perchance it may help me to comprehend this mystery,—how knowest thou the limit beyond which one may, without sin, judge that the Holy Father shall not command obedience of the sons of the Church?"

"I do not say, when it conflicts with that which is in itself against the law of God," Fra Paolo answered him, "this limitation thou also would'st admit; yet it may well-nigh seem to thee a blasphemy to suppose so strange a case, though many of the early fathers do provide against it. But, to take another case, when a command of the Sovereign Pontiff doth conflict with the rule of the Prince in his realm, see'st thou not what confusion should come if the Pope may revoke the laws of princes and replace them by his own in the temporal affairs of their dominions? And if it belong to his Holiness to judge which laws shall be revoked and what may be legislated to replace the old laws, ultimately but one power should everywhere reign— and that an ecclesiastical power. The matter is simple."

Fra Paolo's searching gaze noted the flush of feeling in the face of his friend, which was his only response.

"And thus will the Senate vote when the question shall come before ·them?" Fra Francesco had asked, after a pause; for this conversation had taken place in the earlier days of the struggle, while in many quarters opinions were forming.

"There can be no accurate recital of the manner of a happening before it hath taken place," the Teologo Consultore replied so placidly that his tone conveyed as little reproach as information; yet Fra Francesco could not again have put his question in any form.

Still he lingered, as if something more must be spoken, although Fra Paolo had already sent to summon his secretary. "I also," he said, asserting himself, with an effort which was always painful to his gentle soul, "I also would be faithful to my conscience and my vow; that which I believe— I can teach no other."

"More can one not ask of thee," Fra Paolo answered, suddenly unbending from the stilted mood of his last words. "By the light that is given him must each man choose his path."

"If," said Fra Francesco, speaking sorrowfully, "the blessed law of silence were added to our vow, how would it save a man perplexity and trouble! For that which one believeth must color his speech, though he would fain speak little. Thy light is larger than mine own—I know it to be so—and yet to me it bringeth no vision. I would it had been given us to see and teach alike!"

"In this matter of the confessional," said Fra Paolo, returning and speaking low, "if but thou didst believe with me that, *as a sacrament*, it is oftenest unwise and best left unpractised, thy difficulties might be fewer."

"Nay, Páolo mio, tempt me not. I would I might believe it, but my conscience agreeth to my vow."

"As thou believest, so do; 'for whatsoever is not of faith is sin,' " said Fra Paolo solemnly. "That was a strong word spoken of doctrine to guard the conscience. I would I might scatter all the noble words of that noble Apostle Paul among the people and the priests, in our own tongue!"

"Sometimes thou seemest so like a rebel I know not why I come to thee in trouble"—Fra Francesco looked at him with grieving eyes—"except that in thine heart thou art indeed true."

"So help me God—it is my prayer!" Fra Paolo answered. "And for thee and me alike, however we may differ, there is this other helpful word in that same blessed book which they will not let the starving people share—'God is faithful who will not, suffer you to be tempted above that ye are able, but will with the temptation also make a way to escape, that ye may be able to bear it.' May God be with thee!"

"And Christ and the Holy Mother have thee in their keeping!" Fra Francesco answered, with a yearning look in his loving face, in a tone that lingered on the sweet word "mother" and almost seemed to hint of an omission, as they clasped hands and parted.

This was the last time they had had speech together; but on the evening of the day when Venice had declared her loyalty to her Prince by unanimous vote, there was much animated talk of the matter in the refectory. Fra Francesco had joined the group and listened silently. But as the call to *compline* rang through the cloisters and the friars scattered, he had turned his face to Fra Paolo, who read thereon a very passion of love, reproach, and pain which he could not forget. "When the duties of the Council press me less," he thought, "I will seek him out and reason with him."

But after that night the gentle friar was seen no more in Venice, and inquiry failed to develop a reason for his flight. They missed him in the Servi, where already they were beginning to gather up the pale happenings of his convent life with the kindly recollection which tinged them with a thread of romance, as his brothers of the order rehearsed them in the cloistered ways where he would come no more; for to him some ministry of beauty had always been assigned. The vines drooped for his

267

tending, they said; and the pet stork who wandered in the close languished for his hand to feed the dainty morsel, and for his voice in that indulgent teasing which had provoked its proudest preening.

But this, perhaps, was only fancy, or their way of recognizing a certain grace they missed. But of the reason of his going, which most of them connected in some way with this movement in Venice over which he had often grieved, there was no open recognition among them—partly because they feared that ubiquitous ear of the Senate, which penetrated unseen through many closed doorways, partly because they realized how strange it was that their own sympathies had not confessed his view of right.

Furtively, too, the friars watched Fra Paolo; for the adoration of the gentle Fra Francesco for this idol of their order, from the day when they had entered the convent as boys together, had formed a cloister idyl—none the less that the response of the graver friar was not equally demonstrative, though it was felt to be true; for it was a marvel that two such opposite natures should hold so closely together and that Fra Francesco, for all his gentleness, should apparently retain opinions uninfluenced by the power and learning which all others recognized.

Yet, from those early days, Fra Francesco had abated nothing of his scrupulous and loving conservatism; never had he questioned a rule, nor chosen the least, instead of the most, permitted in an act of humility; and after his Church, the Madonna, and his patron saint, he expended the devotion of his nature upon his friend with a just estimate of his power and daring which filled his soul with anxious happiness. Often, in those earlier days, when the echoes of Fra Paolo's triumphs had penetrated to the refectory of the Servi, Fra Francesco had felt a strange premonition which had kept him long on his knees before the altar in the chapel. "Shield him, O Holy Mother, from danger," he had prayed, "nor let him wander from the lowly path of obedience for pride of that which thou permittest him to know!" And his day-dream of earthly happiness was the spending of his friend's great gifts in the service of the Holy Church, wherein he should ascend from honor to honor, enlarging her borders and strengthening her rule, attaining at last to the supreme position.

Weeks after Fra Francesco had disappeared from the convent a letter was brought by the gastaldo of Nicolotti, Piero Salin, who, in spite of opposition among the brothers, persisted in delivering it with his own hand, though it was rare that any one outside his usual circle was permitted to hold an interview with Fra Paolo; but Piero's masterful ways had not left him, and when he willed to do a thing the wills of others counted little. It was a pity— because the missive was mysterious, crumpled with long carrying—and if a trusty member of their own community had delivered it to Fra Paolo in his cell, there might have been some revelation!

But there was none. Fra Paolo was only a little more grave and silent than of wont; but often now he was so absorbed in government matters that he took less part in the social life of the Servi.

So Piero, laughing at the ease with which he had carried his point for nothing but the asking,—

and it had to be done, since he had promised Marina,—had his interview alone with Fra Paolo, and passed easily through the group of disappointed friars, under those exquisitely wrought arcades to his gondola, thanking them with nonchalance and pressing them to avail themselves more often of the eager service of his barcarioli, that the blessing of the Madonna might be upon their traghetti, to the discomfiture of their rivals the Castellani. For Piero was a faithful gastaldo and lost no opportunity of seeking favor for the faction he represented, and there was a certain grace in his proffer, since priests and friars paid no fares.

Fra Paolo left alone read the message which held the tragedy of a life.

"I could not stay in Venice, dear friend of my whole life, to see thee guide our country into such sad error; for so to my heart it seemeth—may God help us both!

"And when there was no longer hope that my little word might prevail to hold any in that way which alone seemeth to me right—and thou, with thy great gifts, art using them for State and not for Church, Paolo mio, not for our Holy Church— I could not stay, because I love thee! I must have been ever chïding thee had I remained, as if God had made me for no use but to be a thorn in thy flesh—which I could not believe.

"But because He hath made thee great, He hath given thee thy conscience for thy guide, as mine to me; which holdeth me from grief over-much, for I know thee to be true and great.

270

"Therefore for peace, and not for gladness, have I left thee; for reverence to the Holy Father, and for the better keeping of all my vows.

"If perchance, at the feet of the Holy Father, my prayers and penances might, by miracle, avail to turn his wrath from Venice—it could not hurt thee!

"Yet because of this wish, which only holdeth life in me,—so sore is my heart at leaving Venice and thee and our dear home of the Servi,—well I know that never more mine eyes shall see these places of my love—and thee, my friend!

"If we learn by the way of pain, after this life God will forgive our errors!

"FRANCESCO, thy brother of the Servi."

XXIII

A S the cry of the populace rang down the Canal
Grande, following the retreating ranks of the
Jesuits, who, bound by their greater vows to Rome,
had remained steadfast and refused obedience to
the Senate's mandate, the Lady Marina, roused by
the excitement which they dreaded, had started to
her feet with a marvelous return of her former men-
tal power and a fullness of comprehension which
sought for no explanations. She stood for a mo-
ment panting with hot, unspoken speech, turning
from one to another, and then, with a sudden, great
effort, repressed the words she would have spoken,
asking quietly, after a pause in which no reference
had been made to the expulsion of the confra-
ternities:

"Which of the orders have gone? What more
hath happened that I know not?"

"Nay, the orders of the monks and of the friars
have chiefly been faithful to Venice," they told her,
"and all is well. This society, which for long hath
been cause of much disorder in our Republic, it is
well that it leave Venice in peace."

She answered nothing, weighing their words si-
lently. "Is it because they are faithful to their
vows, and to their Church?" she asked at length, in
quiet irony.

"Nay, but because they teach disobedience to princes and would thus undermine the law of the land," Marcantonio hastened to explain, grateful that she could at length discuss the question. "Carina,—blessed be San Marco,—thou art like thyself! We will talk together; we will make all clear to thee; thou shalt grieve no more, carinissima!"

She put up her hand and touched his cheek with an answering caress—the first through all these weary days. "I shall get well, Marco mio," she said, with a sudden conviction that surprised them; but still there was no smile in her eyes, and their hearts were sad, though the change that had come over her was so extraordinary that they hoped much from the explanation which the great Santorio had authorized.

But for whom should they send in this moment, when life and death hung in the balance, to speak that authoritative word.

The Bishop of Aquileia, first and greatest of the Venetian bishops, had incurred the displeasure of the Senate for refusing to perform the duties of his office while the Republic remained under that fulminated but unacknowledged censure, and a new prelate, of opinions approved by the Most Serene Republic, sat in the vacated see. The Bishop of Vicenza had likewise signified his sympathy with the Holy See; and in Brescia their wandering prelate had scarcely yet received that strengthening monition of the watching Senate which was to recall him from his hiding-place and hold him steadfast in his cathedral service.

And for the Patriarch Vendramin, who had been

summoned to Rome to receive the benediction of the Supreme Pontiff, but had been forbidden by the Senate to leave the Venetian domains, this episode, which was a feature of the struggle known to the whole of Venice, placed him so openly on the side of the Republic that it forbade his ministry with the Lady Marina.

But there was one so jealously guarded from all interruption and fatigue that strangers who came from far to see him were refused audience, by order of the Senate, or were received for a few moments only in some protected chamber of the Ducal Palace; for the springs of government moved at his touch, the matters which occupied him were weighty, and for these they would spare his strength. Yet again the Senate signified a rare consideration for the Ca' Giustiniani by permitting the attendance of their Teologo Consultore in the palazzo of the Lady Marina; for who so well could minister to her diseased mind as he who had unanswerably placed the question in its true light before all the Councils of the Republic?

She stood with bowed head and clasped hands as he approached her, her hair falling unbound, as in her maiden days, over the simple white robe which she had preferred in her illness, discarding all her jewels and all emblems of her state—pale as a vision, like a sad dream of the beautiful Madonna del Sorriso which the Veronese had painted for that altar of the Servi at which, each morning, Fra Paolo still dutifully ministered.

"Peace be with thee and to thine house, my daughter," said the Padre Maestro Paolo, spreading out his hands in priestly salutation as he entered the oratory of the palazzo Giustiniani, where the Lady Marina awaited him.

She had desired that the interview should take place in this chapel, which she had not visited since her illness. A faint odor of desolation stole through the dimness of the place to meet him—a breath from the withered rose-petals which had dropped from the golden vases upon the splendid embroidered altar-cloth and mingled with the dust of those many days which had remained guiltless of Mass or service; the altar candles were unlighted; the censer had lost its halo of mystic smoke.

"It were fitter to my mood, most Reverend Father, wert thou to scatter penitential ashes before a desecrated altar which may send no incense of praise to heaven."

"Nay, my daughter; love and faith may still minister, and God, the Unchangeable, accept that service from every altar in Venice! 'The sacrifice of God is a troubled spirit,' it is written in the Holy Book which God hath granted for the comfort of His people. May peace indeed bring thee its benediction—the more that thy need is great."

Was there some strange power of resistance in that fragile, drooping figure which made it difficult to rehearse the argument for Venice with his accustomed mastery?

She listened silently while the learned Counsellor patiently explained that the sentence of Rome was unjust, therefore not incurred and not to be observed by priests nor people; wherefore it was the duty of the Prince to prevent its execution—of the

Prince who, more than any private citizen, is bound
to fear God, to be zealous in the faith and reverent
toward the priests who are permitted to stand in
the place of Christ for the enforcement of his
teaching only; but it is also the more the duty of
the Prince to eschew hypocrisy and superstition, to
preserve his own dignity, and maintain his state
in the exercise of the true religion.

But there was no acquiescence in her eyes.

"I thank thee, most Reverend Father, for thy pa-
tient teaching," she said; "but I lack the learning
to make it helpful. Fra Francesco was more sim-
ple, and he hath taught me by no arguments; but he,
for the exercise of the true religion, hath found it
needful to quit Venice, and doth make his pilgrim-
age to Rome, barefooted, that he may pray the
Holy Father, of his grace, to lift this curse from
our people."

"There is that in her face which maketh argu-
ment useless," Fra Paolo said low to his friend San-
torio, for he was himself no mean physician, having
contributed discoveries of utmost importance to the
medical science, "and there is a physical weakness
combined with this mental assertiveness which doth
make it a danger to oppose her beliefs. Yet I
would I might comfort her, for her soul is tortured."

"It must be that thou shalt convince her!" San-
torio pleaded with him.

Thus urged, Fra Paolo spoke again, in a tone that
pity rendered strangely near to tenderness. "I
would not weary thee, my daughter, having spoken
the truth which I would fain have thee embrace for
thine own healing. Only this would I remind thee
—that none may be excluded from the Holy Catho-

lic Church if he be not first excluded by his own demerits from Divine Grace."

She answered nothing, but there was an unspoken argument in her face.

"See'st thou not that those terrors which thou dost fear shall not come upon Venice, since she hath not sinned? It is this which, for thy peace, we would have thee comprehend."

"My Father, there is but one whose teaching fitteth my reasoning," she answered resolutely, "and he hath fled from Venice that he may be free to believe and to practise his religion as our Holy Church doth require, and to plead against our doom, where prayer may be heard, unhindered by the cloud which keepeth us in Venice from God's favor. He, being a holy man, hath taught me that the law of obedience to the Supreme Head of the Church may not be transgressed—that our doom cometh not undeserved—and my whole heart is sick with fear!"

"There is but One to whom is owed this supreme and inalterable obedience, my daughter; we do not differ in our beliefs; yield it always to him, most reverently and unreservedly," Fra Paolo answered solemnly. "But upon this earth, it hath been taught us by our Lord himself, 'there is none good—nay, not one.' The Head of the Church of God is God himself, the only infallible and just. Thinkest thou that He would have us obey a command conceived in error, with intention to exclude from every benefit of our Holy Church, in the hour when they most need divine comfort and protection, those who would faithfully do him service? Thus read we not the love and mercy of our Heavenly Father!"

"Most Reverend Father," she cried, clasping her

277

hands in extremity. "How shall a weak, untaught woman reason with the Counsellor of Venice! I know not where the words are written—but, somewhere, Fra Francesco hath taught me, yet his soul is loving—there is a thought of the vengeance of God, and it is terrible! Day and night there is no other vision in my soul but this—of the *vengeance of God*, poured out upon the disobedient. For this the blessed Mater Dolorosa of San Donato weepeth ceaselessly. Love is for those who serve him; but vengeance—here and hereafter—for those who disobey. Oh, my Father! for every human soul in Venice—the helpless women, who have no power but prayer, which is but insult while God's face is hidden—the little children who have done no harm —Madre Beatissima, how can we bear it!"

"Nay, nay, my daughter, for our Father is righteous and merciful. 'Vengeance is mine,' he saith; '*I* will repay.' He giveth no man charge to bring his wrath upon us. He hath invested no human power with a supremacy beyond that which abideth in every loving and faithful soul, as to the things of the conscience. Thou, with thy love and faith and pain, art at this moment very near to Him; be comforted, and cease not to believe that He counteth all thy tears, and that thy prayers are dear to Him."

"My Father," she confessed sadly, "it is a part of the shadow that it hides my faith; night and day, with fast and penance, have I not ceased to pray for Venice—and the answer hath been denied me. I could seek for death, but for the horror that cometh after, at the Madonna dell' Orto—the Tintoret

278

—and that which the Michelangelo hath seen in vision— Oh, my God!" ·

"My child, it is not God who faileth thee in answer to thy prayer; and love and faith are yet strong and beautiful within thy soul; only a human weakness is upon thee which cloudeth thy human reason, and for this thy soul is dark. For reason, also, is of God's gift—lower than faith and love, yet a very needful part of man while God leaveth him in his human habitation. There hath come an answer to the prayer, though thou see'st it not."

"Is it written, my father, in the cruel words of the interdict?" she gasped.

"She is tortured out of reverence," Santorio exclaimed apart, and would have hushed her.

But Fra Paolo, overhearing, said gently:

"For this I came, to hearken all thy trouble, if perchance I might give thee rest. The answer to thy prayer is not written in those unjust words. For they—mark well, it is here that thy reason faileth thee—for they were uttered by a human will, striving to coerce obedience in a matter beyond its province. The power which God hath given to priests and princes is not arbitrary, but to be regulated by the law of God; neither is obedience toward those in authority to be stolid and blind, but yielded only when the command is within this divine law. The Holy Father hath no power to command disobedience to the Prince in his rightful realm, —which thus he seeketh to do."

She spread out her hands before her and half-turned away her head, as if in deprecation of some sacrilege, growing very white.

279

"Is *this* the answer, my Father?"

"It is the reason for the answer which hath come by unanimous conviction into the soul of every man of the ruling body of Venice, and hath been voiced by each, in his vote, with a fullness of consent which is of God's sending. Thus are they nerved to declare the censure void—and Venice is unharmed."

"Madre Beatissima! *thus* hast thou answered me?"

"My daughter, may it not comfort thee to know that that which thou, in faith and love, hast prayed for Venice—that in this struggle she should hold God's favor unharmed—hath come to her, though the manner of the benefit accord not with the manner of the grace which thou hast asked?"

"If my reason is clouded with terror," she said very slowly, as if her strength were spent, "God hath vouchsafed me no other reason—but only that which trembles at this broken law of obedience. My Father—I pray thee—I am very weary——"

XXIV

THE nuncio had declared that Venice no longer required his services and had withdrawn, with every ceremony of punctilious and honorable dismissal, to Rome, from whence the Venetian ambassador presently went forth *without* the customary compliments.

But if diplomatic relations were severed between Rome and Venice, there were still chances for private communication which sometimes cast a curious light upon the subject under discussion, but which made no change in that irreproachable suavity of exterior or that invincibility of purpose with which the Venetians held in check any attempt at disaffection through Roman agency, or averted any schismatic movement within their own dependencies.

To Sarpi, the Chief Counsellor, had been committed the censorship of the press; and the supervision of those very papers which had been written by friends of the Republic to scatter broadcast in defense of its rights, formed not the least delicate part of his task. For the government demanded that they should maintain a fine reserve in method, and in spite of examples to the contrary freely given by their opponents, would tolerate neither heresy nor coarseness. Every detail of this world-renowned quarrel was conducted on the part of Venice with an

281

irreproachable dignity and diplomacy that raised it to the height of a negotiation of State, and it formed no part of the policy of the Republic to tolerate any disbelief in her own loyalty; the Venetians should stand before the world as faithful sons of the Church, bearing unmerited sentence of excommunication.

Then Rome, to make an end of the brilliant flow of pamphlets from Sarpi's pen, would have lured him from Venice with flattering promises of churchly preferment. "Nay," said he, "here lieth my duty; and my work hath not deserved honest favor from a Pope who interpreteth the law with other eyes than mine."

Meanwhile the schemes of the enemy were tireless for obtaining secret influence within Venetian borders. Now it was a barefooted friar to be watched for at Mantua, coming with powers plenipotentiary from his Holiness over all the prelates of the rebellious realm; or it might be this same friar, in lay disguise, still armed with those ghostly and secret powers, for whom the trusted servants of Venice were to be on guard. Or there were disaffected brothers, who had left their convents and were roaming through the land inciting to rebellion, to whom it was needful to teach the value of quiet, however summary the process. But Venice, by a broad training in intrigue and cunning, joined to her mastery of the finer principles of statesmanship, still remained mistress of the springs of action and wore her outward dignity, and the disappointments were for her adversaries. But this training was a costly one, for it put a prize on daring, confused the colors of right, and invariably laureled success—if it did no more specific harm to the State.

Piero Salin had been secretly summoned by the Ten and given an indefinite leave of absence from Venice, together with a large discretionary power in the direction of his wanderings, with certain other passes and perquisites which bespoke a curious confidence in one who had been known for a successful and much dreaded bandit gondolier. But if the government in its complicated labors had need of tools of various tempers, it had also the wisdom to discern legitimate uses for certain wild and lawless spirits when they were, like Piero, full of daring and resource.

In the days when they had been dwellers under the same roof Piero had never been able to disregard Marina's will, often as he had chafed under the necessity of yielding to it; and now, since she was Lady of the Giustiniani, it had not been otherwise in the rare instances when it had pleased her to require anything of him. Yet it would have been incongruous to charge Piero with over-sensitiveness on the side of chivalry, though Marina's power over him was still as great as in those old days when, being unable to shake himself free from her influence, he had wished to marry her to make it less.

Piero was not introspective, but he doubtless knew that his ruling passion was to achieve whatever purpose he might choose to set himself. The Nicolotti knew it well when, a few months before, they had unanimously elected him to rule over them —as their chief officers had realized it when they had nominated him, without a dissenting voice, to this position of gastaldo grande—a position of great honor fully recognized by the government. So the rival faction of the Castellani bore marvelous testimony to his mastery when they went over in surprising numbers from along the *Giudecca,* and underwent the strange ceremonial of baptism into the opposition party.

Yet when the rival factions of the people had thus conspired to make him their chief it was Marina who had alone induced him to accept the honor. To all his objections her answer had been ready:

"Nay, Piero, it is meet for thee; they need one strong and brave, of whom they stand in dread, who knoweth their ways——"

"As much bad as good," Piero had interposed frankly, and not without asseverations well known to gondoliers.

"It is well said," she had answered, with the comprehension born of her intimate knowledge of the class; "and to keep them in order—verily, none but thou canst do it."

Piero gave an expressive shrug, having had enough of compliment. *"En avanti—c'è altro!"* he said, laughing. "The taxes are heavy, and their Excellencies the tax-gatherers have less patience than the poor gondoliers bring of *zecchini* to the purse of the Nicolotti. But the gastaldo hath as little liberty of delay, as their Excellencies leave him to decline the burden—I might better make shipwreck in the Canale Orfano."

It was in this canal that the victims of the Inquisition mysteriously disappeared, and Marina had repressed a shudder while she answered, "Thou wilt come to me, Piero, if the purse of the Nicòlotti weighs little; thou shalt not fail, for this, of wearing the honor of gastaldo grande.

"Nay," she had added, quickly disposing of his awkward attempts at thanks, "think not of it again; it is for my pleasure to see thee great among the people, for I also and my father are of them. It is this that I have always wished for thee."

So, chiefly because it had been Marina's will, Piero had waived his unwillingness and become the central figure in the imposing ceremony of the election of the gastaldo grande of the Nicolotti, who were, indeed, almost nobles by antiquity and prestige, not only claiming among themselves the coveted title of *nobili*, but, under the sanction of the government, electing their gastaldo with a degree of ceremonial granted only to high officials, and prescribed in very ancient books of the laws of the traghetti. One of the ducal secretaries, having received official notice of the vacancy of the office carried in person before the Senate by the oldest man of the Nicolotti, came, in purple state, to preside over the election when the bell of San Nicolò had tolled forth the call—taking his seat among the twelve electoral presidents who, already chosen by the people, awaited him, having sworn the inevitable oath of impartiality and fealty to the Republic; they sat behind locked doors until the election was brought to a close—in that solemn semblance of a ducal election which could not fail to impress the people—with complicated, time-using ballotings, and comings and goings of candidates from adjoining chambers to express their views of the responsibilities of the office, or to defend themselves against the freely invited attacks of opponents or malcontents.

And for once Piero had uttered opinions, however clumsily, upon "government" and "reform" from the pulpit of San Nicolò, in the dignified and interested presence of a ducal secretary, the bancali, and the disconcerting throng of gondoliers who were intolerant of speeches and impatient for their vote; and he had retired shamefacedly, like an awkward boy, while his jejune remarks were elaborately discussed by the judges. And because his views—if he had any—had not been over-luminously set forth in this his maiden oration, a party of zealous advocates had nearly caused an uproar by their irrepressible shout of "Non c'e da parlar', ma da fare!" which was, in truth, too sure an indication of the temper of the people to be ignored. "We do not want talking—but doing!"

And for once he had experienced a curious sensation which cowardly men call "fear," but for which Piero had neither name nor tolerance, when all the people who had been worrying him led him in triumph to the altar and forced him down on his stubborn knees to take a solemn oath of allegiance, his great bronzed hand, all unaccustomed to restraint, resting meanwhile in the slippery silken clasp of the ducal secretary.

Here also had the gastaldo received, from those same patrician hands, the unfurled banner of the Nicolotti, with the sacramental words:

"We consign to you the standard of San Nicolò, in the name of the Most Serene Prince and as proof that you are the chief gastaldo and head of the people of San Nicolò and San Raffaele."

And after that had come freedom of breath, with the Te Deum, without which no ceremonial was ever complete in Venice, chanted by all those full-throated gondoliers—a jubilant chorus of men's voices, ringing the more heartily through the church for those unwonted hours of repression.

But when the doors had at last been thrown wide to the sunshine and the babel of life which rose from the eager, thronging populace who had no right of entrance on this solemn occasion—men who had no vote, women and children who had all their lives been Nicolotti of the Nicolotti—a Venetian must indeed have been stolid to feel no thrill of pride as the procession, with great pomp, passed out of the church to a chorus of bells and cannon and shouts of the people, proclaiming him their chosen chief.

Piero Salin was a splendid specimen of the people—tall, broad-shouldered, gifted by nature and trained by wind and wave to the very perfection of his craft; positive, nonchalant, and masterful; affable when not thwarted; of fewer words than most Venetians; an adept at all the intricacies of gondolier intrigue, and fitted by intimate knowledge to circumvent the *tosi.* Moreover, he was in favor with the government, a crowning grace to other qualities not valueless in one of this commanding position.

No wonder that the enthusiasm of the populace was wild enough to bring the frankest delight to his handsome sun-bronzed face as they rushed upon him in a frenzy of appreciation and bore him aloft on their shoulders around the Piazza San Nicolò, almost dizzied with their haste and the smallness of the circle opened to them in the little square by the throng who pressed eagerly around him to grasp his hand—to wave their banners, to shout themselves hoarse for the Nicolotti, for San Nicolò and San Raffaele, for *Piero, gastaldo grande,* for Venezia, for San Marco, with "Bravi," "Felicitazioni," and every possible childish demonstration of delight.

Should not the Nicolotti—blessed be the Madonna!—always overcome the Castellani with Piero at their head, in those party battles on the bridges which had now grown to be as serious a factor in the lives of the gondoliers of Venice as they were disturbing to the citizens at large, and therefore the more to the glory of the combatants?

Was he not their own representative—elected by the very voice of the people, as in those lost days of their freedom the doges had been? And did not the rival faction so stand in awe of the new gastaldo that from the moment of his nomination there had been disaffection in their ranks?

And now, as they shouted around him, many a sturdy red cap tossed his badge disdainfully into the throng and snatched a black bonnet from the nearest head to wave it aloft with cries of "the black cap! The Nicolotti! Viva San Nicolò!"

And again, when Piero essayed to prove himself equal to his honors, his few words dropped without sound upon the storm of vivas—"We do not want talking for our gastaldo—but doing!"

Since this happening Piero had been indeed a

great man among the people—a popular idol, with a degree of power difficult to estimate by one unfamiliar with the customs and traditions of Venice; holding the key, practically, to all the traghetti of Venice, since even before this sweeping disaffection of the Castellani the Nicolotti were invariably acknowledged to be the more powerful faction, so that now it was a trifling matter to coerce a rival offending traghetto; and gondoliers, private and public, were, to say the least, courteous toward these nobles of the Nicolotti, who were dealing with tosi as never before in the history of Venice.

In truth, but for those unknown *observors* in secret service to the terrible Inquisition,—an army sixty thousand strong, one third of the entire population of Venice,—impressed from nobles, gondoliers, ecclesiastics, and people of every grade and profession, from every quarter of the city, and charged to lose nothing of any detail that might aid the dreaded chiefs of the Inquisition in their silent and fearful work—the power of Piero would have been virtually limitless. These three terrible unknown chiefs of the Inquisition were never named among the people except with bated breath, as "i tre di sopra,"*the three above*, lest some echo should condemn the speakers. But the unsought favor of the government was as much a check as an assistance to Piero's schemes, bringing him so frequently into requisition for official intrigues that he had less opportunity for counterplotting, while his knowledge of State secrets which he might not compromise, of the far-reaching vision of Inquisitorial eyes, and of the swift and relentless execution of

those unknown *osservatori* who had been unfaithful
to their primal duty as spies, made him dare less
where others were concerned than he would have
foretold before he had been admitted to these unex-
pected official confidences; while for himself he had
absolutely no fears—having but one life to order or
to lose, and caring less for its length than for the
freedom of its ruling while it remained to him.

And still Marina was, as she had always been,
the gentlest influence in his reckless life,—to some
slight extent an inspiring one,—steadying his daring
yet generous instincts into a course that was occa-
sionally nearer to nobility than he could ever have
chanced upon without her, yet never able to instil a
higher motive power than came from pleasing her.

It was Piero who had escorted Fra Francesco to
the borders of the Roman dominions, guarding him
from pitfalls and discovery until he was free to
undertake his barefooted penitential pilgrimage upon
Roman soil; and from no faith nor sympathy in the
gentle friar's views, but only because he was dear
to Marina.

And through Piero's agents, established under
threats as terrible as those of the Ten themselves,
had come the news which, from time to time, he
unfolded to her; while the same secret agent brought
perhaps a rumor which the gastaldo grande confided
to the Ten, wherewith some convent plotting was
unmasked, or other news so greatly to the keeping
of the peace of the Serene Republic, that Piero
might have bought therewith propitiation for all
those sins against it, of which the government was
happily in ignorance. Now it was a hint of a plot

in embryo to seize the arsenal, involving some members of distinction in the households of resident ambassadors; or word of the whereabouts of that wandering, barefooted emissary with plenary powers, who had hitherto eluded Venetian vigilance.

It was Piero also—although he never confessed to it—who, out of compassion for Marina's priestly proclivities when she lay critically ill, had made it possible for the Jesuits to remove those coffers of treasure which, in spite of strictest orders to the contrary, accompanied them on their flight from Venice; it was not that he took part against Venice in the quarrel, but that the penalty of exile seemed to him sufficient, especially as Marina had a weakness for priests; and he could be generous in his use of power, though a man less daring would not have risked the freak. But there was a masterful pleasure in outwitting the Signoria and the Ten, lessened only by the consciousness that he must keep this triumph to himself, and Piero also knew how to hold his tongue—for discretion was a needful grace in that strange time of barbaric lawlessness shrouded in a more than Eastern splendor.

But even Piero sometimes quickened his step as he passed the beautiful sea façade of the Ducal Palace, whose rose-tinted walls seemed made only to reflect sunshine; for perchance he guessed the name of that victim who hung with covered face between the columns, bearing in bold letters on his breast, by way of warning, the nature of the crime for which he paid such awful penalty—some crime against the State. "To-day," said Piero to himself, "it is this poor devil who cried to me to shield him

when I was forced to denounce him to the Signoria;
to-morrow, for some caprice of their Excellencies—
it may be Piero Salin!"

But the gastaldo relapsed easily into such phi-
losophy as he knew. "By the blessed San Marco
and San Teodoro themselves!" he was ready to cry,
as he reached his gondola, "there must always be a
last 'to-morrow'!"

XXV

L IFE had begun to move again, with slow, clogged wheels, in the Ca' Giustiniani since that sudden favorable change had come to the Lady Marina. Her husband was no longer excused from attendance in the Council Halls of the Republic; and whether to quicken his interest in the affairs of the government or because, in due course, the time had come when a young noble so full of promise should take a prominent place in her councils, he was now constantly called upon to fill important offices in transient committees. Certainly there was some strange, ubiquitous power in that watchful governmental eye; and in the Broglio it had been whispered that if the young Senator were not held constant by multiplied honors and responsibilities the home influence might be fateful to the house of Giustiniani —a house too princely and too important to Venice to be suffered to tolerate any sympathy with Rome. Giustinian the elder, being pronounced in his patriotic partizanship, had replaced the ambassador to his Most Catholic Majesty of Spain, whose attempts at conciliation were so ludicrously inadequate that a court of less astute diplomacy than Venice might have been tempted to withdraw its embassy. Spain and Venice had been stepping through a stately dance, as it were, decorous and

293

princely,—though scarcely misleading,—an interminable round of bows and dignified advances leading no whither, since for a forward step there was a corresponding backward motion to complete the *chassé*, and all in that gracious circle which flatters the actor and the onlooker with a pleasurable sense of progress; but the suspense as to the issue of this minuet was all on the side of Spain, and Venice had patience to spare for these pretty time-filling paces which presented such semblance of careless ease to the watching embassies. England, with an understanding quickened by her own experience, took a serious interest in the quarrel. But his Most Christian Majesty of France was foremost among the princes in efforts to hasten the conciliation of the disputants, and when Henry of France offered to mediate between the powers, Venice said him not nay. For if she would take no personal step toward conciliation, she yet held no code by which the intercession of a monarch might seem to lessen her dignity; and the coming of so princely an envoy as the Cardinal di Gioiosa was celebrated with fêtes meet to grace the reception of so high a dignitary of the Church of Rome.

Hence Venice, under the ban, suggested rather a lively tourney in some field of cloth of gold, than an excommunicated nation in its time of mourning; there were frequent interchanges of diplomatic courtesies—receptions to special embassies which had lost nothing of their punctilious splendor. There had always been time in Venice for absolute decorum, and now there was not less than usual, since her conduct had been denounced—though Venice and her prestige were untarnished and the world was looking on!

Marcantonio, in spite of his deep home anxiety, was becoming more and more absorbed in the affairs of a government which made such claims upon him, and for the honor of his house, by all Venetian tradition, he must give to the full that which was exacted of him. But he worked without the brilliancy and enthusiasm of a few months past—as a man steadied by some great sorrow, striving more strenuously to give of his best where honor is concerned, because he is conscious that the heaviness of his heart makes all duty irksome.

For Marina, with returning health,—the physicians spoke of her thus since they had pronounced her out of danger,—had not fully returned to him; it was less her whiteness and wanness that oppressed him than that nameless change in the face and eyes which suggested a ceaseless, passionate suppression of the deep, impassioned self, under the listless exterior; there was an immeasurable loss in the sweetness of life to them both, though never since the early days of their love had he been so tender and patient, so eager to gladden her in little ways. But she answered his love more often with a mute caress of her hand upon his cheek than with smiles or words—yet with a touch that lingered, as if to assure him that her love was not less, though she herself was changed.

Something terribly real lay between them, of which it seemed better not to speak, since all his efforts to change her point of view had failed. It was utterly sad to have her so nearly herself again, and yet so far from him. Life was hard for this young senator with his multiplied honors, his wealth, and prestige. Marina had always given impetus to his life; now it was he who watched and cared for her, while she seemed to have no will for anything, yet had lost that old charming ingenuousness which had underlain her power. He had promised himself, out of his new pathetic yearning when she had begun to improve, that never again should she know an ungratified wish, yet now he feared that she would give him no opportunity of granting a request, so apathetic had she grown. But one day, when he was trying to rouse her to express a desire, she laid her hand eagerly on his, asking a thing so strange that unconsciously he started away from her.

"Marco, mio, take me to Rome!"

For a moment, in spite of all that had gone before, the young Senator was betrayed into a forgetfulness of his tender mood—it was so strange, this request of a Lady of the Giustiniani, to choose Rome rather than Venice at a time of contest; but her face and manner and speech were luminous with hope; she was radiant again, as she had not been for many months; yet the words escaped from him unintentionally and sternly:

"*To Rome!*"

"Yes, Marco, thou and I and the little one! We should be so happy again in the palazzo Donatello, where baby came to us."

"Marina, a Giustinian abides by Venice. From the days when every man of the Ca' Giustiniani—save only the priest, who might not take up arms—

laid down his life before Lepanto, none hath ever forsaken Venice."

"It is not to forsake our Venice, Marco mio!" she cried, with growing eagerness, "but to serve her—to plead with the Holy Father that he will remove the curse and let all the prayers of Venice ascend again to the Madre Beatissima, who listens no more! It is a service for a Giustinian to render!"

Her whole soul pleaded in face and gesture, beautiful and compelling; he felt her old power reasserting itself; he almost groaned aloud as he put up his hand to shut out this beseeching vision of the wife whom he loved before all things but honor—lest he, being among the trusted rulers of his country, should fail to Venice out of the great joy of granting to Marina the happiness she craved.

Not for an instant did the young Venetian noble question his duty, while with head averted, lest Marina should guess his struggle, he invoked that everpresent image of Venetia regnant, which all her children recognize, to stay him from forgetting it until this temptation were past and he could be strong again; but now he knew that he was weak from an irrepressible yearning to clasp Marina in his arms and grant her heart's desire—at whatever cost; he dared not touch her lest he should yield.

The moment's silence intensified her eagerness and hope; he felt them burning in her eyes, and would not meet their prayer again. But she could not wait, and her hand, fluttering restlessly upon his shoulder, crept up to touch his cheek, thrilling him unbearably, as if each sensitive finger-tip repeated her urgency. He must yield if she kept it there. He snatched her hand to his lips and dropped it quickly, nerving himself to speak steadily, lest he should betray irresolution—so covering the tenderness which would have atoned for the positive refusal.

"Marina, a Venetian may not demean himself to ask forgiveness of the Holy Father in a matter wherein Venice hath not sinned—but Rome.'

"Marco, my beloved, if Venice were mistaken! If thou and I might save her!"

Her voice broke in a sob of agony, and her husband gathered her in his arms, struggling not to weep with her. "Carina—carinissima!" he repeated soothingly; yet, as she grew calmer, brought despair again.

"Nay, Marina, no loyal senator may question the decision of his government; thou presumest too far; but thine illness and thy suffering have made thee irresponsible."

Then, grieving so to cross her in her weakness and pain, with all his tenderness in his voice, he hastened to atone for the firmness of the declaration which had sufficiently proved his staunchness.

"Marina, thou and I—were we not Giustiniani—more than all other Venetians owe our loyalty in time of stress; and for love of thee, beloved, shall Venice find me faithful in her need—I and all my household true, and all my fortune hers in service, if need should be—as thus I vowed, before them all, on that day when the Senate gave thee to me and made thee the sweetest patrician lady in all the land. We will not fail them, beloved!"

He clasped her close, holding her firmly, as if

to infuse her with his faith. "All blessings are for those who do the right, Marina; we need not fear."

Never had she seen his face so inspired, so masterful, so tender; it was a revelation. The whole of their beautiful love story was written on it, mastering all the traditions of Venice, yet binding him more closely to the service of his country.

For a moment she looked at him awestruck, longing to give the submission which would bring her rest; it was not strange that she loved him so; oh, if she might but acquiesce in his view of right! Madre Beatissima, life was hard, and the way of right was the way of the cross—how many holy women had found it so! One hand stole to the little crucifix beneath her robe ánd pressed its roughened surfaces into her breast, for she must not place the sweetness of this earthly love before the duty of the heavenly one. "Santa Maria, save me!" she prayed, while, only for one moment, she drooped her head to his shoulder and nestled close, that he should know her heart was his, whatever came— *whatever came.*

Was it strange that her agony threatened her reason? In that one little moment of comfort, which she yearned to hold free from suffering that its remembrance might uphold her, the powerful vision of the Tintoretto's awful *Judgment* rose beckoningly before her. It was the doom of Venice, and she alone—so impotent—recognized the danger.

The vision pursued her night and day. The River of the Wrath of God, leaping up to meet those frowning skies of His most just anger, and Venice

—superb, disdainful—overwhelmed between; the cloud of innumerable souls, tortured and writhing, fleeing from before the face of the Holy One, no more than a mere film of whirling atoms, falling— falling into an abyss of horrors—the dim, doomed shapes wearing faces that had smiled into hers— With an inarticulate moan she hid her face on her husband's shoulder.

"Marco," she whispered with an effort, for her strength was spent, "not though it were a vision, revealed by the Madonna San Donato, thou wouldest take me to Rome? Not though I could make thee comprehend what it means for me—and thee?"

She waited breathlessly for his answer, with pulses that seemed to pause for the momentous decision, not daring to look at him lest she should falter and retract; for never again would she ask this question, which, even now, she had put in the form of an assertion.

"Nay, Marina, the Madonna asketh naught of thee but that which gracious women must give— submission to their princes—in which, beloved, thou seemest to fail; and duty to thy Church, in which thou, having ever been before all others, art now neglectful. For from the altar of our home no Masses ascend, no fragrance of flowers nor praise. Venice is more faithful in that which she commands, and we, carina, may not longer disregard her will without suspicion of disloyalty. Since Fra Francesco is no longer here, I will apply for some new ministrant. Hast thou a wish in this choice of a priest for the service of our oratory?"

She had started away from him almost resentfully, that he could charge her—whose fealty to her Church was killing her—with neglect of any duty it imposed; but, out of her larger love, she understood him better than he knew her, and she forgave him and nestled back again. He had not been brought up to place the requirements of the Church before the commands of Venice,—few patricians were in those days,—she could not make him realize the awful restrictions of that ban which, by her strict teaching, made it impossible for the faithful to worship in Venice while it remained unwithdrawn; yet he could count it as non-existent!

She was glad that she had felt the tumult of his heart while he answered her so calmly; it made her realize what it cost him to deny her prayer; it assured her that a staunch sense of duty underlay his strength; pitilessly it assured her also that he would not change, and the very firmness which came between them made her love and admire him the more. In the midst of her pain she was proud that he also had conscience on his side, however misguided it seemed to her. Why did the good Madonna permit these differences? How was it possible for Marco, with his quick, intellectual grasp, not to comprehend the truth—not to see the terrors that Venice had brought upon herself! He was suffering also, but only because she suffered; never would he understand her agony; the rudest, cruelest weight of the cross she must lift alone, weary and spent with the bitter struggle.

She summoned all her strength to answer him as though the words were easily spoken. "Since it is not Fra Francesco, whom we love," she said, "I know no other; choose thou, my Marco."

His face flushed with pleasure that her resistance

301

seemed conquered. "And when we have found our confessor, shall we go together—thou and the little one and I," he asked brightly, "to the Island of Sant' Elenà, which thou lovest, and we ourselves bring flowers to deck our chapel? For it hath been long since Mass was said therein."

"Yes, Marco mio," she answered to the love in his voice, struggling to repress every accent of dissent; for in her heart she told herself that the chapel of the palazzo Giustiniani was his, not hers, since their faith was divided; "and for me only, not for him, to worship there is sin. And the beautiful day together, alone on the island with the flowers—it is the gift of the Holy Mother to help me endure!'

And her husband, as he left her, carried with him a smile that satisfied him.

But, turning in the doorway for another glance—so sweet it was to have her all his own again—a pang shot through him, for the glory was gone from her face—or was it the shadow that made it so wan and gray?—and no smile hid the questioning anguish of her eyes. Nay, he himself was fanciful, · for it was too far to see, and he could not shake off the sadness of the days that were past. But he must teach himself to forget them. For Marina had smiled at him, radiantly, as in the sweet, old days; and together they would deck the chapel for a benediction!

XXVI

FRA PAOLO was fast becoming a centre of romance, so many were the attempts from suspicious quarters to manage private interviews which the Senate had thought necessary to frustrate; and the fact that he was known to have declined the escort of guards which the Senate urged upon him as means of safety endowed him with a sort of heroic halo in the eyes of the lesser multitude. "Fate largo a Fra Paolo," they called in the Merceria if the people pressed him too closely—"Make way for Fra Paolo!"—and a strange youthfulness, as of satisfied affections, was beginning to grow upon his calm face. He had had no cravings, feeling that duty sufficed; yet, through this absolute yielding of himself to express the message with which his life was charged, his heart had warmed within him, and now, unsought, the people loved him, magnifying the interest of every minor happening of his life and zealously gathering anecdotes of the days before he was great.

A group of his brother friars were strolling back and forth under the fretted colonnades of the greater court of the Servi one evening before vespers, a glow of relish on their genial, cowled faces, rehearsing the tale of Fra Paolo's unconventional

303

slippers; for it was the hour of small gossip, and the day had been warm.

"They were scarlet, like an eminence's," explained Fra Giulio, who had secured this choice bit for the entertainment of his special cronies; "for all colors are one to Fra Paolo, who hath no distinction for trifles."

"Because he spendeth himself in scheming for honors that belong elsewhere," interposed a disaffected brother who had strolled up and joined the group uninvited; he belonged to another chapter of the Servi, and had but recently come among them; honors had passed him by and duties attracted him less, and he had made no friends within the convent, though he professed great interest in all that concerned Fra Paolo, and had even offered to wait upon him in chapel or in his cell.

"Thou, Fra Antonio, seek thine own friends!" Fra Giulio retorted, with unusual asperity; "for this tale is too good for thine hearing, being another triumph for Fra Paolo in the days when he was only a frate of the Servi."

"*Ebbene,* and then?" urged the eager auditors, crowding around the speaker, for the incongruity of the grave padre, in his frayed and rusty gown attempting to usurp a decoration, lent interest to the petty happening.

"*Ebbene,* and then his Eminence of Borromeo—for it seemeth that only the illustrious play parts in this farce"—Fra Giulio continued with keen enjoyment, "his Eminence of Borromeo hath explained at Rome that Fra Paolo was innocent of contempt of rule."

304

"Verily, the fault might have been counted to one who hath no sins of the body to atone for!" sneered Fra Antonio, who could not be converted to the prevailing tone of admiration for this abnormal being who walked among them not as other men, and toward whom his own attitude was a singular compound of obsequiousness and cynicism. "Even the slippers of your saint can do no wrong," he added venomously.

"But thou, in canonized shoes, couldst walk but wearily, Fra Antonio, lest they should lead thee in unwonted ways!" one of the party retorted maliciously.

"Fra Paolo hath fear of no man, and that which he declareth he knoweth," said another of the frati, lowering his voice and glancing about him furtively. "And it hath chanced to him, more than once, to be wiser than the Serenissimo and the Ten themselves—may San Marco have other uses for his ears! But the day that our famous Signor Bragadin was summoned from his palace on the Giudecca to make his promised gold for the Signoria, I stood with the crowd in the Merceria to see him pass, with his two black dogs and their golden collars looking for all the world like powers of evil! And our gold-maker himself going to the Senate like a noble, with his friends the Cornaro and the Dandolo in crimson robes—the people thronging to see him pass!"

"Ay, Bragadin was a saintly man!" one of them retorted mockingly. "Dost remember the tale how that he fooled the worshipful Signoria to leave him a week in peace, that he might take the blessed sacrament quietly, finding therein 'a holy joy' that should fit him to proceed to the service of Venice—looking, meanwhile, for means of escape?"

"*Davvero!* but this was the hour of his highest favor, and I followed with the rest of the crowd till there was scarce breathing space under the clock tower, where the *Magi* were just coming forth to salute the Madonna and the Bambino at the stroke of the day; and the people were shouting so one could not hear the bell for cries of 'Gold! gold! Bragadin!'

"We surged back against the doorway of the 'Nave d'Oro,' the people struggling with each other lest they should lose the sight as he passed through the Piazza, and suddenly there came a voice,—cold, and scornful, and low, but no man lost the words,— 'Thou art wearied in the multitude of thy counsels. Let now the astrologers, the star-gazers, the monthly prognosticators stand up and save thee from these things that shall come upon thee!' The people stopped their pushing and looked aghast to see who spake, but I could have sworn it was Fra Paolo's voice. I caught a glimpse of him standing quietly just inside the 'Nave d'Oro,' while the other signori who go there to ridotto were out in the Merceria to see the show; and I made haste away lest the crowd should object to my habit for being like Fra Paolo's—they were so crazy for Bragadin, following in the footsteps of the Signoria, like good Venetians!"

"Who told the saying to the Signoria, when it might have crushed Fra Paolo?" Fra Giulio questioned jealously.

"It may well have been his Excellency the Signor Donato, who was of the Council in those days, but a man too strong to have a mind to the folly of the others, and who walked about the chamber giving sign of much displeasure while Bragadin made his gold. And the next day Fra Paolo is commanded before the Signoria to meet the Provveditor of the Mint—being the only man who hath dared speak his mind before the Signoria had proved the worthlessness of Bragadin's promise. And our fine goldmaker exchangeth his palace for a prison; for the test of the crucible is all too easy for Fra Paolo, who speaketh naught that he knoweth not."

"Santa Maria! here cometh the 'bride,'" some one exclaimed warningly; for none of Fra Paolo's friends had the courage for frivolity in his grave presence, harmless as it might appear in his absence, and this watchword was often heard in the cloister as he approached.

He was conversing earnestly with his secretary, Fra Fulgenzio, evidently on business of the Senate, having remained in the convent all day, contrary to his usual custom; Fra Fulgenzio had been to and fro with messages, and once had returned from the Ducal Palace escorting several grave personages who had gone to Fra Paolo's cell for some conference, which gave rise to pleasant comment in the convent—since the Serenissimo could not dispense with the personal service of its Consultore for a single day, and every honor shown to Fra Paolo was dear to the hearts of the Servi.

Fra Paolo paused only for a moment as he passed the group to exchange a greeting, but his keen, quiet glance took in every expression, from the affectionate smile of old Fra Giulio to the jealous discontent of Fra Antonio, whose gaze drooped before him while he hastened to give the accustomed sign of reverence due to one so high in authority.

Fra Paolo considered him seriously for a moment before resuming his stroll. "Fra Antonio," he said, in his passionless voice, "the head of the Roman Chapter hath made inquiry for thee, and knew naught of thy presence here. Thou wilt soon be recalled. That thou doest—do quickly."

A sudden pallor overspread the features of Fra Antonio, who staggered and would have fallen, as he made an effort to steal away unobserved, had not the others come to his assistance.

"What is thy sudden ailment?" one of them asked him roughly, for he was no favorite.

But before the trembling friar could steady his voice or choose his words he was forgotten, for the evening bells began to chime for vespers, and as the brothers came flocking through the cloisters the great bell at the entrance gate on the Fondamenta dei Servi sent back the special deep-toned call, which took precedence of every order within the convent. Those who had already reached the chapel streamed back in wild confusion to answer the summons which filled the court with clanging echoes, while the silvery notes of the chapel chimes sounded faintly in the pauses of the deeper reverberations— like the voice of a timid child crying to be comforted when it does not understand.

In the excitement that followed Fra Antonio was forgotten by all but Fra Giulio, who had been watching him closely as he made his way with difficulty toward the low, arched passage which led in the direction of the dormitory.

"Lean on me," said Fra Giulio, who stood barring the way.

"Nay," replied the other, who seemed scarcely able to stand, "I must needs reach my cell; a sudden illness hath overtaken me."

But Fra Giulio, usually so compassionate that he was called "woman hearted," did not move.

"Later a remedy shall be brought thee," he answered coldly. "Thou hearest the great summons which none of our order may disobey; it is rare and solemn to hear that call. Something of moment hath chanced. *Ecco*, now we shall know!" he added in a tone of relief, as Fra Gianmaria appeared from under the convent entrance, whither he had gone to receive the Chief of the Ten, who now entered the great court with him in formal state, with a secretary and attendants and an officer of the guards.

The tumultuous crowd began to range itself in orderly groups at the command of the superior, and Fra Antonio controlled himself with a supreme effort as a body of palace guards, in brilliant uniforms, scattered themselves among the black-robed friars. The heavy gates closed behind them, and the dismal tolling of the bell ended in a silence through which the heart-beats of Fra Antonio sounded in his ears louder and more ominous than the harsh tones of the summons had done a moment before.

Who were those two terrible gondoliers all in

black, who stood by the water-entrance on the Fondamenta? Was it the shadow of their great black hats that darkened their features like masks? Why were they there?

He glanced stealthily at the faces of the friars; they were more full of interest than dread, while the eyes of the little choristers who stood robed for chapel service shone with delight. Evidently to all that community the interruption was an event filled with possibilities of excitement that was welcomed as breaking the monotony of the daily round. Perhaps no one had noticed those gondoliers! Only Father Gianmaria, the Superior, and the Senator Giustinian Giustiniani, the Chief of the Ten, were stern and angry; and Fra Paolo stood between them—calm and inscrutable as ever.

Now, thought Fra Antonio, before the curiosity of the friars had been satisfied,—while no one was thinking of him,—he must escape! But at every passage leading out of the court a scarlet coat stood guard, save only before the low doorway of the dormitory stair. Fra Giulio's eyes were fixed earnestly, adoringly, upon his beloved Fra Paolo, and he had moved a little way from the wall.

Fra Antonio stole softly in behind him, breathlessly anxious. He was already under the archway when his unsteady foot stumbled in a hollow of the worn brick pavement just within the opening—in another moment he should be safe! But a voice, meant for him alone, leaped through all that crowd and petrified him with horror; it was filled with a sarcastic grace as it offered the courtesy.

"Whoever hath need to leave this cloister before

the Inquiry of Venice is satisfied, shall be served by the gondola of the *Piombi*—which waits."

I Piombi! Those prisons under the leads where the heat was slow torture—this was the meaning of the masked gondoliers!

Surely it was the Chief of the Ten who had spoken! Fra Antonio trembled from head to foot; but was he not already far enough within the narrow, winding passage to be hidden from the cruel gaze of that man of power? Half an inch might make the difference between life and death; he folded his black gown closer about him—stealthily —so that it might not rustle, watching the faint shadow on the pavement in agony—what if his hand had been seen as he passed it behind him to gather up the folds!

Those words could not be meant for him; they were merely a general order; there were twenty men—forty men in that company more wicked than he! He could not turn back and face them to glide into his place again; it would be certain death; but when the Chief of the Ten or Father Gianmaria should begin to speak, he must go on.

He lifted one foot to be ready; a great sweat broke out on his forehead—would this silence never end? He dared not stir until there should be words to hold the crowd; for if he should be caught——

Were they speaking?—His heart thumped so that he could not hear. Santa Maria!—death could not be worse!

"Thou art summoned; they are calling thee,' said Fra Giulio, close beside him, in a low, hard voice that changed to one more compassionate as the friar turned his livid face toward him. "I know not thy fault, but Fra Paolo will plead for thee; for thou art ill, verily."

"Fra Paolo is no man of mercy."

"Nay, but of justice. He will not remember thy discourtesies."

"*Discourtesies!*" ay, it was true; Fra Giulio did not know—nobody knew; he would take courage and plead to be forgiven his manifold "discourtesies" toward this idol of the Servi; it was for this that he was summoned! The palace guards were approaching the low passage, and the extremity of his need steadied him; he rallied all his powers for a last effort, and, shaking off their touch, advanced into the court—his face, withered and pain-stricken, might have plead for him but for the strange hardness of the lines.

"It was a sudden malady that bade me seek my cell," he gasped. "I knew not that your Excellency had need of me."

He was a ghastly thing in his fear.

The inexorable Chief of the Ten surveyed him in silence for a brief moment that seemed unending.

"Ay, Fra Antonio, we *have* need of thee—more than another. For word hath reached Venice, privately, from special friendly sources in Rome, that thou art come hither charged with a message of vital import to a trusted servant of the Republic. Thou hast leave of the Signoria to declare it in this presence."

Fra Antonio opened his dry lips and framed some words of which he heard no echo.

"The Inquiry of Venice is satisfied," said the

Chief. "Thou art the man whom we seek. Conduct him to the gondola of the Piombi."

Fra Antonio fell upon his knees in wild supplication as the guards gathered around him, but the Father Superior detained them with a prohibitory motion.

"I crave your Excellency's pardon. For the better ruling of this community and the clearing of all the innocent among our brotherhood, I have summoned hither every soul under my rule. That no scandal may arise, your Excellency will permit that the charge under which this arrest is made be declared."

Assent was given by an impatient gesture.

"Fra Antonio, while he hath been a recipient of our hospitality," said the Superior, "is described by trustworthy advices from our Chapter in Rome, but just received, as a person who hath designs upon the life of a member of this community."

"It is a false scandal," cried Fra Antonio, who had found his voice at last. "I shall not be condemned without proof!"

"The truth is known,' said Fra Paolo, leaning toward him and speaking low. "It were better for thee to confess—or depart in silence."

But the man was beside himself with fear; he caught at his last, desperate chance of favor, dragging himself to the feet of Fra Paolo and pouring out an abject tale of petty jealousies and offenses for which he obsequiously craved pardon of this "idol of the convent," protesting, with horrible oaths, that he was guilty of nothing more.

The rare shade of compassion that had softened

Fra Paolo's face when he gave his warning, deepened to a glory and his eyes shone with a grace that was like love, as he raised the wretched man and strove to arrest his torrent of words. *"God* heareth thee, my brother," he said pleadingly; "have pity on thine own soul. Kneel to Him alone in thy great need. But spend not thy strength with trifles that demean us both. If thine heart hath aught against me, I forgive it."

Then turning to the Chief he besought that the trial should be short—"For the man is ill, and I would have quiet speech with him."

"For the honor of the Servi, let the matter be dispatched, and let proof be brought," the Superior demanded, surprised and displeased at any softness in Fra Paolo, whose dominant note was justice, rather than mercy.

"We will grant him the favor of a farewell collation ere he taketh leave of his entertainers," said the Giustinian. "Let the refection be brought."

The friars exchanged glances of astonishment and dismay as a dish of fruit and of white bread were brought forward by two of the ducal guards, on a costly salver wrought with the arms of Venice. It was like the simple refreshment they had often carried to Fra Paolo's cell when he had been absorbed by some train of thought, which, according to his wont, he would not suspend for any hour of sleep or meals until the problem had been conquered. Fra Giulio trembled; he would have said those were the very grapes he had chosen to tempt Fra Paolo's slender appetite,—white, with the veins of purple,—all as he had left them on his desk that day, with the plate of fine white bread, when the midday meal was served—but in no lordly dish.

A faint cry escaped Fra Antonio, and he put his hands before his face.

There was a moment of breathless silence; but no compassion anywhere upon all those strained and eager faces, except in the eyes of Fra Paolo, which seemed divine in pity, as he drew nearer the guilty man and put his arm about him to steady him.

"These," said the Chief of the Ten, "fine grapes and wheaten bread, exquisitely flavored with a most precious powder, thou shalt presently enjoy in this presence,—with the compliments of the Signoria, who have most carefully considered this repast,— unless thou dost instantly make frank and full confession of thy deed and thine accomplices.

"And if more be to thy taste," the cruel voice went on, for no answer came, "since in these matters thou hast a consummate knowledge—thou art permitted, by grace of the Signoria, to use the contents of this packet, which hath been found within the lining of thy cassock. This powder hath a marvelous power to still the blood which floweth over-swiftly——"

"We have proof more than sufficient for the arrest, your Excellency," interposed the officer of the guards, as he gave the signal. "And no deposition can be taken here, for the man hath fainted from his fright."

But almost unnoticed the guards bore their burden from the cloister to the gondola of the prisons of the Piombi; for it had taken but a moment to complete the unfinished tale in the minds of the

315

listeners, and with one accord they were gathering about Fra Paolo, eager to express their loyalty, their indignation, their gratitude for his escape.

The court was in a tumult. "Fra Paolo!" "*Our* Fra Paolo!" mingled with bursts of vehement condemnation and rapid questions. "Our Consultore!" "And because he is necessary to Venice!"

The chimes of the chapel sounding joyously broke in upon these demonstrations, and two little choristers came running back to tell them that, by order of Fra Gianmaria, a Te Deum for the safety of Fra Paolo would be sung, in lieu of the interrupted vesper service.

"The Signoria hath had warnings without end," the Chief of the Ten was explaining hastily to Father Gianmaria, as they strolled toward the chapel. "The Holy Father wanteth him out of Venice, since he hath been Consultore—for the man is a marvel! But he would rather have him alive than dead—as the learned Scioppius hath explained, not long since, to Fra Paolo himself! And this whole plot hath been unveiled to us by one who watcheth secretly in Rome for the interest of Venice, since there hath been no open communication. It was hatched in the Orsini palace, in that holy city, not unknown to some of their Eminences; the chief accomplices are friars—we have the names of the other two; and Piero Salin is on the watch. The stakes are high for the friars' game—five thousand *scudi* apiece and a promise of Church preferment; but Piero Salin hath ways of doing his duty! The Senate will send orders for the better protection of its Consultore; meanwhile let him not venture forth without two ducal guards."

"Your Excellency knoweth that Fra Paolo will have no state."

"A cowl over their saintly faces, if it please his fancy! It is the order of the Senate, waiting better plans of safety—a suite in the Ducal Palace or a house connected therewith by some guarded passage. Warning hath been sent us most urgently, by friends of the Republic, of a great price and absolution for him who may bring Fra Paolo to Rome —alive or dead!"

XXVII

THESE days had been important in the Senate. In the deliberations prior to the departure of di Gioiosa the concessions which Rome had persistently asked had been so persistently and diplomatically declined that even the wily cardinal dared no longer press them; and it seemed at last that there was to be truce to the cautious and subtle word-weighing of months past, as di Gioiosa, suddenly realizing that he held the ultimatum of the Republic, had taken his departure for Rome in the night—conceiving it easier, perhaps, to confess his partial defeat to the dignified Signoria by proxy. So he made the announcement through a gentleman of his household the next morning, while he was already journeying toward the expectant Pope, to whom he carried bitter disappointment; and the heart of the cardinal himself had been scarcely less set upon those points of amelioration which he had not obtained. It was a blow to his diplomacy and to his churchman's pride; for the terms which the cardinal was empowered to offer were scarcely less haughty than was the attitude which Venice had assumed throughout the quarrel.

His Holiness had wished that Venice, as a first step, should cancel the "Protest" which she had widely published, declaring the interdict invalid.

But Venice, with cool logic, had declined to accede to this; since the protest, being based upon the censures, was practically annulled by their withdrawal—which must therefore first take place. And, although by this same logic she was led to declare that no act on the part of the Republic would then be necessary to void her protest, she consented to give a writing to that effect, so soon as the censures should have been withdrawn.

The Pope requested that all who had left Venice on account of the interdict should, upon its withdrawal, return and be reinstated in their former privileges—making a special point of including the Jesuits.

But here, also, Venice made and kept to her amendment; all should return, with full privilege and favor—save only the Jesuits, who had in various ways rendered themselves obnoxious to the government.

The revocation of those laws which the Pope demanded was not to be thought of, since this would be questioning the right of Venice to make laws; neither was their suspension possible, for the laws were just. But his Holiness might rest assured that they would be used in moderation and Christian piety only—as they had ever been.

The real concession—the only one—was in the case of the ecclesiastical prisoners—the Abbot of Nervessa and the Canon of Vicenza—whom his Holiness persisted in claiming. But Monsieur du Fresne, the French Ambassador, suggested that the Republic should, "without prejudice to her right of jurisdiction over criminal ecclesiastics," *give* these prisoners to the ambassador as a mark of special favor to his king, the mediator, who might then consign them to the Pope if he chose—they being his to deal with.

Venice, with her powers of subtle reasoning, gladly embraced this way out of the difficulty which had first appeared insuperable. "So to *give* them," she said, appeased, "confirms rather than questions our authority, since no one may 'give' to another that over which he exercises no dominion."

It was not Venice, but France, who was to request that the interdict be withdrawn, that she might not seem to other nations to be under the ban; for the Republic did not acknowledge that this condition of disfavor had gone into effect; she could not therefore personally request the Pope to change an attitude which put only himself in the wrong. But when there was a hint of "absolution," which the cardinal in his zeal would also ask the Holy Father to pronounce, Venice was silent from displeasure. She had done no wrong; she would neither ask nor accept absolution.

The Senate might indeed be weary of these interminable discussions and unending compliments, and glad of a respite in which to turn to other matters. But there were no idle hours in that august assembly, though it might chance that some whimsical phase of statesmanship lightened, by way of entr'acte, the severity of their deliberations. They were, possibly, not unpleasantly aware of the irony of the situation when a letter from their governor in Constantinople announced "the extreme solicitude of the Turkish Government for the life and welfare of the Holy Father," who had so furthered their interests by widely inciting discord among the nations of Christianity that, seeing therein a mark of the special favor of Allah, the sultan had ordered prayers and processions for the continued welfare of his Holiness!

The singular jealousy of the Venetians for the solidarity of their government, with their no less singular jealousy of individual aggrandizement, together with the rare perception of mental characteristics that was fostered by the daily culture of the councils in which every noble took his part, led them constantly to ignore their selfish hopes in order to choose the right man for the place. These sentiments, acting and reacting upon each other, had secured their political prosperity; but a disaffection was beginning to make itself felt in the Senate which led ultimately to over-limitations of power and such multiplied checks and suspicions that noble living and wise ruling became impossible.

It was a time of suppressed excitement, and there had been a grave discussion as to the growing power of the Ten, against which some of the senators had dared to express themselves openly; for many of these strong men were beginning to feel that their government weighed upon them like a Fate, crushing all liberty and individuality; and of secret trials without defense there were tragic memories haunting the annals of that grave tribunal.

But so great were the complications of the involved Venetian machine—so many were the mysteries and fears environing the daily life of these patricians—that each felt the actual to be safer than the untried unknown, and surrendered the hope of change, tightening the cords that upheld the government as their only means of safety.

For there was an under side to all this gold-tissued splendor that was sometimes laid bare to the people, in spite of the deftness with which the Signoria stood tirelessly ready to cover up the flaws; and a recent sad travesty of justice was one of the weird happenings of this time.

Not long since a formal *decree of pardon* had been solemnly declared and published throughout Venetia, at which the people stood aghast. For the man to whom this clemency was graciously extended had been condemned and executed between the columns of San Marco and San Teodoro, ten years before — standing accused of conspiracy against the State. There had been many murmurings when the name of this old patrician, holding honorable office in service of the Republic, had been erased from the Golden Book; and he had suffered his ignominious death protesting that the charge was false, and that all who had aided in his condemnation should die before the year was out. His dying words had proved a grim prophecy, which, encouraged by the pressure of the senators, induced the Signoria to order a re-investigation of his case, whereby the *manes* of this dishonored servant of the State were re-instated in that serene favor now so worthless.

And to-day the people gathered in gloomy silence while the great bell of the campanile tolled the call to the solemn funeral pageant by which the Republic offered reparation over the exhumed body of the

322

victim. The senators, wrapped in mourning cloaks, surrounded the bust of the man they desired to honor as it was carried in triumph to the church where the tomb was prepared; and the three *avvogadori*, who had the keeping of the Golden Book, bore it on a great cushion behind the marble effigy, the leaf bound open where the name was re-in-scribed. Here also walked the domestics of the re-habilitated noble of Venice—the hatchments that had been doomed to oblivion freshly embroidered upon their sleeves above their tokens of crêpe. The Doge and the Signoria all took part in this tragic confession of wrong, doing penance unflinchingly for the sins of their predecessors; for Venice could be munificent in reparation, not shrinking from her own humiliation to appease outraged justice and confirm her power, and there was nothing lacking that might add impressiveness to the pageant.

But the people looked on gloomy and unappeased, filled with a horror which the funeral pomp did little to quiet; they did not follow as the *cortège* descended the steps of the Piazzetta to embark in the waiting gondolas that had been lavishly provided by the Republic. Santissima Maria! they wanted to get back to their own quarters on the Giudecca and breathe a little sunshine! What did one noble matter, less or more? "But it 's a gloomy barcarolle that a dead man sings!"

"And one that hath not died his own death!" a woman answered under her breath, as she crossed herself with a shudder.

The wind inflated the empty folds of the crimson robe that draped the bier, carrying it almost into the water, as the gondolas glided away from the Piazzetta.

"San Marco save us! he wanted none of their pomp," said an onlooker scornfully. "The ten good years of his life and a quiet grave in San Michele—the Signoria would buy them dear, to give them to *him* to-day!"

Yet if some had died unjustly, there was not less need of ceaseless vigilance against unceasing intrigue, within and without that body which held the power; and one morning the Senate was thrown into a state of great agitation by disclosures from one of the brothers of the Frari, indubitably confirmed by the papers which he, delivered into the hands of the Doge.

"It is beyond belief!" Giustinian Giustiniani exclaimed to the Lady Laura, "how Spain findeth method to make traitors in Venice itself! It is a nation treacherous to the core, and it were beyond the diplomacy of any government,—save only ours,—to maintain relations on such a basis of fraud."

"What is there of new to chide them for?" she asked with keen interest.

"Is not the old enough to make one wrathful! Boastful threats of arms against the Republic if she yield not obedience to the Holy Father, with secret promises of armed assistance to his Holiness to keep him firm in his course, at the very moment of her cringing attempts at mediation lest France should carry off the glory!—and because Spain hath neither men to spare for Rome, nor courage to declare against the Republic, nor diplomacy to bring anything to an issue!"

324

"Nay, now thou art returned to Venice forget the disturbing ways of Spain," the Lady Laura answered, with an attempt at conciliation. "I am glad that thy mission in that strange land hath come to an end."

"Ay, but the ways of Spain do make traitors of us all!" Giustinian exclaimed hotly. "When a senator of the Republic hath such amity for the ambassador of his Most Catholic Majesty, forsooth, that at vespers and at matins, in the Frari, they must use the self-same kneeling stool—a tenderness and devotion beautiful to see in men so great; for it is aye one, and aye the other, and never both who tell their beads at once—that, verily, some brother of the Frari doth take cognizance of a thing so rare and saintly and bringeth word thereof to the Serenissimo, *with matter of much interest found within the prie-dieu.*"

"Giustinian!"

"Ay, these minutes of the noble Senator, who acteth so well the spy for favor of Spain, would do honor to a ducal secretary, for accuracy of information concerning weighty private matters before the Council! And due acknowledgment of so rare a courtesy doth not fail us in the very hand of the ambassador himself, for this letter also was intercepted! This frate who hath brought the information verily deserveth honor for so great a service!"

"And the others?"

"Is there more than one treatment for a traitor?" Giustinian exclaimed, with increasing temper. "And for the ambassador—it hath already been courteously signified to him that the air of Venice

325

agreeth not well with one of his devotional tendencies."

"Tell me the name of the traitor," the Lady Laura urged, coming close and laying her hand upon his shoulder.

"Nay," said her husband, shaking off her touch impatiently, "my anger doth unlock my speech to a point I had not dreamed, for the matter may be held before the Inquisition! But it is a name unknown to thee, and new to this dignity, which he weareth like a clown! The freedom is still too great for this entry to the Senate; the serrata hath done its work too lightly if it leave space for one parvenu! To-morrow, when thou takest the air in thy gondola, my Lady Laura, thou shalt look between the columns of the Ducal Palace and know whatever the State will declare to thee of that which concerneth the government alone! The times are perilous."

"They will be better when the interdict is removed——"

"Ay—no—one knows not; it is a matter too grave for women and too little for the Republic to grieve about. His Holiness would have us on our knees, weeping like naughty infants, and abjectly craving his pardon for daring to make our own laws and uphold our prince!"

"Giustinian, there is more to it than that."

"Ay, there *is* more, if it setteth the women up to preach to us and to expound the laws of the Republic—a knowledge in which I knew not that they held the mastery! Take not the tone of Marina, who hath come near to killing herself and making half a fool of Marcantonio."

"Nay, Marco is true to Venice and swerveth not. And for our daughter—she hath suffered till it breaks my heart to look into her face, poor child! And thou, Giustinian, wert little like thyself, when she lay almost dying! The Signor Nani hath confessed to me that in Rome there was much intriguing for her favor—of which she suspected naught. It was a harm to them that they went to Rome; I would not have had it so."

"Ay, thou would'st not have had it so; thou would'st have had it all thine own way!" retorted Giustinian, who was becoming impossible to please, now that the paths of government were growing more thorny and exacting, and the Lion showed no sign of climbing to his portal. "That father confessor of hers hath much to answer for. Keep the little one well out of the way of their craft—dost thou hear? He is to be trained for Venice, after the ways of the Ca' Giustiniani. And Marcantonio —who knows?"

He had drifted into his favorite reverie, and wandered abstractedly out upon the balcony looking longingly toward the rose-colored palace where his every ambition centred; but he felt the glittering, jeweled eyes of the patron saint of Venice glare upon him mockingly from his vantage point upon the column, while the very twist of the out-thrust tongue insinuated a personal message of malice and defeat.

XXVIII

VENICE was flooded with moonlight. The long line of palaces down the Canal Grande shone back from the breast of the water, starred with lights, repeated again and again in the rippling surface.

A ceaseless melody filled the air, braided of sounds familiar only to this magic city—echoes of laughter from balconies high in air, silvery tintinnabulations falling like drippings of water from speeding oars, franker bursts of merriment from the open windows of the palaces, low murmured tones of lovers in content from gliding gondolas, hoarse shouts of quick imperious orders from gondoliers to offending gondoliers, as they passed—apostrophes to liquid names of guardian saints, too melodious for denunciations, hurled back with triple expletives and forgotten the next moment in friendly persiflage; here and there a strain of ordered music, in serenade, from a group of friendly gondolas swaying only with the tranquil movement of the water; or the mysterious tone of a violin, uttering a soul-prayer meant for some single listener, which yet steals tremblingly forth upon the night air—more passionate, more beautiful and true than that other human voice which breaks the quiet of a neighboring calle with some monotonous love song of the people.

And far away, perhaps, in the quainter squares of the more primitive island villages—in Burano or Chioggia—before the Duomo, some reader lies at full length in the brilliant moonlight under the banner of San Marco, his "Boccaccio" open before him, repeating in a half-chant, monotonous and droning, some favorite tale from the well-worn pages to listeners who pause in groups in their evening stroll and linger until another story is begun; this time it is some strophe from the "Gerusalemme," to which a passing gondolier may chant the answering strain—for this is the very poem of the people, echoing familiarly from lip to lip, and tales from the Tasso are not seldom wrought into the ebony carvings of their barks. Meanwhile the younger men and maidens, on a neighboring fondamenta, keep step to the music of some strolling player who lives, content, on the trifling harvest of these moonlight festivities.

In the great Piazza of San Marco, with its hundreds of lights and its hurrying throng, life is gayer than in the day. Crowds come and go under the arcades, loiter at the tables closely set before the brilliant cafés, or stroll with laughter and snatches of song and free Venetian banter where there is less restraint, up and down the broad space of the Piazza, between the colonnade and the burnished Eastern magnificence of San Marco, beyond the reach of the yellow lamp flames—their laughing faces grotesque and weird in the white glare of the moon. But under the shadow of the Broglio and those great

329

columns of the Ducal Palace there are only slow-moving figures here and there, wrapped in cloaks, and dark under the low, unlighted arches, talking in undertones which even the watchful Lion—so near, so cunning—does not always overhear.

But in the calles, half in moonlight and half in shadow, night wears a more poetic air of mystery and quiet; and if a fear but come in passing some dread spot of tragic memory, a gentle Virgin at every turning, with a dingy, flickering flame beneath her image, is waiting to grant her grace—for is not Venice the Virgin City? And on the splendid palaces in the broad canals the watching Madonna stands glorified in exquisite sculpture and cunningest blendings of color,—ofttimes a crown of light above her, or rays of stars, symbolic, beneath her feet,—casting her benediction far out on the water, which, ever in motion, repeats it in shimmering, widening circles—all-embracing—in which the stars of heaven shine, tangled and confused with these stars of a paradise in which earth has so large a part.

Yet in the glory and charm of this Venetian night how should there be space for sorrow or thought of care, or cause for the tears which brimmed the eyes of the Lady Marina, as she sat in her sculptured balcony at the bend of the Canal Grande, watching for the coming of Marcantonio, who lingered late at the Senate when every moment was precious to her!

Ever since her husband had left her she had sat with her little one gathered convulsively in her arms, showering upon him a tenderness so passionate and so unlike herself in its uncontrolled ex-

330

pression, that the child, wondering and afraid, was but half-beguiled by the rare treat of the music and the lights of the Canal Grande, and clamored for his nurse.

And now he was gone, with a kiss upon his sweet, round baby-mouth that was like a benediction and a dirge in which a whole heart of wild mother love sobbed itself out in renunciation—but to him it was only strange. And she herself had hushed the grieving quiver of his lip, and quickly filled his dimpled hands with flowers to win the farewell caress of that dancing smile which irradiated his face like an April sunbeam, parting the pink lips over a vision of pearly infant teeth.

Below, in the chapel, her maidens were decking it as for a festa with vines and blossoms which she and Marco had brought that day—that heavenly day—from the beautiful island of Sant' Elenà, wandering alone, like rustic lovers, over the luxuriant flower-starred meadows and through the cloistered gardens of its ancient convent, lingering awhile in the chapel of the Giustiniani, while he rehearsed the deeds of those of his own name who slept there so tranquilly under their marble effigies—primate, ambassadors, statesmen, and generals; ay, and more than these—lovers, mothers, and little ones!

And now, while she sat alone in this holy moonlight, the voices of her maidens came in sounds of merriment through the fretted stonework of the great window, and a sweet odor of altar candles and incense mingled with the breath of the blossoms that was wafted up to her; for to-morrow, for the first time since her illness, there would be matins

331

in the chapel of the palazzo, and Marcantonio had assured her that the new father confessor was much like Fra Francesco—coming, also, from the convent of the Servi, that he might seem nearer to her who had so loved the gentle confessor.

Ay, she had loved him, with a holy reverence, for his goodness and gentleness and faith; for his inflexible grasp of duty, according to. his views of right; for his teachings, which she could understand and which she believed the Holy Mother had taught him—for his self-denial and suffering.

And now, for a few moments, she forgot herself —forgot to watch for Marco, her thoughts busied with the sad tale of Fra Francesco, which Piero, always *in viaggio* for business of the Senate, had told her but a few days before—news that had reached him from the frontier. The gentle confessor had indeed completed his pilgrimage, barefooted, to Rome, but had gained no favor with the Holy Father; having at first been welcomed as a deserter from the enemy's camp, flattered, and plied with questions, to which Fra Francesco gave no answers —wishing no harm to Venice nor to any who sat in the councils of the Republic. Whereupon his lodgings had been changed and all communications with the brothers of the Servite chapel in Rome had been forbidden. And again, and more than once, he had been brought forth to be questioned; and again there had been nothing told of that which they sought, for they asked him of his friends, and his heart was true. But it was told that he had used strange words. "Each man is answerable to his own soul and to God for that which he believeth. He answereth not for the faith of another man—nor shall he bring danger upon his friend—who hath also his conscience and God for judge of his faith and actions."

"But what of Fra Paolo?" he had been asked; "How doth he defend himself for leading thus the cause of Venice against Rome?"

"Am I my brother's keeper?" the gentle Fra Francesco had answered; and had said no more.

"Thou shalt at least show us how one may obtain speech with him, for the furtherance of his soul's salvation—apart from the vigilance of the Senate, and without suspicion in the convent that the message cometh from Rome, else were it not received in that unholy city."

And in this also Fra Francesco was obdurate. And then, for disobedience to authority, acknowledged lawful by his own submission, came prison—wherein he languished, always obdurate,—and death, —perhaps from discontent or homesickness, one knows not; or from failure of his plans; or—there was a question of torture, but one knows not if it were true.

"No, no, it was not true!" Marina had exclaimed, quivering, when Piero had told her the story. "It is wicked to say these things—and they are not true!"

But now, alone—apart from all the brightness about her, from every hope of happiness except those few brief hours with Marco—she did not know if it might not be true; her heart was too sad to deny any pain that had been or that might be; but Fra Francesco's sad and gentle eyes seemed to

333

smile upon her through whatever distance might be between them—of this, or of any other world—without reproach for those who had bidden him suffer, and charging her to keep her faith.

"If it be true," she said, "the end of pain is reached, and he hath won his happiness.— Why cometh not my Marco?"

A gondola of the Nicolotti detached itself from a group of serenaders just above the palace, was caught for a few moments among the *pali* before the Ca' Giustiniani, and then floated leisurely down toward the Piazzetta. She noted it idly while she sat waiting for Marco, for in the gondola there was a graceful figure, closely wrapped, clasping her mantle yet more closely with a hand that was white and slender enough for one of the nobility; yet the gondolier wore the black sash of the Nicolotti with the great hat of a bravo shading his face. "It is some intrigue," she said, almost unconsciously, in the midst of her sad dreaming.

"Oh, Marco, thou art come! It hath been long without thee."

"The Senate is but just dismissed," he answered, smiling fondly at the eagerness which gave to her pale face a passing flush of health. "But why is the Lady Beata not with thee?" he questioned abruptly.

"She is in the chapel, making it fair with flowers."

"Thou knowest it, Marina?"

"She came to me with a question but a little while ago, when Marconino was with me—and I wished to be alone. Marco, he was so beautiful! And the day has been a dream; I wished for no one but for thee alone."

He held her hand in a mute caress, but with preoccupation, while his eyes wandered back to the Piazzetta searchingly.

"It is strange," he muttered to himself, still watching from the end of the balcony. "It was an echo of the Lady Beata's voice that startled me, crossing the Piazzetta saying two words only—'In Padua.'"

Then rousing himself, he turned brightly to his wife. "Carina, I have news for thee, for the time hath been momentous for us in Venice. Di Gioiosa hath gone forward, these many days, with terms from Venice; and soon, it is thought, there will be peace."

Terms from Venice to Rome!—but the words did not move her from her resolve to let no shadow of their difference mar the beauty of this night.

She looked at him wearily. "It is ever the same," she said, "through this long, dreary year—ever the same! Let us forget it all for this one night. Let us talk together of our Marconino!"

And as if there had been no questions—no interdict—no pain—while the night sounds died into silence and the moon withdrew her glamor and left them alone to the solemn mystery of the starlight, they sat and talked together of love and their little one and their hopes for him, and of things that lie too deep for utterance—save by one to one—far into that beautiful Venetian night, with the odor of flowers and incense blown up to them on the breath of the sea.

335

XXIX

THE yellow lamp flames were burning late in the cabinet of Girolamo Magagnati, who took less note of the difference between evening hours and those of early dawn since there was no longer in his household a beloved one to guard from weariness. Nay, the night was rather the time in which he might forget himself and plunge more whole-heartedly into his schemes of work—financial or creative. For the world was surely on the eve of discoveries important to his art, and it would be well if he might secure them, before his working days should pass, for the Stabilimento Magagnati.

Piero Salin stood in the doorway as he glanced up from the drawings that littered his table—the dark oak table which had seemed a centre of cheer to Girolamo, when, in this very chamber, his child had made a radiance for him in which the lines of his life shone large and satisfying.

Girolamo never seemed to remember that this son-in-law was a great man among the people; to him he was only Piero Salin, barcariol; the single token of the old man's favor was that in his thought he no longer added the despicable word *toso;* and it was a proof that he was mellowing with the years, for Girolamo never forgot this unwelcome and dishonorable past, and Piero was always ill at ease in his presence.

"Messer Magagnati," he began awkwardly, twirling his black cap in his hand rather after the fashion of a gondolier than of the Chief of the Nicolotti, "I must crave, by dawn of the morrow, the blessing of San Nicolò—of holy memory."

"Enter," said Girolamo, with a reluctance not wholly concealed by his attempt at courtesy, for he felt the moments to be the more precious that the dawn was near; but the invocation of the sailor's patron saint portended a journey. "Verily, Piero, thy comings and goings have been, of late, so frequent that one learns the wisdom of not mourning over-much when thou dost crave an ave at the shrine of San Nicolò. May he grant thee favoring breezes! Thou art in favor with the Ten, they tell me."

Piero shrugged his shoulders. "Favor or disfavor," he said, "it is but the turning of the head—and both may lead to that place of unsought distinction between San Marco and San Teodoro, if the orders of their Excellencies bring not the end they sought. But it matters little—a candle flame is better blown out than dying spent."

"And whither art thou bent on the morrow?"

"Nay, Messer Girolamo, that is not mine own secret. But this word would I leave with thee; if, perchance, I return not before many days, seek me on the border-land—at the point nearest Roman dominions." He had come close to the old merchant, and uttered the last words in a tone very low and full of meaning.

Girolamo started. "On the border-land of Rome!" he echoed. "This mission of thine is then weighty; and thou fearest——"

"Nay, I fear naught," said Piero haughtily. "But the times are perilous; and later, if thou would'st seek me, thou hast the clew. But of the mission, to which I am sworn in secrecy, let it not be known that I have so much as named it—it would argue ill for me and thee. And the clew is for thy using only. Meanwhile, forget that I have spoken. The Ave Maria will soon waken the fishers of Murano. *Addio!*"

But he still waited as if he had not uttered all his mind. Girolamo studied his face closely.

"There is more," he said. "Speak!"

"By the Holy Madonna of San Donato!" said Piero, casting off his restraint with a sudden impulse, "if I come not back, I would have thee know that if ever there came a chance to me to serve Marina—the Lady Marina of the Giustiniani—I, Piero, barcariol or gastaldo, would serve her as a soldier may serve a saint. For she hath been good to the Zuanino. Ay, though it cost me my life, I would serve her like a saint in heaven!" he repeated. Then, flushed with the shame of such unwonted speech and confession, he hastened to the door, and his steps were already resounding on the stone floor of the passage when Girolamo recovered from his astonishment sufficiently to follow him into the shadow and command him to stop.

"Thou hast seen my daughter—thou hast news of her?"

"Ay, yestere'en, at the Ave Maria, I spoke with

her, in Santa Maria dell' Orto, coming upon her kneeling before the great picture of Jacopo Robusti —she, saint enough already to wear a gloria and looking as if the heart of her were worn away from grief! She hath need of thee daily, for her love for thee is great, and death not far."

"Tell it plainly!" commanded Girolamo, hastening after the retreating figure and violently grasping his arm to detain him. "Have I failed to her in aught? She is soul of my soul! Maledetto! why dost thou break my heart?"

"Look to thine other son-in-law!" Piero retorted wrathfully; "him of the crimson robe who sits in the Councils of Venice, and findeth no cure for thy daughter—dying of terror beside him."

"It is a base slander!" cried old Girolamo, trembling with anger and fear. "Never was wife more beloved and petted! Marcantonio hath no thought, save for Marina and Venice!"

"Ay, 'for Marina and Venice,'" was the scornful answer, *"but Venice first.* Splendor and gifts and the pleasing of every whim, if he could but guess it—gold for her asking, and her palace no better than a cross for her dwelling; for the one thing she needeth for her peace and life he giveth not!"

"What meanest thou?" cried Girolamo, furiously. "Hath he not spent a fortune on physicians—sparing nothing, save to torment her no more, since their skill is but weariness to her! She is eating her heart out for this quarrel with Rome—which no man may help, and it is but foolishness for women to meddle with; and she hath ever been too much

339

under priestly sway. Why camest thou hither this night?"

"For this cause and for no other," said Piero solemnly, "that thou mightest find me, if need should be for any service to *her*. And to swear to thee, by the Madonna and every saint of Venice, that I would give my life for her!"

But old Girolamo grew the angrier for Piero's professions of loyalty. "Shall her father do less than thou?" he questioned, wrathfully. "On the morrow will I go to her, and leave her no more until she forgets."

"By all the saints in heaven, and every Madonna in Venice, and our Lady of every traghetto!" Piero exclaimed, as he wrenched himself away from Girolamo's angry grasp, while the old man staggered against the wall, still holding a bit of cloth from the gondolier's cloak in his closed hand, "I am vowed to my mission before this dawn! What I have spoken is for duty to thine house, and not in anger—though I could color my stiletto in good patrician blood and die for it gaily, if that would help her!"

But Girolamo could not yet find his voice, and Piero, with his hand on the latch of the great iron gates of the water-story, turned and called back: "Women are not like men, and Marina is like no other woman that ever was born in Venice. Whether it be the priests that have bewitched her— may the Holy Madonna have mercy, and curse them for it!—or whether she be truly the Blessed Virgin of San Donato come to earth again, one knows not. But, Messer Magagnati,"—and the voice came solemnly from the dark figure dimly outlined against the gray darkness beyond the iron bars,—"thy daughter is dying for this curse of the Most Holy Father—'il mal anno che Dio le dia!' (may heaven make him suffer for it!)—and she hath no peace in Venice. *She will never forget nor change.* If thy love be great, as thou hast said, thou wilt find some way to help her. *For in Venice she hath no peace.*"

The old merchant, dazed by Piero's hot words, was a pitiful figure, standing, desolate, behind the closed bars of his gate, the night wind lifting his long beard and parting the thin gray locks that flowed from under his cap, while he called and beckoned impotently to Piero to return, repeating meanwhile mechanically, with no perception of their meaning, those strange words of Piero's—*"In Venice she hath no peace."* He stood, peering out into the gray gloom and listening to the lessening plash of the oar, until the gondola of the gastaldo was already far on the way to San Marco, where sat the Ten.

But it was not of Piero's mission he was thinking, but of his child—saying over and over again those fateful words, "In Venice she hath no peace." Had Piero said that?

Suddenly the entire speech recurred to him—insistent, tense with meaning. She could not live in Venice. Marina had no peace in Venice. She would never forget nor change. She had need of him—of her father's love; and if he loved enough, *he would find a way!*

Chilled and heart-sick he turned, and with no

341

torch and missing the voice which had guided him through the long, dark passage, he groped his way to his cabinet and sat down to confront a graver problem than any he had ever conquered with Marina's aid. He *would* find a way—but "it must not be in Venice!" How could they leave Venice? Were they not Venetians born, and was not Venice in trouble? To leave her now were to deny her. *It could not be!*

He put the argument many times, feverishly at first, then more calmly—coming always to the same conclusion, "it could not be." It was a comfort to reach so sensible and positive a decision. To-morrow he would go to his daughter, and meanwhile he must continue his work; he needed to reassert his power, for he had been strangely shaken.

He drew the scattered papers together, but the lines, blurred and confused, carried no meaning; the fragments of broken glass in the little trays beside him were a dull, untranslucent gray, and written all over papers and fragments, in vivid letters that burned into his brain, were those other terrible words of Piero's which he had tried in vain to forget—"Thy daughter is dying for this curse." *Marina—dying!*

How should Piero know more about Marina than her own father knew? Did he profess to be a physician that one should credit his every word? What did he mean by his impudent boast of "dying for her, if need should be!" Had she not her husband and father to care for her? Her husband "who was denying her the only thing that could give her life and peace," Piero had said.—What was the matter with his insulting words, that he could not forget them?—Had she not her father, who was going to her on the morrow, when he had matured his plans, and would do whatever she wished—"in Venice"? Her father "who loved her, as his own soul"—that was what he had said to Piero, with the memory of all those dear years when they had been all in all to each other, in this home.

Was it for hours or moments only that he sat in torture—enduring, reasoning, placing love against pride, Marina against Venice, Venice against a father's weakness, duty to the Republic before the need of this only child who was "soul of his soul"?

The last of his race—inheriting the traditions and passionate attachments of that long line of loyal men who had founded and built up the stabilimento which was the pride of Murano; of the people, yet ennobled by the proffer of the Senate, and grandsire to the son of one of the highest nobles of the Republic—what was there left in life for him away from Venice? How should he bear to die dishonored and disinherited by the country which he had deserted in her hour of struggle? For never any more might one return who should desert. Venice for Rome!

And those panes of brilliant, crystal clarity which he had dreamed of adding to the honors of the Stabilimento Magagnati—so strong that a single sheet might be framed in the great spaces of the windows of the palaces and show neither curve nor flaw—so pure that their only trace of color should come from a chance reflection which would but lend added charm—these might not be the discovery of his later

343

days, though the time was near in which this gift *must* come to Venice. He had not dreamed that he could ever say, while strength yet remained to think and plan, "The house of Magagnati has touched its height, and others may come forward to do the rest for Venice."

And the secret lay so near—scarcely eluding him! It was no mere empty jealousy, nor trivial wish for fame, nor greed of recompense—of which he had enough—that forced the veins out on the strong forehead of this master-worker, as he struggled with this question of surrendering all for his daughter's peace. It was the art in which his ancestors had taken the lead from the earliest industrial triumphs of the Republic—an art in which Venice stood first —and in his simple belief it was not less to their glory than the work of a Titian or a Sansovino. In this field he wrought whole-hearted, with the passion of an artist who has achieved, and his place and part in the Republic, as in life, was bounded for him by his art. "To stand with folded hands— always, hereafter, to be unnecessary to Venice!"

How should one who had not been born in Venice ever guess the strange fascination of that magic city for her sons, or dream with what a passion the blood of generations of Venetian ancestry surged in one's veins, compelling patriotism, so that it was not possible to do aught with one's gifts and life that did not enhance the greatness of so fair a kingdom! It was the wonderful secret of the empire of Venice that here the pride of self was counted only as a factor in the superior pride of her dominion.

Marina had been proud of his cabinet, and he took the little antique lamp she used to hold for him and unlocked the door with a tremulous hand, standing unsteadily before it and trying to hearten himself, as he ruthlessly flashed the light so that each fantastic bit came out in perfect beauty, glowing with the wonderful coloring of transparent gems.

But suddenly those fearful words of Piero's played riot among them, obliterating every trace of beauty, every claim of Venice, every question as to his own judgment or Marina's reasoning—even the ignominy of the secret flight. *"Thy daughter dying!"*

The letters blazed like stars, gleaming among his papers—glittering around the chair where Marina used to sit, climbing up into the air, closing nearer to him—wavering, writhing lines of living fire, tracing those awful words he could not forget——

"My God!" he cried, "is not Marina more than all!" There was no longer anything in life that he willed to do but to win peace for her, according to her whim.

"Stino!" he shrieked, with a voice louder than the clang of the rude iron bell whose rope had broken in his impetuous hand.

"Light me a fire in the brazier, and burn me this rubbish!" he commanded of the foreman who entered, aghast at the imperious summons, and yet more amazed at the destruction of those precious pages over which his master had spent days of brooding; but he ventured no protest.

"And here," said Girolamo, with a look of relief,

345

as the last paper shrivelled and curled into smoke, "are the keys of these cabinets—thou knowest their contents, and that they are precious. And here shalt thou remain, as master, until my return—keeping all in order, as thou knowest how, and loyally serving the interest of the stabilimento. All moneys which I may send for thou shalt instantly remit by trusty messenger."

"How long doth the Master remain away?"

"So long as it may please the Lady Marina, who hath need of change. And if I return not," Girolamo resumed, after a moment's pause which gave solemnity to his words, "my will shall be found filed with the Avvogadori del Commun; and thou, Stino, shalt answer to the summons they will send thee—if I come no more."

"Master!" cried the faithful Stino, greatly troubled, for these preparations filled him with dread, and were strange indeed for so old a man who had never yet left Venice for a night. "Life is other than we know it away from Venice; and the heart of us goes mourning for the sight and sound of the sea and the color of our skies!"

"Nay, Stino, I have said it," his master answered, unmoved by his imploring eyes.

"When goest thou—that all may be ready?"

"Now; ere the dawn!" Girolamo cried with sudden resolution. "I would say my Ave Maria in the chapel of the Lady Marina. Rouse the gondolier, and lift the curtain that I may see how soon the day cometh."

"Master, dear Master," said Stino tenderly, as he drew the heavy draperies aside. "Already the sun is high, and the household hath been, these many hours, awake."

"So!" Girolamo answered with deep gravity, for the battle had been longer than he had dreamed, yet with his habitual control. "I knew not the time—my thoughts held me. Stino, if I return not, may the saints bless thee for all thou hast been to me since the Lady Marina hath dwelt in the palazzo Giustiniani. And in my will thou art not forgotten."

As Girolamo issued from his own portal, closely followed by Stino and the other superintendents of the great stabilimento who were filled with foreboding at this sudden and surprising decision of their good master, several gondolas wearing the colors of the Giustiniani floated into the waterway from the broad lagoon; and with them, like a flock of sea-birds in their habits of gray and their cowls of white, came the sisters of San Donato, returning from that early chanted Mass at the palazzo Giustiniani which had been a dream of the Lady Marina's happier days.

The young Senator had urged his boatmen to feverish speed, and his own gondola was far in advance of the train. He bounded from his bark the moment it neared the steps, and, rushing blindly toward the dwelling, encountered his father-in-law on the threshold.

"She is here—Marina?" he questioned, half crazed with grief; and, forgetful of the usual courtesies, would have pushed him aside to enter. "I have come with her maidens and her child to take her home. Let me go to her!"

And, as Girolamo stood, dumb and dazed, "I beseech thee—conceal her not!"

Looking into each other's faces for one anguished moment, they knew, without need of further speech, that she had gone from them both.

Girolamo gave a great and bitter cry, "My son!" folding his arms about the younger man in measureless grief and compassion.

And when they could trust their footsteps they went desolately into the house together.

. . . .

"Nay," Girolamo had answered to every argument. "It is for thee to remain in Venice with her child, that the Signoria be not wroth with the Ca' Giustiniani, and for me to seek and care for her— mayhap, if heaven be merciful, to bring her to thee again! She cannot be far to seek."

"In Padua!" cried Marcantonio, with sudden conviction. "They will sleep in Padua to-night. It *was* the voice of the Lady Beata!"

XXX

"ART thou sure, Marina?"
"Ay, Piero, though it were death to me; and death were sweeter——"

Her hair lay like a wreath of snow across her forehead, from stress of the night's vigil, her lip trembled like a grieved child's, but in her exquisite face there was the grace of a spirit strong and tender.

He helped her silently into the gondola and steered it carefully between the pali which rose like a scattered sheaf, glowing with the colors of the Giustiniani, in the water before her palace. And thus, in the early dawn—unattended, with the sadness of death in her pallid face—the lady of the Giustiniani floated away from her beautiful home—away from happiness and love—into a future cheerless and dim as the dawn lights that were faintly tinging the sea. For the day was breaking, full of gloom, under a sky of clouds, and the wind blew chill from across the Lido.

She sat with her gray mantle shrouding her face, and neither of them spoke, while the gondola, under Piero's deft guidance, quickly gained the steps of the Piazzetta and passed on to San Giorgio. Then she touched his arm entreatingly.

"Oh, let us wait one moment before we lose sight

349

of the palazzo! Madre Beatissima, have them in thy keeping!"

She stretched out her hands unconsciously, with a gesture of petition, and her mantle slipped back, exposing her pallid, pain-stricken face and her whitened tresses.

Piero was startled at the havoc the night had made, for he had seen her only the day before, in answer to her summons, when she had been far more like herself.

"Santa Maria!" he exclaimed, crossing himself, and awkward under the unaccustomed sense of an overwhelming compassion. "The Holy Mother must shrive me for breaking my vow, for if San Marco and San Teodoro would give me a place between them before the matins ring again—mistaking me for a traitor—I cannot take thee from Venice. We will return," and already the gondola was yielding to his stroke. "Let Marcantonio bring thee himself to Rome."

"Piero, thou hast sworn to me! Thou shalt abide by thy promise!" she cried, seizing the oar in her trembling hand.

"Ay, Marina, I have sworn to thee," he answered, with slow pauses, "and by our Holy Mother of San Giorgio, I will serve thee like a saint in heaven. Yet I would thou wert in thy home again—already thou hast broken thy heart for love of it."

The gondolas of the people were gathering about the steps of the palaces, bringing their burdens for the day's ongoings in those luxurious homes; the bells were calling to early Mass; the stir of life was beginning in the city; soon, in her own palace, her little one would wake, and Marco— She stood with straining eyes, yearning for the chance of a face in her palace window—the bare last chance of another sight of his dear face. She did not know that Piero was watching her—compassionate and comprehending—while she was struggling to out-live the agony for the very love's sake which made it so keen.

It was the only sweetness left in life for her, that this cruel parting was yet for Marco's sake; that she might still plead with the Holy Father for this desperate need of which Marco seemed unconscious —since, in a vision never to be forgotten, the blessed Madre of San Donato had confided this mission to her. She could bear everything to win such a bless-ing for her beloved ones, only she must reach Rome—surely the Madre Beatissima would let her live to reach the Holy City!

The tide was brimming the canals, rising over the water steps; the growing light gleamed coldly on the polished marbles of her palace, burnishing the rich gold fretwork of frieze and tracery—but not any face of any dear one responded to her hun-gry longing, watching for her in the deep spaces of the windows, in token of the love from which she was fleeing.

This also—this last longing—she must surrender!

Her white face grew brave again; she sat down and drew her veil—the ample *fazzuolo* of the Mu-ranese—more closely about her. "I am ready," she said, and turned her face resolutely forward.

As they rounded San Giorgio, turning into the broad Giudecca, a shoal of little boats came over the water from Murano.

"They are the nuns of San Donato!" she said in

amazement, and drawing her veil closer. "Piero, canst thou not ask their whither?"

It was so strange, on this morning of all others, to see them turn in the direction of Ca' Giustiniani; there came a vision of her chapel, which her maidens were decking—of the dear altar, at which she should kneel no more—and she held her breath to hear the answer.

"Will the most Reverend Mother bless the boat of a gondolier of the people; and his sister, who hath been ill and craveth the morning air?" Piero, who had discarded every emblem of his office, and wore only the simple dress of the Nicolotti, put the question easily, without fear of recognition. "And there is no great trouble in the city which calleth these illustrious ladies so early from Murano?"

"Nay; but the Senator Giustiniani hath prayed us for a grace to his sweet lady, for the chapel hath been closed while she hath been too ill for service; and to-day it will be opened, dressed with flowers, and we—because she loveth greatly our Madonna of San Donato and hath shown bounty, with munificent gifts, to all the parish—will chant the matins in her oratory."

They gave the benediction and passed.

While Marcantonio, with his tender thought for Marina fresh in his heart, was waking to find only her note of farewell.

"Only because I love thee, Marco mio, I have the strength to leave thee. And it is the Madonna who hath called me. Forgive, and forget not thy sad Marina."

"Marina—" Piero began awkwardly, for argument was not his forte, and Marina had always conquered him. " 'Chi troppo abbraccia nulla stringe,' one gains nothing who grasps too much. Thou wast ever one for duty, and if the Senator Marcantonio will not take thee to Rome———"

"No, Piero, he cannot; he is one of the rulers of Venice."

"Thou, then—his wife———"

How could he venture to counsel her, of whose will and wisdom he had always stood in awe? It seemed to Piero that he had already delivered an oration; yet he felt that there was more to say, but his thoughts grew confused in seeking for expression, and it was a relief to him to communicate his uncertainty to the motion of his gondola.

The unsteady movement said more to her than words, for Piero was an unfailing stroke.

"It is the men only of whom the Republic hath need," she explained, unflinchingly; "but for the women there is no conflict of duty—the Holy Church is first. 'Prayers for the women and deeds for the men'—thou hast seen it written."

"And thy father?" Piero questioned, unconvinced, recalling the interview of a few hours before.

A quick, tender light flashed and passed in her eyes; a ray of color trembled on her cheek. "I shall grieve him," she said, "but he will forgive, for ever hath he bidden me choose the right." Her voice broke and she was silent, while she sought for some token in the folds of her robe. "Thou wilt take him this when thou returnest, that he may know I hold him dear.'

"Marina!" he pleaded, growing eloquent, with a last desperate effort, "thou wast ever an angel to the Zuanino—thou canst not leave thine own bimbo!"

She did not answer immediately, but she clasped and unclasped her hands passionately. "He is safe," she said at last, very low and struggling for control. "He hath the blessing of the Holy Father, given when it might avail; and the little ones are ever in the care of the Blessed Mother. It is not for my baby that I needs must go—but for Marco and my father, and for Venice. Santissima Maria, because thou sendest me, shalt thou not grant the strength!"

There was a silence between them while they floated on, for Piero had many things to think of. He was accustomed to accomplish whatever he undertook, for he was not a man to fail from lack of resource, nor to be overcome by fears and scruples. By means of his passes and his favor with the government he could reach the borders of the Venetian dominions without suspicion, from whence he would escort Marina to the nearest convent and place her in safety with the Mother Superior, to whom he would confide the story of her distinguished guest and secure for her the treatment due to a Venetian princess; which, under the circumstances, would be an easy matter, as no member of a noble Venetian house espousing the side of Rome would be met with any but the most flattering reception. To provide Marina with companionship, Piero had confided her intended flight to the Lady Beata Tagliapietra, being sure of her devotion; and she would be waiting for them at Padua with two trusted gondoliers and whatever might be needful from the wardrobe of the Lady of the Giustiniani. The fact that he had broken his promise of secrecy did not trouble him, since it was in Marina's service, which made the action honorable; and were it not so, the little perjury was well atoned for by a keg of oil anonymously sent to the traghetto of San Nicolò è San Raffaele, "pel luminar al Madonna";[1] and Piero had much faith in anonymous gifts, for confessions were not always convenient for an officer of his dignity. But it was perhaps too much to expect that these poor little traghetto lamps should be more than dimly luminous, since the oil was so largely provided by fines for delinquencies!

With an easy conscience, also, he had helped himself to the requisite funds for their journey, amply estimated, from the treasury of the Nicolotti, which was in his keeping; and his reasoning savored of Venetian subtlety, with a hint of his toso training. Had not the Lady of the Giustiniani offered to guarantee the funds necessary for the assessments of the state, when Piero, doubtful of their resources, would have declined the position of gastaldo grande, cumbered as it was with the uncomfortable requirement that the chief should be personally responsible for all dues and taxes levied upon the traghetti? Piero was not the first gastaldo who had wished to escape an honor that weighed so heavily, and a very serious penalty was already decreed for such contempt of office by that tribunal tireless in vigilance.

So, without compunction, Piero had taken the

[1] To light the Madonna.

needful, sure that when he returned Marina's husband or her father would repay it.

Could he return—after helping a patrician to escape from Venice into the heart of the country with which the Republic was at war? It looked doubtful even to Piero, with his indomitable temperament, but he wasted no sentiment upon this question; for if he might not return there were other countries in which a man could live. Or, should he be pursued and lighted upon by the far-seeing eye of the Ten, he could die but once and get into trouble no more! He crossed himself decorously as he dismissed the matter; but it was not an event that he could change by pondering.

There was another question that interested him more keenly at this moment; when Messer Girolamo should know that his daughter was not in Venice, could he fail to comprehend the hint he had given a few hours before, and would he not follow them to Rome, as Piero devoutly hoped, for he wished to leave Marina in her father's care. It was not easy to predict what Messer Girolamo might do—the case had been too doubtful for a more explicit confession, and Piero had been wise in his generation.

He turned now to Marina with the question: "If thou hadst told thy father of thy wish mayhap he might have come with thee?"

She shook her head sadly and made no answer, but after awhile she said, "He is like the others. They cannot understand the need, for to them the Madonna hath not revealed the desperate state of Venice."

"Yet thou knowest, Marina, that already the great cardinal—but lately come from France—hath started for Rome to make up this quarrel?"

"That is what the Senate will not understand!" she cried, with flashing eyes. "The Holy Father will have submission and penance, in place of embassies and pomp. One must go to him quite simply, from the people, saying, 'We have sinned; have mercy upon Venice!' Piero, thou knowest that awful vision of the Tintoret? It is Venice that he hath painted in her doom—the great floods bursting in upon her—all the agony and the anguish and the desolation of God's wrath! Santa Maria! I cannot bear it!" She closed her eyes, shuddering and sick with terror.

"It was the way with Jacopo," said Pietro irreverently. "He was full of freaks, and some demon hath tormented him. He was a man like others—not one for a revelation."

"Hush, Piero!" she implored; "it breaks my heart! This also may be counted against Venice, for it is the Holy Madonna who hath granted me the vision."

If Piero was silent he was only restrained by deference to Marina from invoking the aid of every saint in the calendar, in copious malediction, on this miserable Jacopo who had so increased the trouble in Marina's eyes—since women had such foolish faith in pictures.

"Jacopo Robusti, posing for a seer, and foretelling the end of the world, like a prophet or a saint! *Goffone!*[1] Piero was paddling furiously. "Ja-

[1] Great fool!

357

copo, of the Fondamenta dei Mori—not better than others—with that boastful sentence blazoned on his door!—'The coloring of Titian, with the drawing of Angelo!'"

But he forgot even his resentment against Jacopo in his anxiety as he watched Marina, asking himself if it would be possible for her to pray herself back into healthful life again, even in the dominions of the Holy Father; for he realized that nothing could help her but this one thing on which her heart was set—while he was yet, if possible, more utterly without sympathy for the fear that moved her than her father or Marcantonio had been. But if the one woman in Venice had but one desire, however desperate and incomprehensible,—"*Basta!* It is enough," said Piero to himself,—she should not die with it unfulfilled, if he could compass it.

Yet, at the thought of death his heart sank. "It was the Madonna which thou beheldest in thy vision —not the cross?" he asked her quickly, making the fateful sign as he spoke, to avert this dread presage of death, and afraid of her answer; for Marina was failing before his eyes, and doubtless, in her vision, there had been some apparition of a cross; and even the less devout among the gondoliers were still dominated by some of the superstitions which gave a picturesque color to the habits of the people.

But she, too earnest in her faith to take any note of a less serious mood, answered simply:

"It was the very Madonna herself, as thou knowest her in San Donato, who came to me in the palazzo one night when I slept not, and gave me the mission to save Venice,—scarce able to speak for her great sadness, and the tears dropping, as thou knowest her in San Donato,—commanding me to go before the Holy Father and pray for mercy to Venice. She it was who told me that our prayers pass not up beyond the clouds which hang above a city under doom of interdict. Oh, Piero, hasten; for my strength is little, and Rome is far!"

When the Lady of the Giustiniani had sent for Piero to meet her in Santa Maria dell' Orto, to ask him to manage her escape to Rome, it had not been possible to refuse her; all his attempts at reasoning were in vain. "I must go," she said, with that invincible persistence which he never could combat. "If thou wilt not help me, I go alone." She was kneeling before the terrible "Judgment" of the Tintoret, and the face she had lifted to him in appeal was white with agonized comprehension.

The journey had been long and wearisome; all day they had been slowly toiling against the tide; and long since Piero had summoned to his aid a trusted gondolier who had been ordered to follow them at a little distance, and who, at a sign from the gastaldo, had silently left his bark to drift and taken his place at the other end of the gondola in which the fugitives were making their way to Padua.

They had passed the domain of the Laguna Morta, weird and half-forbidding, with tangles of sea-plants and upspringing wild fowl calling to each other with hoarse cries across the marshes—with armies of water beetles zigzagging in the shallows, and crabs and lizards crawling upon the scattered sand heaps among the coarse sea-grasses, while small fish brought unexpected dimples to the deeper pools that lay between. And the mingled odor of waters fresh and salt was broken into a breath now pungent and pleasant, now almost noisome, as the light breeze stirred the shallows of this strange domain which was neither land nor sea. Yet even here the pale sea-holly and the evening primrose made redeeming spots of beauty, with their faint hues of violet and yellow; and a distant water-meadow shimmered like the sea, with the tender blue of the spreading lavender.

They had passed Fusina, and the lagoon lay silvery, like a trail of moonlight behind them—Venice in the distance, opalesque, radiant, a city of dreams. The clouds above them, beautiful with changing sunset lights, were no longer mirrored on a still lagoon, but mottled the broken surfaces of the river with hues of bronze and purple, between the leaves of the creeping water-plants which clogged the movement of the oars; for they had exchanged the liquid azure pavement of their "Città Nobilissima" for the brown tide of the Brenta. On the river's brink the rushes were starred with lilies and iris and ranunculus, and the fragrance of sheeted flowers from the water-meadows came to them fresh and delicious, mingled with the salt breath of the sea, while swallows — dusky, violet-winged — circled about their bows, teasing their progress with mystic eliptical flight—like persistent problems perpetually recurring, yet to be solved by fate alone.

It was the hour of the Ave Maria, and Marina roused herself from her sad reverie. The clouds piled themselves in luminous masses and drifted into the hollows of the wonderful Euganean hills, and a crimson sunset tinged peaks and clouds with glory, as Padua with its low arcaded streets, and San Antonio—cousin to San Marco in minarets and Eastern splendor—and the Lion of Saint Mark upon his lofty column, closed the vista of their weary day.

The chimes of Venice were too far for sound, but from every campanile of this quaint city the vesper bells, solemn and sweet, pealed forth their call to prayer—as if no threat of Rome's displeasure made a discord in their harmony.

XXXI

PIERO had watched all night before the little inn of the "Buon Pesce," impatient to meet and conquer his fate, while above, in an upper room, the ladies Marina and Beata tried to sleep; but before the dawn they were off again, down by the way of the brown, rolling river, taking the weary length to Brondolo and the sea.

There were two gondolas now, and the men in each pulled as if the prize of a great regatta awaited them—Nicolotti against Castellani—and silently, saving voice and strength for a great need.

It might have seemed a pleasure party, save for the stress of their speed, as they swept by the groves of poplar and catalpa, which bordered the broad flood, to the sound of the waters only and the song of the birds in the wood; water-lilies floated in the pools along the shore; currents of fragrance were blown out to them on wandering winds; and in the felze, as they were nearing Brondolo, Marina and the Lady Beata, soothed by the gliding motion and the monotonous plash of the oars into the needed sleep which the night had failed to bring them, were unaware of the colloquy between Piero and his gondolier.

"Antonio!" Piero called cautiously to the man who was rowing behind the felze, "I have somewhat to say to thee; are there those within thy vision who may hear our speech?"

"Padrone, no; but the time is short for speaking much, for we reach the lock with another turn of the Brenta."

"May the blessed San Nicolò send sunshine to dazzle the jewels in the eyes of Messer San Marco till we are safe beyond it and out of Chioggia!" Piero exclaimed fervently. "And thou, Antonio, swear me again thy faith—or swear it not, as thou wilt. But thou shalt choose this moment whom thou wilt serve; and it shall go ill with thee if thou keep not thy troth."

"By San Marco and San Teodoro," Antonio responded readily, crossing himself devoutly as he spoke, "I swear to do thy bidding, Messer Gastaldo."

"And thou wilt die for· the people against the nobles if need should be?"

"If thou leadest, Gastaldo Grande."

"Hast thou a pouch beneath thy stiletto where thou mayest defend with thy life what I shall give thee?"

Antonio displayed it silently.

"This for the need of the cause in thy hand," said Piero, passing him a purse of gold. "But gold is worthless to this token which shall win thee the hearing of the bancali, and the aid of every loyal son of San Nicolò, and shall be proof that thou bearest my orders and my trust."

The trust was great—the bancali were the governing board of the traghetti.

Antonio unfastened his doublet and secured the precious token under his belt.

363

"Command then, cáro padrone."

"Slacken thy pace, for this may be our last speech together. Are those who follow true as thou?"

"Messer Gastaldo," Antonio answered with reluctance, "by signs which be but trifles to relate,—by a word dropped in Padua, and not for mine ear,—one of them—I know not which—hath, perchance, affair with a master mightier than thou." He made the usual gesture which indicated the Three of that terrible Inquisition whose name was better left unsaid—a sign much used in Venice where the very walls had ears.

It was a blow to Piero, but he wasted no words.

"They then—both—are apart from this and all my counsel. It shall be for thee alone, Antonio."

"So safer, Messer Gastaldo. I listen—and forget, save as it shall serve thee."

"First, then, Antonio; I have sworn to escort the Lady of the Giustiniani in safety to Rome, from which naught shall keep me—save if the Ten have other plans, the Madonna doth forgive the broken vow!"

It was a strange admission from a man stalwart and fearless like Piero, but he made it without shame, as a soldier acquiescing in destiny.

"Santissima Maria!" Antonio ejaculated with unusual fervor and crossing himself in full realization of the meaning.

"At Brondolo a brig is waiting—orange and yellow of sail, device of a blazing sun; a hunchback, with doublet of orange above the mast for luck, and a fine figure of a *gobbo* upon the deck—a living hunchback—by which thou shalt know it for mine, and bound to my order whether it come by me or by my token. If we reach and board her it shall be well—and Rome, so will it heaven, before us all! But if the dreaded ones are on the search and overtake us——"

Again the sign.

The tragedy of the situation was in his face as he looked steadily at Antonio, who did not flinch.

"Thy duty, then, Antonio, shall lie elsewhere. Thou must escape, unseen, while they lay hands upon the lady and me, whom first they will secure before they give thee a thought."

Antonio instantly touched his stiletto, and looked his question with a fearless glance.

"Nay," said the gastaldo scornfully, and drawing a line quickly about his own throat. "Thou wilt serve me better with thy head in its place. Thou shalt return to Venice—by Fusina or Brondolo, as thy wit shall serve thee—leaving the precions gondolieri to prove whether their silken sashes be badges of men or traitors! Art thou listening?"

"Command me, padrone!"

"Within two days, if I be free, the bancali shall have news of me. Listen well, Antonio,"—again the hand and eyes went up with the dreaded unmistakable sign,—"if thou seest THEM seize me before thou takest leave, wait no longer than to plan with the bancali to come and demand my release. Thou shalt tell the bancali that I sent thee; thou shalt tell them there are affairs of moment for the Nicolotti which shall go hard for the traghetti if I be not there to work them—Art listening, Antonio?" he questioned feverishly.

Antonio's eyes were fastened upon his. "Padrone, yes!" he answered breathlessly.

"With my token thou canst command the loyalty of every Nicolotto—is it thine oar that made that rustle?—and perchance, if'there were a rising of the traghetti to demand aught of the Signoria—come nearer, Antonio!—the Castellani also, if they willed to join with their traghetti in asking for justice—would not serve under my token the less heartily for the word, confided low to their bancali—dost understand?—*that if their taxes and their fines oppress them*, these also, I being free, will pay this year to the maledetto Avvogadoro del Commun."

Antonio gravely bowed his head in assent.

"This at thy discretion—thou understandest, Antonio—and so that no violence come from the massing of the people, but only the proof of its will and of the numbers who make the demand. Only—if it be not granted, they shall make a stand at the traghetti and *fight*——"

"Padrone, yes!"

"For—thou dost mark me, Antonio?—this Lady of the Giustiniani hath been a saint among the people; she hath given them much in gifts—she hath given almost her life in prayers and penances, that heaven may avert its wrath from Venice, which she in truth believeth the Holy Father—may the saints make him suffer for it!—hath brought upon the people by his curse—may heaven forbid! And she, being now noble, hath preferred the cause of the *people* to the cause of the *nobles*, and bringeth upon her the displeasure of the Signoria by her flight to

Rome. For—see it well, Antonio!—if the Senate hold the Lady of the Giustiniani for fault in this,"—Piero paused and uttered the last words with a slow, mysterious emphasis, while Antonio listened with an intensity that missed no shading of meaning,—*"it will be the cause of the people against the nobles."*

"If they harm her not," he resumed in his usual tone, after a moment's pause, "my fate shall be avenged in the judgment and command of the bancali of the Nicolotti only. They shall not risk the people's good for the poor life of one leader!"

"Padrone!" Antonio cried, with flashing eyes. "Commandi altro?" ("Hast thou other commands?")

"None, save that if I return not—and not otherwise—thou shalt seek with my token the Master Girolamo Magagnati; thou shalt tell him of this my confidence, holding nothing back; and thou shalt pray him, of his honor, to discharge the debt which may be found lacking in the treasury of the Nicolotti,—since the moneys have been taken for the need of the lady on her journey,—the which, if I return, I have means, and more, to repay."

The two men grasped hands and looked into each other's eyes for a brief recording moment, having each touched that *best* in the other which was not shown to all men, and so begotten trust each in each.

"By the Holy Madonna and San Nicolò, I will not fail!" Antonio promised, and in a moment had seized his oar again and was springing forward on the bridge of his gondola, as if his thoughts were light and rhythmic as his motions.

They sped on with a few swift, silent strokes—then, "Brondolo!" he cried brightly; but a sudden desperate steadying of resolution was felt in the fierce stroke which sent the gondola forward with a jerk.

The fishing-skiffs of Chioggia fluttered like gaudy butterflies before them, dipping their wings of orange and crimson and every conceivable sunset tint to catch the breeze; and the air was suddenly vibrant with sounds of traffic and busy life. Men called to each other with song and jest from heavily laden barks, while they waited the hour of sailing; or lay at ease on the top of their wares, smoking luxurious draughts of content from their comrade pipes,—lords of their craft, though their couch was but a pile of cabbages or market produce,—exchanging some whimsical comment upon the affairs of busier neighbors which brimmed these frequent hours of *dolce far niente* with unflagging interest.

And there, among the lighter shipping, was the brig bound to the order of the gastaldo grande, with the yellow sails and device of the rising sun—with the gobbo in orange doublet on the masthead for good luck, and the gobbo on the deck to make it sure. Piero turned and looked for it, as they passed the lock. And there too——

"Corpo di San Marco!" ejaculated Antonio under his breath, for he stood higher than Piero upon the bridge of the gondola and facing forward.

There, full in sight, and riding proudly at anchor, the beautiful curves of her swan-like prows made cannon proof with plates of shining steel,—and below, in lieu of figurehead to promise victory, those

letters of dread omen, *C.D.X.*,—with thirty oars-
men from the arsenal of Venice, to ensure her speed,
each ready at his oar-lock to wield his oar, with a
band of marksmen trained to finest tempered arms
to quell the resistance which no Venetian would
dare offer with those letters on the prow; the gold
and scarlet banner of San Marco, for good fortune,
at her masthead; the wind swelling her impatient
sail, as the curb but frets the steed—*the galley of
the Ten was not waiting without a purpose!*

The shock of the boats as they passed through
the lock had roused the sleepers rudely, and Piero
had time but for a swift glance of command to
Antonio, bidding him escape, when a gondola bear-
ing the ducal colors floated out from the sea of small
waiting craft and saluted them courteously. The
dignified signor who addressed them wore the violet
robe and stole of a secretary of the Doge, and his
face was the face of that secretary in whose silken
hand the gastaldo's had lain prisoned when he took
the oath of office!

Resistance was impossible.

"Messer Gastaldo," said the secretary suavely,
"it hath pleased those who have ever the welfare of
Venice at heart to provide for the most noble Lady
of the Giustiniani an escort which better fitteth her
rank than the size of thy *barchetta* permitteth, and
a dwelling more honorable than the 'Osteria del
Buon Pesce,' where, in company of the Lady Beata
Tagliapietra, she hath passed the night."

The secretary paused and placidly noted the
effect of his words upon Piero, who could have
gnashed his teeth for anger at those talking walls

24   *369*

of Venice which had betrayed him—so cautiously had he told his secret to the Lady Beata only, in that short moonlight stroll!

At a sign from the secretary a second gondola, wearing the ducal livery and filled with the gorgeons costumes of the palace guards, came out from the floating mass and approached the gondola of the people, where the Lady Marina sat trembling like a frightened fawn.

There was a struggle among the lesser craft to draw closer to this dramatic centre; they jostled each other unceremoniously; a splash, like a falling oar, was heard, but scarce noted in the absorbing interest of the moment; only a bare-legged boy jumped off from a tiny fishing-skiff near which the oar had floated, and swam with it to to the gondola from which it had fallen—since it was this boat which was making the carnival for them! Piero, alone, had slightly turned his head and noted that no one now stood on the *ponte piede* behind the felze of his gondola.

"The galley waits to receive the noble ladies to whom I am commissioned *by those who have sent me* to offer my respectful homage," said the secretary, bowing low before the felze. "The noble ladies will proceed thither in the ducal gondola which attends them. And thou, Messer Gastaldo, wilt graciously aid me in their escort—since, verily, they owe much to thy chivalry."

It was a pleasant scene for the onlookers.

But the Lady Marina sat motionless, and gave neither word nor sign in response to the invitation of the ducal secretary.

"Shall the pleasure of the lady of this noble house not be consulted?" Piero questioned, struggling to cover his defiance under a tone of deference.

But his answer was only in the secretary's eyes, —smiling, imperious,—more defiant than his own impotent will; and in the courtly waiting attitude, which had not changed, and which seemed unbearably to lengthen out the passing seconds.

The Lady Beata, winding compassionate arms around her friend, had raised her veil, whispering words of tenderness.

But there was no recognition in the glance that met hers—only the immeasurable pathos of a hopeless surrender; the fervent passion of Marina's will and faith had made all things seem possible of achievement, though Venice was against her, for had not the mission been given her in a vision by the Holy Madonna of San Donato—Mother of Sorrows—and was not the issue sure? And yielding all thought of self she had braced every faculty to accomplish the holy task of which she alone felt the urgency. But the overtaxed heart and brain could endure no longer thwarting; their activity and unquestioning purpose had been her only power; and the moment she ceased to struggle will and reason fled together.

Pitifully acquiescent, she went with them unresisting.

. . . . . . - .

A haze that was not luminous hung in the sky; night was creeping on without a sunset, as they battled their way up the Giudecca against the current which rushed like a boiling torrent around San Giorgio—the blue calm of the waters turned to a frenzied, foam-lashed green.

The men rowed fast, with tight-furled sail, but the storm came faster; ranks of threatening clouds were hurrying from the east, gathering like armies of vengeful spirits, darker, closer about them, shutting off every breath of air; an oppression, throbbing with nameless fears, was upon them—a hush, as if life had ceased; then the scorching, withering torment of a fierce sirocco, and the moan of the wind, like a soul in pain.

Marina grew faint and wide-eyed for terror, but they could not soothe her by word or touch; she sat with clasped hands, gasping for breath, listening to the low, long boom on the shores of the Lido, like muffled thunder, ceaselessly recurring—the terrible noise of the great waves beating against the sea-walls—beating and breaking in fury, tossing their spray high in air and whirling it in clouds, like rain mists, far across the lagoon. Would the barriers stand—or yield and leave them to their doom? Were the great waters of the Adriatic uprising in vengeance to overwhelm this city in her sin? Boom upon boom sounded through all the voices of the storm. Santa Maria! was it this that the Tintoretto had foretold!

A dazzling, frenzied flash of light,—a vast peal of thunder that was like the wrath of a mighty, offended God,—then darkness, and a torrent of rain —the waters in the shifting path of the wind leaping up to meet the waters from the sky!

The vesper bells of Venice came sobbing through

the storm, tossed and broken by the tornado into a wraith of a dirge; and now, by some fantastic freak of nature, as the winds rose higher, the iron tongues from every campanile—for a brief moment of horror—came wrangling and discordant, as if tortured by some demon of despair.

"Ave Maria, Gratia plena!"

the women cried together, falling on their knees, while the men toiled and struggled to hold the invincible galley of the Ten outside the whirling path of the storm—advancing and retreating at the will of the elements, against which their own splendid, human strength was like the feeble, untaught effort of a helpless infant.

"Mater Dei, Ora pro nobis peccatoribus, nunc et in hora mortis nostræ."

The words rose in a wail between the gusts.

For measureless moments, mighty as hours, they battled between San Marco and San Giorgio, tossed to and fro—now nearer the haven of the great white dome, now—as a lightning flash unveiled San Marco —near enough to see a cloud of frightened doves go whirling over the flood which swept the Piazza from end to end and poured out under the great gates of the Ducal Palace into the lagoon.

"Summa Parens clementiæ — nocte surgentes——"

373

XXXII

A DAY momentous for Venice—or was it Rome?
—had come and passed; it chronicled the right
of the Crown to make its own laws within its own
realm, without reference to ecclesiastical claims
which had hitherto been found hampering; it de-
fined the limits of Church and State, as no protest
had hitherto done.

But Venice was calm in her triumph as she had
been unmoved in disaster, and would not reflect the
jubilant tone of the cardinal when he had returned
from Rome empowered to withdraw the censures
upon the terms stipulated by the Republic.

Yet, at this latest moment, the cardinal mediator,
from lack of discretion, had come near to failure;
for the terms being less favorable than he had de-
sired to obtain for the Holy Father, he could not
resist attempting to win some little further grace
before pronouncing the final word, when the Sig-
noria, weary of temporizing, told him plainly that
his Holiness must come at once to a decision, or
Venice would forget that she had so far yielded as
to listen to any negotiations.

There was no pageant at the close of this long
drama of which the princes of Europe had been in-
terested spectators. Venice sat smiling and un-
ruffled under her April skies when the ducal secre-

374

tary escorted the two famous prisoners from the dungeons of the Palace to the residence of the French ambassador, and there, *without prejudice to the Republic's right of jurisdiction over criminal ecclesiastics*, explicitly stipulated, bestowed this gift —so fitting for the gratification of a "Most Christian Majesty"—upon the representative of France, who must indeed have breathed more freely when this testimonial of favor, with its precious burden of nameless crimes, had been consigned by him to one who waited as an appointee of the Pope.

The Doge and the Signoria sat in their accustomed places in their stately Assembly Chamber when the cardinal came with congratulations upon the withdrawal of the interdict, and the words of the Serenissimo, as he gave the promised parchment, were few and dignified.

"I thank the Lord our God that his Holiness hath assured himself of the purity of our intentions and the sincerity of our deeds."

And the writing of that parchment, sealed with the seal of Saint Mark, stood thus:

"Essendo state levate le Censure è restato parimente rivocato il Protesto." ("The censures having been taken off the protest remains equally revoked.")

It was whispered low that the cardinal, under his cape, made the sign of the cross and murmured a word of absolution. But if the Signoria suspected his intention there was no movement of acquiescence; only, when the short ceremony of the passing of the document was completed, they observed the usual forms of courtesy with which the audience of so princely an envoy is closed when his mission is accomplished.

If Paul V had surrendered with reluctance his hope of a sumptuous ceremony in San Pietro, where delegates of penitent Venetians should kneel in public and confess and be graciously absolved—if the Cardinal di Gioiosa had indulged flattering visions of a procession of priests and people to the patriarchal church in the Piazza, with pæans of joy-bells and shouts of gladness that Venice was again free to resume her worship, and that her penitent people were pardoned sons of the Church—he was doomed to disappointment. The cardinals of Spain and France, attended only by their households, celebrated Mass in the ducal chapel of San Marco; and the people came and went—as they did before and after, through that day and all the days since the interdict had been pronounced, in this and all the churches of Venice—and scarcely knew that their doom was lifted, as they had hardly realized that the curse had ever penetrated from those distant doors of San Pietro to the sanctuary of San Marco!

But the world knew and never forgot how that stately court of Venice had met the thunder of the Vatican and lessened its power forever.

The cause had been won in moderation and dignity upon a basis of civil justice that was none the less accredited because the Teologo Consultore who sat in chancelor's robes behind the throne was a zealous advocate of the primitive principles of Christianity, and defended, without fear of obloquy or death, the right of the individual conscience to interpret for itself the laws of right,—as founded upon the words of Christ,—because the extraordinary keenness, fineness, and breadth of his masterly mind enabled him to conceive with unusual definiteness the limits of civil and spiritual authority, and to ascribe the overgrowth of error upon the Church he loved to the misconception and weakness of human nature. He did not place Venice, the superb, —with her pride and pomp and power and intellectual astuteness, with her faults and worldliness and her magnificent statesmanship,—against the *spiritual* kingdom of Christ's Church on earth and declare for Venice *against* the Church.

But he weighed in the clear poise of his brain the Book of the Divine Law—which none knew better than he—with the laws of the princes of this world —which also few knew better—and declared that *One*, lowly and great, had defined the limits of the Church's jurisdiction when He said, "My kingdom is not of this world."

But in Rome the reasoning was not so simple, and threats of vengeance pursued this "terrible friar," whose bold judgments had ruled the councils of rebellious Venice.

But though peace was declared with Rome the labors of the Senate were scarcely lessened; there were still adjustments to be made which were not whispered abroad—there were embassies to be dissolved and appointed, gifts to be voted, honors to be heaped upon the head of the man whose counsels had led to such results, and in whose person the Senate now united the three offices of the Counsellors to the Doge, making Fra Paolo sole Teologo Consultore.

It was the first time in the history of the Republic that such honors had been voted, for Venice was not wont to be over-generous in recognition of individual service; and this friend of statesmen, scholars, and princes temporal and spiritual, pre-served the greatness of his simplicity unspoiled in prosperity and power—as was possible only to a spirit ruled by inflexible principle and faith.

When the Senate voted him a palace near San Marco he preferred his simple quarters among his brethren of the Servi. When, in proof of their appreciation, they doubled his salary and would have trebled it again—"Nay," said he, "it is but my duty that I have done. May the honorable words of the Senate's recognition but hold before me that which, by God's help, I may yet accomplish"; and he would take but so much as he might bestow in charity and gifts to his convent, having for himself no need nor tastes that were not met by the modest provision of his order.

And when, having refused to go to Rome for reconciliation—being not penitent—or for preferment, which would not come without penitence, Fra Paolo still pursued, unmoved, the quiet tenor of his daily round, from convent to palace, without pause or tremor, in spite of continued warning;—"My life," he said, "is in the hands of God. My duty hath he confided to mine own effort."

The Lady Marina was a guest in the Ducal Palace, detained under surveillance, yet treated with much honor; her friends might see her in the presence of the ducal guards who watched within the doors of her sumptuous chambers, but she was not free to go to her own, who had guarded her with such laxity that in striving to reach the court of the enemy she had imperiled the dignity of the Republic by her silent censure. Marcantonio had trembled more when, the morning after the storm, news had reached him that the fugitive was in the keeping of the Signoria, than if the message had announced her death. What might he not expect of their jealousy!

But a ducal secretary had received him with courtesy and conducted him at once into the audience chamber of the Doge, who bade him send for her maidens that she might be cared for tenderly, for her stay at the Palace would be indefinite. It was a royal command, against which pleading or rebellion were alike useless.

"Most Serene Prince!" cried Marcantonio in agony, "I beseech thee leave me that gift which a gracious Senate once so generously bestowed! I have never swerved in loyalty—though my heart was nigh to breaking that I might not grant her prayer!"

But one in attendance spoke quickly; for the face of the good Leonardo Donato wás full of compassion, and he might not be trusted to serve the higher interests of the Republic.

"It is of the clemency of the Serenissimo," said that inflexible voice, "that the Lady Marina reaps not the penalty of her flight and of her disloyalty to the State, since she hath sought to place her private judgment beyond the wisdom of the rulers of Venice."

The figure stood motionless in the shadow of a column, muffled in a long black mantle, a black beretta partially concealing the face.

There was an icy inflection in the tones which sent a chill to Marcantonio's heart as he listened. One of the Chiefs of the Ten was always a member of the still more dreaded Inquisition, whose identity was never known, and the passionless voice held a hint of indisputable authority—was his suffering wife to rely upon the mercy of the most puissant member of this terrible commission!

"Take my life for hers!" he implored, so beside himself with grief and terror that he disclosed his fear for Marina; "and bid her return to care for our little one."

"Not so," said the emotionless voice; "the Lady Marina hath disproved her right to care for a noble of Venice. It would be to imperil his loyalty to leave the child under his mother's influence."

"My God!" cried Marcantonio bitterly; "take me to her and let us die together—if the Republic may grant us so much grace!"

Again the Doge would have spoken compassionate words, but the other interposed:

"The State hath little use for the lady's life—save in her keeping. And she herself, perchance, hath less. For so hath her strange whim wrought upon her that she knoweth naught of that which passeth around her, and one face to her is like another."

The young Senator turned from the cruel speaker to the Doge in mute appealing agony. The old man grasped his hand in a steadying clasp.

"Let us go to her," said Leonardo, very low,

when he could command his voice. "She is like a lovely child—resisting nothing. It is some shock—it will pass."

   .   .   .   -   .   .

And now there came a day when the proud heart of Venice was stirred to its core, for a messenger dashed breathless into the Council Chamber—an excited, protesting throng of the populace surging in through the open door behind him. "Fra Paolo! Il caro Padre! Morto!"

"*Dead!*" They started to their feet with ready imprecations. Fra Paolo, who had left them an hour before, with the Signor Malipiero and his devoted secretary! They exchanged glances of terrible comprehension—the triumph of Venice was avenged upon the faithful servant of the State!

The Consiglio broke up in confusion.

"Eccellentissimi," the messenger explained to the horror-stricken questioners, "they were five,—rushing out from the dark of the convent wall against him when he came alone down the steps of the Ponte della Pugna,—the villains held the others down. And Fra Paolo lay dead on the Fondamenta—stabbed in many places, as if one would cut him in bits—and the stiletto still in his forehead! And they sent me——"

" 'Alone'? you ask me, Illustrissimi?—Santissima Vergine! the whole city pouring in to the cries of those that found him; and the murderers off before one could touch them, and never a guard near! They carried him into the Servi.—And the people—furious—are storming the palazzo of the nuncio as

I pass; and some one cries that the envoy is off to the Lido, with his fine friends, who start for Rome. A thousand devils!—May the good San Nicolò send them to feed the fishes!"

The Senate, to testify its honor, grief, and sympathy for the beloved Counsellor, had instantly adjourned, and its members repaired in great numbers to the convent to make personal inquiries, returning to a new session prolonged through the night; for Fra Paolo, who had fainted from loss of blood on his pallet in the Servite cell, had recovered consciousness and hovered between life and death—his humble bed attended by the most famous physicians and surgeons whom the Republic could summon to her aid. The secretaries, meanwhile, were busy in preparing resolutions of affection by which to honor him in the sight of the Venetian people; letters of announcement to foreign courts, as if he had been of the blood royal; proclamations of reward for the persons of the criminals, alive or dead, which, before the day had dawned, the Signori della Notte had affixed to the doors of San Marco, along the Rialto, on the breast of Ser Robia, that all might read. And for means of bringing the offenders to justice they plotted and schemed as none but Venetians could do.

It was three days since the storm, and the gastaldo had not yet been released; he also was simply detained, without ignominy or discomfort, in rooms set apart for prisoners of State before they had been brought to trial; for the events of these days had been too absorbing to permit of an examination of his case. And now, in the gray dawn which broke

upon that night of anxiety and excitement, alter-
nating between hope and fear as frequent messen-
gers, each guarded by a detachment of palace
guards, appeared with fresh news from the convent,
the weary senators strolled up and down in the
great chambers opening on the sea façade of the
Ducal Palace discussing the event in a more desul-
tory way—its meaning, its dangers, the achieve-
ments of the great man who might, even now, be
receiving the viaticum in the convent of the Servi.

He was first named with terms of endearment
strange upon the lips of that stately assembly—"Il
caro Padre," "Teologo amato di Venezia"—yet the
guards had failed to seize those villains who lay in
wait at the Ponte della Pugna! The bridges and
traghetti must be closely watched.—Ah—the gas-
taldo grande!"

"Hath one yet been named *Condottiere* for this
frontier service?" questioned one of the older sen-
ators, among a group of the more important men
who had detached themselves from the others and
strolled out into the great loggia on the sea façade
for a reviving breath of the morning air. "For
such an employ there is none like Piero Salin for
daring and intrigue; and the assassins may linger
long in hiding on the route to Rome."

And so they first remembered Piero in these
crowded days and discussed his fault with a degree
of leniency that would have been foreign to the tra-
ditions of Venice had he not been needed for im-
portant secret service.

Meanwhile, Fra Paolo was still the theme among
the senators at large in the Council Chamber. "Il

miracolo del suo secolo," they called him, as they rehearsed the opinions of the learned men of their age in every field of science.

"It cannot be from knowledge, acquired as all men learn, that he taketh this position in such varied sciences," said the Senator Morosini; "for a lifetime doth suffice to few men for such attainment in one field as he hath reached in all. It must be that the marvel of his mind doth hold some central truth which maketh all science cognate."

"Else were he not 'friend and master' to Galileo of Padua."

"And it is told that Acquapendente, who hath been summoned by the Signoria to bestow his skill, hath learned of him some matters which he taught in the medical school of Bologna. The world hath not his equal for learning."

"By the blessed San Marco!" ejaculated one under his breath, who had been idly leaning on the balustrade, as he crossed himself and looked furtively around to note whether he had been overheard.

But the others of the group, keenly alive to danger, had instantly joined him.

"Was this some new intrigue?" "Was the night not already full with horror?" they questioned of each other, thrilled with dread and superstition.

Dawn was growing over the water, and the gray and oily surface of the lagoon was closely dotted with gondolas, distinct and black in the morning twilight; they came sweeping on from San Nicolò and Castello—black and red, breast to breast—gathering impetus as they neared the Piazzetta, in numbers which must have left every traghetto of Venice deserted; Nicolotti and Castellani—*allies,* since they never had been friends! It was some intrigue of the people, or some favor they had come to ask— *to-day,* when the Senate might not spare one thought for disorder among the masses!

Weary and overwrought, after their night of sorrowful labor, they looked at each other in consternation.

"It is their gastaldo whom they are come to seek," a secretary of the Ten confided by inspiration to his Chief, as an old man, wearing the robe of a bancalo, was escorted from the landing by a band of gondoliers with black and crimson sashes, who disappeared under the entrance to the palace courtyard.

"Let him be summoned and honorably discharged; he hath done no harm that may be compared with the disaffection of the traghetti."

"Rather, let them receive him back, appointed by the Senate to honor, as Condottiere of the border forces"; a second Chief hastened to respond, for the moment was grave, "and the command will most excellently fit the gastaldo."

"And for the Lady of the Giustiniani, it matters little—Rome or Venice," said an old senator, compassionately, as he followed his colleagues into the Council Chamber. "She hath so spent herself in grieving that she knoweth naught. For the Senator Marcantonio hath vainly sought to teach her that the interdict hath been lifted; yet even this she comprehendeth not."

"We are come, your Excellencies, for news of our Gastaldo Grande, whose presence is verily needful for the traghetti," said the white-haired bancalo, when an audience had been granted him.

"How many of you have come as escort?" the secretary questioned carelessly.

"Eccellenza, we are enough," the bancalo answered fearlessly, and with a significant pause, *"to prove the will of the people—as well Nicolotti as Castellani.* And to escort our Gastaldo Grande with honor, since it hath pleased your excellencies to receive him—*as a guest*—in the Ducal Palace."

He was the eldest of the officers of the traghetti, accustomed to respect, upheld by the united forces of the people; this man of the people and this mouthpiece of the nobles measured each other fearlessly as they looked into each other's faces—each coolly choosing his phrases to carry so much as the other might count wise.

"It is well," said the secretary of the Ten, after a brief private conference with his Chiefs, "that ye are come in numbers to do him honor. Since the Senate hath need of his brave service and hath named Piero Salin, for exigencies of the Republic, Condottiere, with honors and men of artillery to do him service."

And so it chanced, that because of the stress of the time, Piero Salin floated off in triumph to Murano, named General of the Border Forces, with secret orders from the Ten.

XXXIII

THE great bell in the tower of the arsenal told twelve of the day, and already the broader waters near the rios which led to the high machico-lated walls surrounding this famous Venetian stronghold were crowded with gondolas of the peo-ple and barges from the islands filled with men, women, and children, jubilant with holiday speech and brilliant in gala colors; for this was one of those perpetually recurring festas which so endeared this City of the Sea to its pleasure-loving people.

This splendid ceremony of inspection by the Doge was a day of annual triumph, for nowhere in all the world was there such an arsenal, and nowhere such an army of workmen,—thirty-five thousand men trained to the cunning from father to son in lifelong service,—with sailors, sixteeen thousand more, who should presently make a brave review within those battlemented walls, to tickle the fancy of the Serenissimo and his guests. For these pa-geants of Venice were not guiltless of timely hints to the onlookers of the futility of opposition to a naval force so great and so admirably controlled; and well might the Republic be proud of the foun-dry, the docks, the galleys, which the Doge and the Signoria came each year in state to visit, with all

387

the nobles of the Maggior Consiglio and many of the high officials.

This year it was to be a fête more magnificent than usual, for the households of the ambassadors were bidden to the banquet which was prepared in the Great Hall of the arsenal—the attractions of which were invitingly rehearsed, as the speakers leaned across from gondola to gondola, to exchange their pleasant bits of gossip with dramatic exaggerations. "And the gondolas of the ambassadors! Santa Maria! the Signori, 'i provveditori alle pompe' have nothing to say, for there is a dispensation! the velvets and satins and golden fringes—it will be a true glimpse of the *paradiso!*"

"And the great Signor medico, Acquapendente, will be made this day Cavalière of the Republic, since he hath had the wonderful fortune to save the life of our Padre Maestro Paolo; for it is well known there was little hope of matins or vespers more for him, the night the *maledetti bravi* left the stiletto in his face!"

"And thou, Giuseppe!" cried a smiling mother from Mazzorbo, proudly indicating her boy as an object of interest, and pushing him into a more prominent position—"the bambino hath seen it with his own eyes, since he is prentice at the metal graver's shop of Messer Maffeo Olivieri on the Rialto; thou, tell us, Giuseppe, of this great goblet of graven silver which the Master Olivieri hath ready for the presentation, by order of the Signoria. È bello, ah? *Bellissimo!* And the Lion of San Marco on the crown of it—*è vero* Giuseppe?—with wings—*magnifico!* And jewels of rubino in the eyes of it; and a tongue——"

"Cosi!" interposed Giuseppe, with dramatic effectiveness, thrusting out his own with relish. *"Thus!"*

"Ma c'è altro!" cried a gondolier from Murano. "There is more yet! For the magnificent galley which the little one of the Ca' Giustiniani—he that is grandson to our Messer Girolamo Magagnati—hath given to the Republic will be floated out from the basin of the arsenal and christened this day!"

The spirits of the light-hearted crowd effervesced in a jubilant cheer.

"I Giustiniani!"

On every page of the history of Venice the name of the Giustiniani stood brilliantly forth, and the stained and tattered banners in the great hall of the arsenal were so many laurel leaves for this patrician house, keeping the memory of the brilliant victory of Lepanto green in the hearts of the Venetians. It was a Giustinian, "Gonfalonière," *standard bearer*, who had brought the glorious news on his triumphant galley, the solemn Lion of San Marco waving his banner above the drooping crescent of the Turk from every green wreathed mast. It was this Giustinian who had been carried in triumph on the shoulders of the people, before the Doge and the Signoria—who had been the hero when that solemn Mass, in honor of the victory, had been offered up in the ducal chapel—when the Rialto and the Merceria, for the extravagant joy of Venice, were draped in blue and scarlet and gold, bound with laurel wreaths and decorated with the art treasures of Titian and Giorgone. It was a name which the people were accustomed to honor. "I Giustiniani!" they shouted.

There was a sudden hush, for the bells of the

Campanile of San Marco had given the signal, and there was a great stir before the Piazza—a train of gondolas was sweeping into line far down the Canal Grande; the guards on the watch-towers of the arsenal were full of animation; the gondolas of the orderlies were buzzing like bees about the barge of the grand admiral, who awaited the coming of the Doge, in all his magnificence of satin ceremonial robes.   He was like a noble to-day, this man of the people. *Viva San Marco!*

The moment was approaching; orderlies glided back and forth among the excited people, prescribing their distance; the raft of small craft shifted its position and presently a salute was fired from all the cannon of the arsenal; the Doge, in his great State barge, was near.

The people shouted themselves hoarse when the smoke cleared away and revealed the splendid train of private barges from Venice; there were banners of the Republic and streaming pennons of the nobles; the gondoliers wore the colors of their house, and were welcomed by the people on these days of pageant as a distinct addition to the glories of the festa—though on other days the barcarioli of the traghetti poured out full vials of contempt upon their sashes of rose and silver and the blazonry of arms upon their silken sleeves.

The gondolas and barges of the people drifted back again, close about the train of magnates from Venice.

"I Giustiniani," they shouted; "il Marconino!"

There was a movement on one of the splendid barges bearing the colors of the Giustiniani; a little child was caught up and held for a moment high in the air; he waved his tiny hands gleefully—it was such beautiful play!

"It is the grandson of Messer Girolamo Magagnati, of the Stabilimenti!" they cried from the barges of Murano, surging nearer in the waterway. "He belongs to us—to the people!" for the story was well known, and the people of Venice were not less proud than the nobles who ruled them. "Viva Messer Magagnati!"

The group upon the deck parted and disclosed an old man with bowed head and faltering movements, supported by the young Senator Giustiniani, who gravely recognized their salute; but there was no answering smile upon his face; and Girolamo Magagnati, who had proudly confronted the senators in their Council Chamber when he had declined their proffer of nobility, in this day of triumph scarcely raised his eyes.

The mothers on the barges lifted their little ones in their arms and taught them to call a name—"Il Marconino!" they ventured, in hesitant, treble tones.

But now the splendid moment was near. The admiral, in his crimson robes of state, had mounted to his place on the Doge's barge, and all the floating crowd had fallen into ordered position, in a hush of vibrant suspense, as, with slow majesty and grace, one by one the galleys of Venice came forth in procession from the great basin of the arsenal, sweeping round from the Punta della Motta into the lagoon, and passing the Signoria with a salute. And now the great bell sounded again from the arsenal tower, and was answered from the Campanile of

391

San Marco, and the suppressed excitement of the eager spectators burst forth in cries of greeting to the *Marconino*—just set afloat—as she came gracefully around in front of the Doge's barge, full manned and saluting, magnificently equipped, the colors of the Giustiniani waving below the crimson banner of San Marco, with its regnant Lion, and on her prow the beautiful sculptured figure of a little child.

"Il Marconino! Il Marconino!"

There was a brief moment of confusion from the coming and going of barges,—a short delay which brimmed their excitement to the fever pitch,—then the waters cleared again ôf their floating craft, and the Senator Marcantonio Giustiniani stepped forth on the deck to christen the gift of his child.

The people looked, and would have shouted—but forebore—gazing awestruck.

As he stood, firmly planted upon the prow, the crimson drapery of his senator's robe parted and disclosed the firm young vigor of his limbs, in their silken hose, and his very attitude showed power. But he wore the face of a young Greek god who had lightly dreamed that he could fashion Life out of grace and sunshine, and had waked to carve Endurance out of Agony.

The child, held high in his arms, was radiant in the sunshine; its rosebud mouth parting over pearly teeth in dimpling glee, the breeze lifting the light rings of hair that caressed his soft, round throat, the hands waving in childish ecstasy and grace. As they stood, just over the beautiful bust of the "Marconino" which Vittorio had carved upon the prow,

392

child and father were an embodiment of the play of the crested foam over the deep trouble of the waves beneath.

"Was it thus that the nobles took their triumphs?" the people questioned low of each other. "And where was the Lady Marina, the daughter of Messer Magagnati—*their* lady, who had been good to the people?"

"She was there—within," some one answered; "she was not strong—the salutes were too much for her. She was waiting within, with her maidens."

"To miss such a beautiful festa! Santa Maria!" —the strong peasant mothers, clasping their infants in their arms, with prattling, barefooted children clinging to their mantles—so glad for this glimpse of holiday—looked again at the beautiful, stern face of this father who had youth and gifts and wealth, his seat in the Consiglio, his boy in his arms—but no smile for the people pressing around him ready to shout his name; and they crossed themselves with a nameless yearning and dread.

But the nobles, with more understanding, looked upon him and forgot their jealousy.

For the Lady Marina was within, waiting with her maidens in a private chamber of the arsenal until the hour of the banquet, when her presence had been required by the Signoria. Only so much had her father—the giver of the gift—and Marcantonio, on this day of honor to his name—been able to obtain of the imperious Republic. There were rumors afloat, questions were asked, and the body of nobles must bear witness to the clemency of the State, who could be gracious in forgiving. If the Lady of the

Giustiniani might not have the custody of her child, it was not that because of her transgressions they would refuse her any grace or honor.

Meanwhile Giustinian Giustiniani, standing proudly erect among the nobles of the Doge's suite, searched the crowd for further homage, and wondered at the silence when the charming figure of the baby Marconino danced in his father's arms—a very embodiment of life and glee.

It was over in a moment, and the crowd of smaller barges fell back in disorder, for the Doge was passing through the gates of the arsenal; the galleys were returning back by San Pietro in Castello, and that which was to follow of the glories of the day was only for the great ones now gathering behind that charmèd gate, where the golden chair was waiting in which the Serenissimo should make his royal progress. There was nothing more for the people until the hour of the Ave Maria should call the stately procession forth on its homeward way.

But the brilliant memories of this morning would gladden many a less golden day—Viva San Marco! Their voluble tongues were suddenly unloosed, and those who had been favored with near glimpses of the heroes of the day became centres of animated discussion. Life was good in Venice! "And thou, Nino, forget not that the Madonna hath been 'gentile' to thee! Thou shalt tell thy little ones, when thou art old, that thou hast this day seen, with thine own eyes, the Marconino, who hath given the great galley to the Republic!"

The banquet was over, and there was a stir among the Signoria when the infant Giustinian was called for that he might receive the thanks of the Republic for his princely gift; and a murmur of admiration circled from lip to lip as the blooming child was brought into the banquet hall. All eyes were now turned upon the Lady Marina, who had hitherto remained surrounded by her household and inconspicuous among the group of noble Venetian ladies who gave distinction to this festa.

It was Marcantonio who, with a tenderness that was pathetic and a touch that was a caress, led her down from her place and folded the little one's hand in hers. He would have led her to the throne; but a gesture that was scarcely more than a glance conveyed a command he dared not disobey.

They looked to see a flush of pride on her beautiful face as, in answer to the Doge's summons, she came slowly forward, with the tiny hand of the boy clasped in hers—his unsteady, childish footsteps echoing unevenly on the marble pavement between her measured movements. But she walked as in a dream, as if she were no longer one of this bright company, yet strangely beautiful to see, with a face like some noble spirit,—pale and grieving,—and in her eyes a great trouble that was full of dignity and love. Over the dark velvet of her robe the bountiful, white waves of her hair streamed like a bridal veil, wreathing her brows and her young, pathetic face with silken rings of drifted snow.

But before she had reached the dais prepared for the Signoria at the end of the great hall she paused, as if unable to proceed further, swaying slightly and throwing out her hands to steady herself; a sudden change swept over her face, and for a moment it seemed that she would fall; the child, losing hold of her hand, clung sobbing to her skirts, hiding his pretty head.

Her husband sprang to her aid, tenderly supporting her, but as instantly she seemed to recover her strength, smiling upon him graciously, while she gently disengaged herself from his hold, leaving the little one with him, and gliding rapidly forward, looked around her with unrecognizing eyes.

It had pleased the whim of the Republic to make some ecclesiastical parade on this festa of Venice which followed so closely upon the prosaic closing scene of the quarrel with Rome, wherein no churchly pomp had been permitted; and as Marinà's bewildered gaze steadied itself upon the noble group of the Signoria, with whom to-day, in great state, sat the Patriarch of Venice with mitre and hierarchical robes and all the attendant group of Venetian bishops, a look of intense relief suddenly flashed over the trouble in her eyes—as if that which she had sought with such long suffering no longer eluded her.

"Madre Beatissima!" she cried, clasping her crucifix closely to her breast, and raising her eyes to heaven, "I thank thee!"

The light grew upon her face.

As her whole life had been merged in this struggle which had only conquered her overwrought heart and brain when she had felt that the Madonna had deserted her and delivered her to the wrath of Venice, so now, in her hallucination,—since the Madonna had brought her to Rome,—her faith and power of speech suddenly returned, and she rallied all her strength to fulfil her mission.

In that great and sumptuous Hall, flaunting and gay with banners which chronicled the victories and the power of the Republic—in the impregnable stronghold of the realm, under the astonished gaze of the entire Venetian court and the brilliant throng of the households of nobles and ambassadors who looked down from the circling galleries, expectant and awestruck under the spell of so strange a vision —this pale, slight champion of a desperate spiritual struggle, with no host to help her save her prayers and faith, with no standard but the cross clasped to her breast, knelt at the feet of the Patriarch, while the sunset light through the broad western window made a radiance where she knelt—as if Heaven at last had smiled upon her.

"Oh, Holy Father!" she implored, "have mercy upon Venice! Forgive her unfaithfulness, because she hath meant no sin!

"The Madonna hath granted me to reach Rome at last, because she hath laid her command upon me in a vision and it could not fail. But all those, my loved ones, have I lost by the weary way; and save for her mercy I could not have reached thee.

"With prayers and penance have I striven—and ceased not—since the anguish of thy displeasure came upon Venice. Oh, Holy Father! for all the mothers who understand and grieve, and for our innocent little ones, and for all those, our beloved, who are good and noble—and yet know not the hard way of submission, because the Lord hath taught them some other way—lift thy wrath from Venice, that our Heavenly Father hide not his face in clouds too heavy for our prayers to reach him!

"It is the will of the Madonna San Donato—thou canst not refuse to lift the doom!"

The words leaped over each other like a torrent —impetuous, passionate, as if the moments for speech were few.

"These do I bring—and these, for an offering!" she cried, feverishly unclasping the lustrous pearls from her throat and girdle and laying them at the feet of the Patriarch. "And all the dear happiness of my life have I given, that I might reach thee with this prayer for Venice! Oh, Holy Father, accept my sacrifice!"

She reverently pressed the hem of the priestly robe to her lips, and those who knew of her flight from Venice understood that she fancied she had reached the Roman Court and was kneeling in the presence of the Sovereign Pontiff; but in their amazement that she alone, who was dying from the grief of it, did not know that the interdict had been removed, it had not seemed possible to answer her.

But there was no room for anger as they listened —though her plea was a judgment on the court of Venice—for her voice thrilled them with its unearthly sadness, and, looking into her beautiful, spirit face, they saw that all her consciousness was merged in her intense realization of the utmost terror of the curse, and in her one burning hope—to which all things else were as nothing and in which she herself was wholly lost.

The Patriarch, moved with immeasurable compassion, raised her tenderly. "My daughter," he said, in a voice that trembled with feeling, "Venice is restored to favor. The Interdict is removed!"

Through the stern assembly a wave of sympathy surged irresistibly, impelling them to comfort this lovely, grieving lady, distraught by anguished brooding. Scarcely knowing that their emotion expressed itself in words, they caught up the Patriarch's answer and echoed it from group to group —from gallery to gallery—until it gathered impetus and rolled like a Hallelujah Chorus through the vast, vaulted chamber.

"Venice is restored to favor; the Interdict is removed!"

The light grew upon her face.

How should it seem strange to her that her prayer at the feet of the Holy Father had wrought this pardon for Venice—was it not for this that the blessed Madonna of San Donato had sent her? She had promised blessing for sacrifice!

She stood for a moment, radiant, while the chorus of many voices throbbed around her—her face like an angel's for joy and love—a glorified vision in the parting rays of the evening sun—then her faint fluttering breath died in a *Benedicite!*

. . . .

The vesper bells of Venice came softly through the twilight, calling to Ave Maria.

SD - #0070 - 281222 - C0 - 229/152/22 - PB - 9781331101147 - Gloss Lamination